TRUST: REASON, ROUTINE, REFLEXIVITY

TRUST: REASON, ROUTINE, REFLEXIVITY

Guido Möllering
Max Planck Institute for the Study of Societies
Cologne, Germany

Elsevier

Amsterdam – Boston – Heidelberg – London – New York – Oxford
Paris – San Diego – San Francisco – Singapore – Sydney – Tokyo

Elsevier
The Boulevard, Langford Lane, Kidlington, Oxford OX5 1GB, UK
Radarweg 29, PO Box 211, 1000 AE Amsterdam, The Netherlands

μℳ First edition 2006

British Library Cataloguing in Publication Data
A catalogue record for this book is available from the British Library

Library of Congress Cataloging-in-Publication Data
A catalog record for this book is available from the Library of Congress

ISBN-13: 978-0-08-044855-8
ISBN-10: 0-08-044855-0

> For information on all Elsevier publications
> visit our website at books.elsevier.com

Printed and bound in Great Britain
06 07 08 09 10 10 9 8 7 6 5 4 3 2 1

Working together to grow
libraries in developing countries

www.elsevier.com | www.bookaid.org | www.sabre.org

ELSEVIER   BOOK AID
             International   Sabre Foundation

PREFACE

What makes trust such a powerful concept? This question has been at the back of my mind for about nine years now while I have been researching trust both in highly abstract terms and in more practical settings. It is with great pleasure and satisfaction, but also with a sense of vulnerability and uncertainty, of course, that I present in this book what I believe to be the most important approaches to understanding trust in the social sciences as well as core original insights into the leap of faith as the essential element at the heart of trust.

Young scholars are increasingly discouraged from writing books and advised to focus their efforts on journal articles. Personally, I am glad that people around me have encouraged me to compose and publish this work. The opportunity to develop and describe my scholarly understanding of trust more thoroughly has been immensely valuable to me because in this book I can connect my most recent thoughts with some ideas that I have presented separately in articles and chapters elsewhere. As a result, a bigger picture emerges not just for me, but also for the reader. I have noticed that key inspirations have often come from books rather than articles on trust, which might reflect the fact that trust is a complex topic that does not lend itself well to merely incremental or fragmented contributions. Books, however, can integrate a broad range of ideas and move the field in new directions.

The authors whose writings have enabled me to develop my own argument are duly cited in this book. Of those who have encouraged, inspired and assisted me in my work on trust over the years in person, I would like to thank specifically: Mats Alvesson, Reinhard Bachmann, Jens Beckert, Katinka Bijlsma-Frankema, Sandro Castaldo, John Child, Nicole Gillespie, Chris Grey, Rod Kramer, Christel Lane, Frédérique Six, Denise Skinner, Jörg Sydow, Malin Tillmar, Antoinette Weibel, Arnold Windeler and Aks Zaheer. Countless others have also helped me through constructive dialogue and exchanges of ideas. I am grateful to all of them and hope that this work provokes further lively discussion to which I already look forward.

The book owes much to the amazing enthusiasm and professional support of the people at Elsevier Science. Mary Malin fuelled my initiative, Julie Walker was an excellent editorial advisor and AnnHelen Lindeholm reassured me on the marketing side. Moreover, I received terrific assistance in manuscript preparation from the Max Planck Institute for the Study of Societies in Cologne, in particular from Astrid Dünkelmann, Thomas Pott, Christel Schommertz and Sabine Stumpf. We commissioned the external services of Jeanette Störtte, who did a magnificent job in typesetting the camera-ready manuscript, and John Booth, who copy-edited the whole text and polished my English carefully with a great sense of humour and understanding. Overall, I am impressed by the professionalism that all these people demonstrated and flattered by their genuine interest in the content of my work, confirming the feeling that trust matters to all of us.

I thank the British Printing Industries Federation, London, and the respondents of my long field interviews for their kind cooperation, which enabled me to generate the empirical cases described in the last part of the book.

The book's cover features the painting 'Leap of Faith' by Margaret Smithers-Crump (2004), which resonates extremely well with my ideas. Acknowledging the artist's authorship and copyright, I am very grateful for the permission to use the artwork here.

I dedicate this book to my wife Martina Möllering and to our families because the meaning of trust is particularly clear to me whenever I realize how fortunate I am in enjoying their love and support.

Cologne, Germany, November 2005   *Guido Möllering*

CONTENTS

Preface   v

Figures   ix

1   Allured by Trust?
1.1   Topicality of Trust: Blessing or Burden?   1
1.2   Key Concepts and Challenges   7
1.3   Overview of the Book   10

2   Trust and Reason
2.1   The Rationalist Paradigm   13
2.2   Trust in Rational Choice Perspectives   15
2.3   Trust in Economic Theories   24
2.4   The Rationality of Emotions   44
2.5   Indicators of Trustworthiness   46

3   Trust and Routine
3.1   Taken-for-Grantedness   51
3.2   Trust as a Form of Natural Attitude   54
3.3   Trust as a Form of Institutional Isomorphism   61
3.4   Rules, Roles and Routines   65
3.5   Trust in Institutions   71

4   Trust and Reflexivity
4.1   Adopting a Process View   77
4.2   The Functionality of 'Blind' Trust   80
4.3   Experience and the 'Principle of Gradualness'   84
4.4   Familiarity, Unfamiliarity, Familiarization   94
4.5   Active Trust and Reflexive Structuration   99

5   The Leap of Faith
5.1 The Missing Element: Suspension   105
5.2 As if: Trust as Fiction   112
5.3 Bracketing: Just Do It   115
5.4 The Will to Believe   119
5.5 Evidence of Suspension   121

6   Studying Trust
6.1 Overview of Empirical Approaches   127
6.2 Quantitative Studies: Measuring Trust   135
6.3 Qualitative Studies: Understanding Trust   140
6.4 Comparative Studies: Context and History   145
6.5 Calling for Interpretative Studies   151

7   Experiencing Trust
7.1 An Exploratory Study of Buyer–Supplier Relations   155
7.2 Case I: Uni Press, Brass Plate Paper and Scott Mills   160
7.3 Case II: Bluechip Print and Merch Papers   170
7.4 Case III: Retail Group Print Unit and Repute Papers   176
7.5 Interpreting Trust Relationships: Lessons from the Cases   185

8   Positive Expectations
8.1 Core Insights and Contributions   191
8.2 Reconnecting to Bigger Research Agendas   193
8.3 Avenues for Further Trust Research   196

Bibliography   **199**

Index   **217**

FIGURES

2.1 The Trustor's Bet   16
2.2 Effect of Trust on Transaction Costs   28
2.3 The Trust Game   34
2.4 The Trust Game with Contractual Penalty and Incentives   35
2.5 Trust Game with (Un)Trustworthy Trustees   42

3.1 Types of Isomorphism   63

4.1 Spiral Reinforcement Model of Trust   86
4.2 Process Framework of the Development of Cooperative IORs   91
4.3 Duality and Recursiveness in the Constitution of Trust   101

5.1 The Trust Wheel – An Integrative Framework   110

6.1 Heuristics for Categorizing Empirical Work on Trust   129
6.2 Perceptions of Trust in the Cambridge Contracting Study   148

7.1 Typology of Supplier Relations   158

1

ALLURED BY TRUST?

1.1 TOPICALITY OF TRUST: BLESSING OR BURDEN?

Trust belongs to the same class of abstract concepts as freedom, justice, knowledge, power, prosperity, solidarity or truth, which are all highly evocative, but also highly 'elusive' (Gambetta, 1988b), and which keep on fascinating not only generations of scholars but anybody with at least a slight proclivity for social philosophical questions. The initial cue that makes trust appear an attractive concept that one wants to read or, for that matter, write about can come from almost anywhere. In my case it was the question of how interorganizational cooperation can be successful. Others start, for example, with problems in the family, disappointments in the political system, the challenges of teamwork, or the remarkable economic success of certain regions or communities. At the beginning of my own research on trust somebody warned me that this was a slippery slope and, if they meant by this that there is an infinite amount of issues within and around trust that one can get drawn into, then they definitely had a point. In this book, I want to demonstrate systematically the many facets of trust, the value of taking different perspectives on trust, and also the possibility of getting to the bottom of the phenomenon, pointing to the key idea that unites all abstract conceptions and practical applications of trust.

Research has to be relevant and, in keeping with this spirit of striving for legitimacy, virtually all contributions to the trust literature begin by pointing out the topicality of trust. The general line taken is that not only has trust always been relevant; it is of particular importance today (see,

for example, Deutsch, 1973; Gambetta, 1988b; Sztompka, 1999; Nooteboom, 2002; McEvily et al., 2003). Rather than simply replicating such
common and well-rehearsed claims, this first section of the book is intended as a comment on the apparent topicality of trust and on the question of whether this topicality is a blessing or burden from the point of
view of a scholarly interest in trust. I will look into the claim that trust is
currently problematic and into allegations that the interest in trust is
'mere' rhetoric, and I will offer my own thoughts on the essential ambivalence of trust, which makes the concept an attractive long runner, too.

We often hear about crises of trust and there is a general feeling that
trust may have become problematic, which is bewildering if Georg Simmel ([1907] 1990) was correct when he said that 'without the general
trust people have in each other, society itself would disintegrate' (p. 178),
not to mention Confucius who regarded trust as a precondition for all
worthwhile social relations 2,500 years ago (see Hann, 1968). Talking
specifically about the bases for business, Alfred Marshall (1920), often
seen mainly as a founding father of neoclassical economics (rather than
as an economic sociologist), made a similarly broad claim that trust is
fundamental to the workings of society and that it 'permeates all life, like
the air we breathe: and its services are apt to be taken for granted and ignored, like those of fresh air, until attention is forcibly attracted by their
failure' (p. 165; see also Aspers, 1999, 2001). This statement suggests
that trust is strongly related to taken-for-grantedness (as I will argue in
Chapter 3) and thus explains why trust tends to become topical when it is
problematic (and may then involve deliberation and reasoning, about
which see Chapter 2; see also Barber, 1983). As Doris Brothers (1995)
puts it: 'We are no more likely to ask ourselves how trusting we are at a
given moment in time than to inquire if gravity is still keeping the planets
in orbit. However, when trust is disturbed it claims our attention as ur-
gently as would any irregularity in the gravitational field' (p. 3, also cited
by Kramer, 2001).

Building on these observations – highlighting that there must be a perceived failure – current claims that refer to the shortage of trust can be
divided into at least two main lines of argument, which are ultimately
connected. On the one hand, some authors see an erosion of trust and
trustworthiness (Barber, 1983; Coleman, 1990; Putnam, 1995; Cook, 2001).
On the other hand, there are authors who argue that there is an explosion
in the demand for trust (Giddens, 1994b; Misztal, 1996; Seligman, 1997;
Sztompka, 1999; Adler, 2001; Bijlsma and Koopmann, 2003; Bijlsma-

Frankema and Klein Woolthuis, 2005). While the first group fear that a given demand of trust can no longer be supplied ('the wells are drying up'), the second group claim that we require more trust because it has to be used in more and more areas of life ('the pumps cannot keep up'). Ultimately, the effect perceived by both groups is a lack of trust, but the suggested visions of future social life are diametrically opposed: in the pessimistic scenario people have to learn to live without trust, while in the optimistic scenario they have to learn to build trust at a faster rate and on a greater scale. Their common interest lies in understanding trust better so that it can be preserved, rebuilt and/or extended more effectively at a time when it becomes both more important and more problematic (Lane, 1998).

Another way of looking at the topicality of trust would be to question that there is any real substance to it. The discourses on trust that we find may be little more than a rhetoric that disguises some kind of helplessness or hypocrisy. The plea 'Trust me!' certainly sounds helpless and/or raises suspicion in most practical situations, irrespective of whether it is uttered by a loved one or the leader of a nation – and is therefore generally not to be recommended except as a very last resort, if only because it draws attention to a potential failure as mentioned above. However, as will become clear in the following chapters, trust always involves a certain kind of helplessness on the part of the one who trusts (*trustor*) as well as the one who is trusted (*trustee*) because trust necessarily implies one's own lack of certainty and the other's room for autonomy. This is why Niklas Luhmann (1979) points out that trust needs to be 'perceptive' (p. 68) and tactful, meaning that actors who are aware of the precariousness of trust seek to avoid causing the embarrassment that comes with the element of helplessness in trust. Annette Baier (1986) concludes from this that trust should not be put to the test lightly or unnecessarily. In other words, even though we may recognize the helpless rhetoric, pointing it out might jeopardize genuine trust.

A different kind of helplessness can also be observed in academic writings on trust whenever scholars introduce trust as a quick fix or catch-all solution without explaining exactly what they mean by trust. For instance, the burgeoning literature on the formation of international joint ventures and strategic alliances in the 1990s regularly included a paragraph or short section, just before the conclusion, stating more or less in passing that – besides all sorts of economic and technical matters that have to be considered carefully before entering a partnership – mutual trust has to be built, too (see also, more generally, Gambetta, 1988b). Incidentally, I became so frustrated with this that I spoke to John Child about it, decided to investigate the issue more thoroughly and ended up writing my doctoral dissertation about trust. (See also Child and Faulkner, 1998, who recognize this issue as well, devote a whole chapter to trust and thus represent the exception that proves the rule).

More generally, rational choice theory, game theory and other rationalist theories reviewed in Chapter 2 of this book come across as helpless whenever they are confronted with the fact that they explain trust away, explain anything but trust and/or introduce trust as an explanation for the 'non-rational' phenomena they cannot account for themselves (see James, 2002). Similarly, a certain helplessness could be attributed to the very common idea that trust needs to be built up in small steps over time and that the main concern is to simply initiate the process somehow – 'just do it' (see Chapter 4). However, this latter approach is not so much helpless in itself but acknowledges the helplessness implied in all trust as mentioned above. There is a huge difference between bringing in trust as a black-boxed, catch-all concept to fill major holes in a theory, on the one hand, and seriously investigating the complexity and ambiguity underlying the concept of trust, on the other.

Moreover, the rhetoric of trust may be hypocritical, disguising ulterior motives on the part of those who either invoke the socially desirable notion of trust or induce paralysing feelings of distrust in order to manipulate others in a way that serves their own interests. For instance, companies hope that customer trust will increase sales and that employee trust will increase productivity. Politicians hope to win votes by portraying themselves as trustworthy people (instead of laying out their intended policies in detail). And there are many examples of actors forcing their own 'trust' on others in order to compel them into a form of loyalty and responsibility that stretches beyond the ordinary (see Simmel, 1950, on secret societies; Fox, 1974, on spurious trust in the workplace; Eisenstadt and Roniger, 1984, on patron–client relationships; Gambetta, 1988c, on the Italian mafia).

Such rhetoric is evidence for the politics of trust, which is often recognized as a problem but rarely investigated in detail (see Bachmann et al., 2001). Can trust be requested, created or, at least, manipulated in such a way that people trust against their own will and interests? Later in this book, I will refer to several sources that doubt this. In order to make progress on this question and more generally on understanding the politics of trust, it will be important to distinguish between genuine trust and trust-like façades in discourse and behaviour. For this, we will need a good understanding of 'proper' trust to start with. Hypocritical or not, the rhetorical aspects of trust remind us that trust has consequences and affects interests.

Apart from helplessness and hypocrisy, trust is also a highly attractive and powerful concept because of its inherent 'connectability'. Trust is a concept that many people can relate to from personal experience; it is a topic that interests everybody in some way and regularly crops up in public discourse; it is also highly convenient in that many social science disciplines can connect to it because it is generally not defined in an overly technical or narrow way; it refers to basic but non-trivial problems of most forms of social interaction and association; and it also carries moral and emotional elements, making it a far from dispassionate issue. We can find preliminary evidence for this connectability thesis in the high level of interdisciplinarity of the contributions to edited volumes on trust (for example, Gambetta, 1988a; Kramer and Tyler, 1996; Lane and Bachmann, 1998; Cook, 2001; Bijlsma-Frankema and Klein Woolthuis, 2005), in the participant lists of conferences on trust and, not least, in the bibliographies of literature on trust (as in my own list of references at the end of this book).

By way of illustration, Niklas Luhmann is not exactly a social theorist whom most scholars would find easy to relate to in their own work, but his impressive little book on trust has inspired trust researchers across a broad range of disciplines and it is also highly interdisciplinary in itself (Luhmann, 1979). However, in the foreword to his seminal volume on trust and cooperation, Diego Gambetta (1988b) reminds us that interdisciplinarity is a challenge: 'the sense of discomfort and isolation that scholars in the social sciences sometimes feel in connection with the limitations of their subject ... does not imply that they are ready to embrace each other fraternally as soon as they are given the chance.'

Nevertheless, even Gambetta recognizes points of convergence, and trust may be topical because social scientists have (re)discovered it recently as a concept that captures common questions and enables researchers and practitioners from very many different traditions to talk to each other – mostly without hostility, in my experience. This is wonderful, but it also raises the suspicion that the topic of trust may be no more than a fashion or fad of the kind that is criticized, for example, in management research (see Abrahamson, 1991, 1996; Kieser, 1997). The words 'fashion' and 'fad' as such connote that a new idea is transient, insubstantive and restricted to a particular place and time. Especially when presented with a certain exaggerated enthusiasm, any new or newly revived idea is prone to be called a fad, but will subsequently have to either pass into extinction (traces of them remaining like 'embarrassing teenage photographs', Morris, 1998, p. 11) or be deemed valid knowledge (for instance when backed up by solid research, at least until better ideas are presented). At times, I have also had the feeling that the topic of trust has merely been a recurrent interlude between major waves of research on 'culture', 'knowledge', 'networks' and perhaps, recently, 'identity'. However, as many serious publications keep coming out, largely unaffected by the faddish pamphlets that are also on the market, I believe that the connectability of trust is a good thing. It may even connect the other 'waves' just mentioned.

This brings us, finally, from the crisis and rhetoric of trust to the concept of trust as such and to the core question explored in this book: what makes trust such a powerful concept? Before going into more detail in the next section, a first approximation to my answer is that I regard the inherent ambivalence of trust as the main feature that makes the concept so interesting and unusual. Trust has both highly uncomfortable and highly positive connotations. It reminds actors of the harm others might cause them in principle. Yet, at the same time, trust also implies that this vulnerability and uncertainty need not be problematic in practice.

Trust is ambivalent because it solves a basic problem of social relations *without* eliminating the problem. This ambivalence applies to the current topicality of trust, too: it expresses the ongoing possibility and necessity of a favourable state of expectation towards others in the face of a heightened awareness of vulnerability and uncertainty raised by negative experiences, ranging from everyday lies and deceit to terrorism and war, as well as by positive new possibilities, created through individual empowerment and global media of communication and interaction.

As will be emphasized in Chapter 5 in particular, in order to describe the typical experience of trust we often refer to the fact that actors trust *despite* their vulnerability and uncertainty, *although* they cannot be absolutely sure what will happen. They act *as if* the situation they face was unproblematic and, although they recognize their own limitations, they trust *nevertheless*. This ambivalence (expressed by words like 'despite', 'although', 'as if' and 'nevertheless') is not some quirky defect of an otherwise sound concept, but rather the powerful essence of the concept –

the particular trick of trust, as it were. I propose that this can be captured by the concept of suspension (the leap of faith, see Chapter 5 and Möllering, 2001).

1.2 KEY CONCEPTS AND CHALLENGES

Instead of proceeding straight to the main conclusions, which I propose to reach after I have reviewed a broad range of trust research that I group into three main perspectives over the following chapters, it is first of all necessary to introduce some key concepts that are required to circumscribe what the topic of trust entails.

As a starting point, Denise Rousseau and her colleagues (1998) offer a widely supported definition of trust as 'a psychological state comprising the intention to accept vulnerability based upon positive expectations of the intentions or behavior of another' (p. 395). From this we can already derive that trust is essentially the state of expectation of a trustor (see also Gambetta, 1988d; Bradach and Eccles, 1989; Sako, 1992; Mayer et al., 1995). It must not be confounded with the bases from which it is reached (antecedents), nor with the actions (enactment) resulting from trustful expectations (see Hardin, 2001). Manifestations of trust are any empirical incidents in which this state of expectation is reached, irrespective of whether the trustor is conscious of this or whether it is directly observable by others in any way.

The carrier of trust is the actor as an entity that can have expectations and in the broadest sense refer to them in action (see Bachmann, 1998). The trustor expects favourable intentions and actions on the part of the object of trust – another actor referred to as the trustee (see Baier, 1986; Gambetta, 1988d). Going beyond Rousseau et al.'s strictly psychological definition, not only individual persons but also collective or even non-human entities could be classified as trusting or trusted actors as long as it is possible to ascribe expectations and actions to them meaningfully (see, for example, Nooteboom, 2002). To what extent this is the case, for example, with reference to a social group, an organization, a political system, an animal or a god is a moot point, though. Avoiding this debate here, the main conceptual requirement is simply that we need to be able to identify trustors and trustees in order to be able to speak of trust.

The relevance of trust is due to the principal vulnerability and uncertainty of the trustor towards the trustee (see Luhmann, 1979; Bigley and

Pearce, 1998; Lane, 1998; Rousseau et al., 1998; Heimer, 2001). The trustee could harm the trustor, who cannot be absolutely sure whether this will happen or not, but his own action partly determines whether or not and, if so, to what extent the trustee can actually harm him (see Luhmann, 1979; Dasgupta, 1988; Gambetta, 1988d). The actions of the trustor and the trustee are therefore interdependent. This view implies that trust is a social phenomenon and does not cover the actors' vulnerability and uncertainty in matters not (primarily) attributable to the actions of others, for example self-inflicted accidents, technical failures or natural disasters (see also Lewis and Weigert, 1985; Luhmann, 1988; Craswell, 1993).

Moreover, for trust to be relevant, social vulnerability and uncertainty have to be irreducible, because the trustor's expectations about the other's actions are imperfect, reflecting not simply the cognitive limitations in processing information, but more crucially the agency of both trustor and trustee, who are autonomous in that their states of mind and actions are not fully determined, the result being that neither manifestations of trust nor the honouring of trust can ultimately be forced or guaranteed (see Gambetta, 1988d; Brenkert, 1998; Bachmann, 1998). Note that uncertainty is used here in the sense introduced by Frank Knight ([1921] 1971), who distinguished between *risk* as randomness, on the one hand, where the probabilities of alternative outcomes can be assigned, and *uncertainty*, on the other hand, where neither the alternatives nor the probabilities are known by the actor. Hence, trust is indeed 'risky' (Luhmann, 1979, p. 24) in a general sense of the word, but it is irreducible to calculation and therefore more than simply a probabilistic investment decision under risk (see Chapter 2). Instead, trust would fall into the category of Knightian uncertainty.

It is also important to note how exactly vulnerability is understood in the context of trust. Referring back to the basic ambivalence noted earlier, vulnerability is a precondition for trust because the trustor could be harmed in principle, but when the trustor reaches a state of trust it means that the trustor no longer expects to be harmed. The definition of trust by Rousseau et al. (see above) is sometimes misunderstood in this respect, as is the following definition by Roger Mayer and his colleagues (1995), who propose that trust is 'the willingness of a party to be vulnerable to the action of another party based on an expectation that the other party will perform a particular action important to the trustor, irrespective of the ability to monitor or control that other party' (p. 712). The 'intention to accept vulnerability' (Rousseau et al., 1998) and the 'willingness to be vulnerable' (Mayer et al., 1995) should *not* to be understood as 'willing-ness to be hurt' (indicating a somewhat masochistic desire), but as highly optimistic expectations that vulnerability is not a problem and no harm will be done. Trust differs in this very crucial point from other social pro-cesses that are about avoiding or eliminating vulnerability, or resigning to it, rather than positively accepting it.

Moreover, it is also important to recognize that the trustor and the trustee are embedded in a social context which influences how exactly they can define themselves as actors and enact their agency (see Meyer and Jepperson, 2000): through networks of social relationships (see Gra-novetter, 1985; Burt, 1993) and through institutionalized rules (Berger and Luckmann, 1966; Giddens, 1984; Powell and DiMaggio, 1991). It follows that trust is practically never a purely dyadic phenomenon be-tween two isolated actors; there is usually always a context and a history, and there are also other actors that matter (see Chapters 3 and 4).

In sum, and put differently, without actors, expectations, vulnerability, uncertainty, agency and social embeddedness, the problem of trust does not arise and, if this were the case, the conceptualization of trust would be pretty meaningless or superfluous. The main challenge in trust research lies in devising a rigorous theoretical framework for understanding trust, drawing on existing theoretical perspectives and traditions. More specifi-cally, it is a challenge to use theory in such a way that trust is not ex-plained away, because otherwise there is a temptation to treat trust as just another form of expectation and/or action that fits established rational choice models (see Chapter 2), reproduces well-known institutionalized patterns (see Chapter 3) or emerges in a self-reinforcing process (see Chapter 4). Instead, the conceptualization of trust offers an opportunity to push the limits of rational, institutional and processual theories. This im-plies, of course, that there is some unique element in the concept of trust that existing theories are not able to capture. Thus, the biggest challenge is to try and identify this element (see Chapter 5). It will then be neces-sary to show that a theoretical framework that includes such an element also has implications for empirical research (see Chapters 6 and 7) and contributes to broader research agendas (see Chapter 8). As indicated, these challenges are reflected in the composition of this book, which I present next.

1.3 OVERVIEW OF THE BOOK

The book is structured as follows. Following this introduction, Chapter 2 on 'Trust and Reason' reviews the vast literature that frames trust as being essentially based on reason. Specifically, I look at the work of James Coleman, Jon Elster, Russell Hardin and Piotr Sztompka as indicative examples of an extended rational choice approach to trust. I then move on to present trust-relevant aspects in economic theories in particular transaction cost economics, principal–agent theory, game theory and signalling theory. I also discuss the 'rationality of emotion' (de Sousa, 1987) and the efforts of many researchers to identify indicators of trustworthiness. In the course of the chapter, I note repeatedly that rationalist explanations of trust run into paradoxes. I conclude that there may be an element of reason in all trust, but that trust as such would not be required if it could be explained solely and wholly by reason.

Following on from this, Chapter 3 on 'Trust and Routine' takes a radically different approach by building on that part of the trust literature which points out the taken-for-granted nature of trust in many practical situations. Often, trusting and being trustful appear to resemble a routine that people follow habitually, rather than a conscious choice. This can be conceptualized using theories such as sociological phenomenology, ethnomethodology and, first and foremost, neoinstitutionalist sociology. In this chapter, I present Alfred Schütz's concept of the natural attitude and Harold Garfinkel's work on constitutive expectancies and normalizing. Then I progress via Lynne Zucker to neoinstitutionalist sociology and the idea that trust may be a form of institutional isomorphism. It follows that when institutions serve as a source of trust between actors those institutions also become objects of trust, which raises a number of further issues. Overall, this neoinstitutionalist approach to trust highlights the important influence institutions have on trust, but it does not deny agency either (which would eliminate the relevance of trust). Hence, a more processual perspective suggests itself.

This is taken up in Chapter 4 on 'Trust and Reflexivity'. Searching further for perspectives that enhance our understanding of trust, I discuss in this chapter a number of diverse ideas about trust, whose common thread is that they see trust as a reflexive process that depends on ongoing interactions between actors. Such interactions may be started relatively blindly or accidentally, but then there is a possibility that they become self-reinforcing. Trust typically undergoes gradual growth and transformations in a process of reflexive familiarization and structuration. I argue that actors play an active role in this, which is expressed most strongly in Anthony Giddens' concept of 'active trust'. This means, however, that actors are assumed to 'just do it' and initiate potentially harmful trust-building processes somehow. The process view as such cannot explain how actors are able to achieve this.

Chapter 5 is entitled 'The Leap of Faith'. It starts by acknowledging that all three perspectives introduced in the preceding chapters highlight important aspects of trust. I summarize the previous discussion and explain in detail what is meant by trust as a phenomenon that manifests itself *between* reason, routine and reflexivity. It means that all three elements are needed, but neither can explain trust alone, and all three need to be complemented by a conceptualization of the leap of faith required for all trust – the 'as-if' element which Georg Simmel drew attention to and which I prefer to call suspension. This chapter offers various ways of making sense of suspension: trust as fiction, trust a bracketing out and trust as the will to believe. I also present a number of empirical studies that have applied the notion of the leap of faith and represent evidence for its practical relevance. This chapter takes the first steps in a new direction of trust research, placing the suspension of uncertainty and vulnerability at the heart of the concept of trust.

Chapter 6 on 'Studying Trust' takes a closer look at how trust has been studied empirically and what we can infer from different perspectives on trust for studying the phenomenon in the future. This is done on the basis of six heuristics for distinguishing between the vast number of highly diverse empirical studies of trust that have been undertaken to date. The main heuristic is the distinction between quantitative, qualitative and comparative studies and these are discussed in detail. The chapter closes with a call for interpretative approaches that adopt a process perspective, obtain a rich picture of actual trust experiences, understand the embeddedness of the relationships under investigation and take into account the reflexivity not only in trust development as such but also in the research interaction.

The fact that it is possible to get close to the ideal presented in the preceding chapter is demonstrated in Chapter 7 on 'Experiencing Trust'. Here I present three qualitative cases of interorganizational relationships in the British printing industry. The cases are instructive in the way they reveal the concurrent simplicity, complexity and ambivalence of experienced trust. And they allow critical reflection on the limits of accessing trust in empirical research. The chapter gives empirical meaning to the abstract conceptualizations of the earlier chapters and therefore furthers our understanding of the concept of trust in this way, too.

In the final chapter (Chapter 8, 'Positive Expectations') I summarize the key insights from this book once again and suggest how my approach can enhance the relevance of trust research and its contributions to broader research agendas. In particular, I argue that trust research is ultimately part of the general investigation into the question of how actors can form positive expectations of others. Trust is only one answer to this question and we need to be able to say how it relates to other answers such as 'control'. In this spirit, I suggest avenues for further research and conclude, optimistically, that trust is indeed a truly powerful concept in understanding past, present and future developments at different levels within and between our economies and societies.

It may be helpful to know that I have written the book with two kinds of readership in mind. First, I hope that the book can serve as a general introduction for advanced students and scholars in the social sciences, especially in economics, sociology, psychology and management studies. This means that I cover a fairly wide range of literature, try to include all the 'classics', realizing, though, that I cannot mention everything that would be worth mentioning. Many accounts also have to be highly simplified, to say the least. I am also aware that, due to my own disciplinary background, the ground that I cover is biased towards sociological organization theory and empirical applications from business studies.

Second, for more experienced researchers, I want to provide a challenging and provocative critique of the field and a new approach to understanding trust. This is why I do not hide my own opinion on previous conceptualizations of trust and I go into more detail in those more unusual areas where I personally find new, original ideas that are ignored or underexplored in the existing literature. Overall, this is still a relatively short book and I definitely do not claim that my argument is exhaustive. I am confident, though, that my main message is substantiated enough to give plenty of food for thought: the leap of faith is at the heart of the concept of trust, but present theories of trust fail to grasp it so far. Indeed, I expect that those who read this book with a more practical rather than theoretical interest will be able to relate to the ideas presented here relatively easily by reference to their own daily experiences of trust, whereas theorists tend to think in abstract frameworks which are not so easy to challenge and revise.

2

TRUST AND REASON

2.1 THE RATIONALIST PARADIGM

'A natural and common account of trust is that certain people are trustworthy and can therefore be trusted' (Hardin, 2001, p. 18). This simple observation by Russell Hardin expresses three important ideas. First, trust is selective: we can only trust certain people, not everybody. Second, trust is reasonable: we look for good reasons and, in particular, we assess the other's trustworthiness before we trust. Third, trust is decisive: we trust by taking a step in one direction, not the other, thereby reaching a certain state of expectation, performing corresponding actions, if required, and facing consequences. Altogether, in this approach, trust represents a choice made 'within reason' (Hollis, 1998).

While this may truly be a natural and common account of trust in many of our everyday experiences, it also circumscribes the paradigm for the current mainstream of trust research. Against the background assumption of methodological individualism and self-interested utility maximization, trust (as the dependent variable) is seen as a rational or, at least, reasonable choice based on the trustor's perception of the trustee's trustworthiness (as the independent variable). Sometimes acknowledging the potential influence of contextual factors such as predispositions and embeddedness, models of trust express trust primarily and essentially as a function of perceived trustworthiness, predicting a positive sign: the more trustworthy others appear to us, the more likely we are to trust them at all, the stronger our trust will be and the more we will be prepared to enact this trust.

Once this general hypothesis is established, researchers in this tradition are interested in how trustors are able to recognize trustworthiness in potential trustees: what makes a trustee trustworthy in the eyes of a particular trustor? Overall, if the trustee is more likely to honour than to exploit trust, this makes him trustworthy in the eyes of the trustor, who also needs to be aware of the gains and losses at stake. This emphasis on probability is expressed by Diego Gambetta, who concludes that 'there is a degree of convergence on the definition of trust' which turns on the idea of subjective probability: 'When we say we trust someone or that someone is trustworthy, we implicitly mean that the probability that he will perform an action that is beneficial or at least not detrimental to us is high enough for us to consider engaging in some form of cooperation with him' (Gambetta, 1988d, p. 217).

One line of research looks at the trustee's specific incentives to honour or exploit trust in a given situation. Another line of research identifies more general and less situation-specific indicators of trustworthiness. These mostly concern the character that the trustor attributes to the trustee. In principle, the two lines should be connected because, whenever the choice of trust needs to be made, incentives and character need to be considered together.

To give just two brief examples, which will be taken up again in more detailed analyses later, much research aiming to predict trust is often based on models of the trustor's net expected values, as for example in the work of Robert Axelrod and James Coleman. This approach would be more common in economics and sociology. Research identifying indicators of perceived trustworthiness which, together, predict trust can be found a lot in psychology and management studies. Probably the most famous and certainly one of the most cited models of trust has been proposed by Roger Mayer, James Davis and David Schoorman (1995). Integrating much of the previous literature, they propose: 'Trust for a trustee will be a function of the trustee's perceived ability, benevolence, and integrity and of the trustor's propensity to trust' (p. 720). Although the authors do not emphasize this point, they naturally assume that it is reasonable to trust a trustee who is competent, means well and adheres to acceptable principles. All such catalogues of trustworthiness indicators presume that they are applied more or less consciously by intendedly rational trustors in choosing whether to trust or not.

In this relatively long chapter, I will present in detail the fundamental ideas underlying the view that trust is a matter of reason. First, fundamental work in the more general rational choice tradition of the social sciences offers a good starting point for outlining the basic problems and also the key challenges in the relationship between trust and reason. This will be reinforced by the second section, in which I discuss several economic theories of trust that certainly advance our understanding but run into even more difficult paradoxes. Third, perhaps somewhat provocatively, I offer some ideas on the rationality of emotions in the context of trust. At the end of the chapter, I take a closer look at indicators of trustworthiness in order to summarize what it means to say that trust is reasonable and to prepare the ground for the other perspectives on trust that follow.

2.2 TRUST IN RATIONAL CHOICE PERSPECTIVES

Certainly the most prominent and typical, albeit not the first, best or definitive conceptualization of trust in the rational choice tradition has been offered by James Coleman (see also Misztal, 1996, pp. 77–88). Drawing on earlier work in which he already expressed that his interest in trust is 'part of a larger theory of social action' (Coleman, 1982, p. 281), he uses the problem of trust to illustrate and elaborate his social theory (Coleman, 1990), seeing trust as a typical example of transitions between micro-level individual action and macro-level states of the system.

At the micro level of purposive actors, Coleman regards the issue of trust as the subclass of decisions under risk, in which the risk taken by one actor depends on the future actions of another. Thus, the involvement of at least two purposive actors – a trustor A and a trustee B – and a time lag are preconditions for the problem of trust to arise. Moreover, there has to be a potential gain $G > 0$ for the trustor, if he places trust and it is honoured by the trustee, but also a potential loss $L > 0$ for the trustor, if trust is placed but the trustee is not trustworthy. G and L have to be seen in comparison to the option of not placing trust, which presumably does not change the trustor's utility. This precondition matches Daniel Kahneman and Amos Tversky's (1979) prospect theory, where outcomes are expected as positive or negative deviations from a neutral reference, which is assigned a value of zero.

Two further preconditions require that the trustee gains from the placement of trust by the trustor and that the trusting action as the 'unilateral transfer of control over resources or actions or events' (Coleman, 1982, p. 283) is voluntary in so far as neither the trustor A is strictly forced to place trust

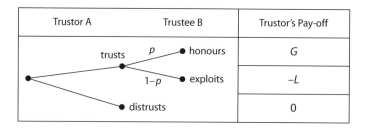

Figure 2.1 The Trustor's Bet

nor the trustee B is obliged to honour that trust. The placement and honouring of trust is presented as a matter of rational choice for both the
trustee and the trustor. Coleman is interested in how they make the choice
and, first and foremost, in the considerations involved in A's decision
which has to come first in sequence and is therefore the primary problem
in practice.

The central and oft-cited contention is that the trustor's decision is
essentially like placing a bet: 'If the *chance of winning*, relative to the
chance of losing, is greater than the *amount that would be lost* (if he loses)
relative to the *amount that would be won* (if he wins), then by placing the
bet he has an expected gain; and if he is rational, he should place it'
(Coleman, 1990, p. 99, emphasis in original). Hence, the trustor needs to
know the potential gain G, the potential loss L and an estimate of the
probability p $(0 < p < 1)$ that the trustee will be trustworthy (Figure 2.1).

A purposive actor will place trust if $p/(1-p) > L/G$. This inequality
represents a simple transformation of a comparison of Bayesian expected
values, where the potential loss or gain is multiplied by the corresponding
probability of occurrence and the net expected value $E = pG - (1-p)L$.
Rational actors will only place trust if E is positive (Coleman, 1990,
p. 747). This notion of expressing a potential trustee's trustworthiness as
perceived by a potential trustor in terms of a probability which effectively
determines whether or not trust is placed represents the principal heuristic
and therefore the core of this paradigm: a trustor will rationally trust a
trustee if he perceives the probability of the trustee's trustworthiness to be
high enough to yield a net expected gain.

Coleman recognizes that from this plausible paradigm follows a far
from trivial question: how does the trustor gain the required information
and estimates? He notes that in various circumstances p, L and G are

known to different extents and, further, that often p is the least well known of them. A purposive actor will therefore try to obtain more information as long as the effort of searching for further information is rational: 'The search should continue so long as the cost of an additional increment of information is less than the benefit it is expected to bring' (p. 104). Here, he conveniently ignores the economic paradox of information famously identified by George Stigler (1961), if not, for that matter, already by Plato: in order to assess the value of information and thus determine what cost a rational actor should incur for obtaining it, the actor would have to already know the information. A first fundamental issue in the rational choice conception of trust is thus already evident. I will emphasize in later chapters that the essence of trust is how to bracket the unknowable, meaning in rational choice terms the lack of conclusive information on p, G and L.

Further, Coleman argues that in order to obtain a good estimate of B's trustworthiness p the trustor A must seek to understand B's motives and, in the words of Partha Dasgupta (1988), 'look at the world from his perspective' (p. 51). When estimating p, the trustor has to consider, for example, whether B has a longer-term interest in the relationship. Another very important question is whether the trust is mutual, in which case it is generally rational for trustors to assume higher p values. The problem remains, though, that the trustor's rational bet revolves around a value of p which may not be – and in most practically relevant cases will not be – rationally attainable.

Even if this problem cannot easily be resolved, the framework can be extended and refined. For example, the trustee B also needs to be seen in relation to potential trustors other than the one who has placed trust in him in a particular instance (Coleman, 1990). If the result of breaking trustor A1's trust might be that certain other trustors A2, A3 etc. withdraw or withhold their trust in the future, then B should forego the benefits of breaking A1's trust, presuming that B's future benefits of being trusted by A2, A3 etc. are larger. This mechanism only works if there is a relatively close community of trustors A1, A2, A3 etc. who maintain B's reputation. Thus when a trustor A1 estimates p, he needs to take into account B's reputation, B's interest in having a good reputation in a relevant community and, finally, the effectiveness of communication between trustors in that community (see also Dasgupta, 1988).

Moreover, other trustors in the role of intermediaries feature strongly in Coleman's (1990) further ideas about the trustor's choice. Intermediaries may come into the relationship between A and B as guarantor, adviser or entrepreneur. In 'chains of trust' the intermediary may take over the whole risk, provide a recommendation or pool the resources of a number of trustors and entrust them to various trustees. In all cases, trust becomes possible where it would not have been in a simple, direct relationship between A and B. Furthermore, third-party obligations could encourage A to trust B. Intermediary and third-party mechanisms, however, also increase the complexity of the trust decision because the trustor no longer needs to estimate just one p value for the decision to trust one trustee, but multiple p values for the intermediaries, too. And the core underlying logic remains a calculation of net expected values.

Coleman describes how the mechanisms identified above operate equally in 'large systems involving trust'. Thereby he aims to address the theoretical requirement of explaining the micro-to-macro transition of trust. He shows that the mechanisms work more effectively the larger the number of actors involved, but that they can also lead to expansions or contractions of trust within the system. One consequence of this is that the system level could be quite misleading for a trustor when estimating p because certain dynamics sometimes inflate or deflate the perceived trustworthiness of some trustees.

Coleman also discusses the role of institutions and social norms, but in the rational choice framework – as opposed to, for example, neoinstitutionalist theories – these are part of the actor's purposive choices and therefore part of the problem. As Barbara Misztal (1996, p. 80) comments, in Coleman's view 'self-interest exploits social norms to punish untrustworthiness'. Norms do not stand outside of utility considerations. Equally, Christel Lane and Reinhard Bachmann (1996) point out: 'Social institutions matter in the Rational Choice perspective because and in so far as they are parameters in social actors' calculations of whether or not to trust' (p. 370). Overall, Coleman's rational choice approach to trust is paradigmatic for a stream of trust research that assumes purposive actors for whom trust is a decision based primarily on an estimate of the probability that the trustee will honour the trust placed in him. The problems associated with this approach will help us to formulate requirements for alternative approaches later. Next, however, it is worth looking at other contributions in the rational choice tradition that have already refined and extended it.

Jon Elster's work developed in parallel to James Coleman's but not without exchanges of ideas and, at times, even in the same place (University of Chicago). Elster's project, stretching across numerous publications, has been to explore the limits of rationality from within the rational choice paradigm, pointing out that 'the first task of rational-choice theory must be to circumscribe its own limits' (Elster, 1989a, p. 85). Elster's work does not feature a specific and detailed concept of trust, but I would follow Misztal (1996) in that an insightful framework can be inferred from the few remarks he makes on trust and in particular on the analogy between trust and credibility (Elster, 1989a).

Accordingly, in one respect trust is firmly a matter of self-interest and rational choice by actors given the foreseeable outcomes of alternative courses of action. Elster argues, however, that even when both the trustor and the trustee know that the pay-off structure indicates that the trustee should rationally break the trust if it is placed by the trustor, there are ways of inducing the purposive trustor to place trust anyway and to make the trustee trustworthy. One possibility, also recognized by Coleman, is to invoke the long-term interest of the trustee in trust being placed in him again in the future. Another strategy suggested by Elster (1989a) is that the trustee could make 'credible promises', precommitments which transform his pay-offs in such a way that breaking the trust would no longer be rational. A third possibility of interest when placing trust is whether the actors concerned actually conform to the behavioural assumptions of rational choice theory, namely that they are rational, self-interested utility maximizers. Elster (1984) explicitly recognizes that actors may (sometimes) be irrational or deliberately seek to act in a way that enhances the utility of others. By inference, a trustor who sees that the trustee is irrational or altruistic may trust him on that basis. Similarly, the trustor himself may irrationally or altruistically place trust. Elster emphasizes that these possibilities are realistic, but that it is unrealistic (and methodologically ineffective) to assume altruism and irrationality as the dominant features of social action.

Finally, a useful insight from Elster's work on rationality is that he recognizes the limits of instrumentality for certain conditions of social actions to arise, notably friendship, love and respect, which are essentially a by-product of rational interaction over time and themselves cannot be willed, because this would destroy them: 'Altruism, trust and solidarity are genuine phenomena that cannot be dissolved into ultra-subtle forms of self-interest' (Elster, 1984, p. 146).

His realization that the rational choice paradigm cannot capture all aspects of social action leads him to consider social norms as a source of motivation, including the possibility that trust springs from a code of honour or norms of reciprocity and cooperation (Elster, 1989a). He notes that social norms usually imply sanctions which make them effective, but argues that this does not make the adherence to norms and their existence reducible to rational interest. Norms are ultimately 'autonomous' and 'real', not merely instruments of self-interested utility maximizers. I will return to this point in Chapter 3.

Elster therefore suggests that trust may be placed and honoured even when the pay-offs do not suggest so, if the motivation to follow a norm of trust overrides the rationality and self-interest of the actors involved. His concept of trust therefore lies partly outside of the rational choice perspective and, overall, it can be summarized as follows: trust is predominantly a rational choice, given alternative courses of action and their prospective outcomes for the trustor and trustee; but the placement and honouring of trust may also be motivated beyond the limits of rationality, in particular when social norms are followed.

Unlike Coleman, Elster rejects a Bayesian probabilistic solution to these complications, because in line with Amos Tversky and Daniel Kahneman (1981) he has little faith in the human capacity to apply stochastic methods in ordinary decision-making. Yet, although he recognizes many limitations, he still believes that 'rational-choice theory will probably remain privileged, by virtue of the simplicity and power of the maximising assumption' (Elster, 1989b, p. 35).

In 1992–93, the German social science periodical *Analyse & Kritik* (Analysis & Criticism) devoted two issues to a symposium on Coleman (1990). The first one featured an influential article by Russell Hardin, which was soon reprinted in *Politics & Society*. Hardin was also a professorial colleague of Coleman and Elster at the University of Chicago, where he held academic positions from 1979 to 1993. During this time he developed his original ideas on trust (Hardin 1991, 1993), on which even his most recent contributions to the trust literature are still largely based (see Hardin 2001, 2002). Hardin (1993) picks up the discussion on trust where Coleman left off by stating that a 'widely held view is that trust and distrust are essentially rational' and that a rational choice theory of trust needs to address two central aspects: 'incentives of the trusted to fulfil trust and knowledge to allow the truster to trust' (p. 505). The first aspect gives rise to Hardin's concept of trust as encapsulated interest while the second aspect requires what he calls a street-level epistemology of the trustor's knowledge of trustworthiness.

Hardin identifies as a basic precondition for any concept of (rational) trust to make sense, first of all, that trust is a three-part relationship: A trusts B to do X. In this respect – but not in many others – he follows Annette Baier (1986). Hardin argues repeatedly that a self-interested trustor always needs to consider whom he is supposed to trust and what this trustee is to be trusted with: it is rarely rational for A to trust B in all respects and situations or even that A simply trusts everybody with everything. Secondly, trust is not a behavioural but a cognitive category: 'Trust is not an action' (Hardin, 2001, p. 17) and 'it is not trusting that is risky, *it is acting on trust that is risky*' (p. 10, emphasis in the original). Thirdly, if trust is a kind of knowledge by the trustor about the trustworthiness of a trustee, then the trustor's trust and the trustee's trustworthiness must not be confused or conflated, although trustworthiness commonly begets trust. When an actor entrusts then the trustee must have a genuine choice, too, between honouring and breaking the trust. The resultant uncertainty and vulnerability on the trustor's part is a defining precondition for the concept of trust to be an issue at all. Note that, although purposive actors intend to be rational, 'we are in the murky in-between land that is neither deterministic nor fully indeterminate' (p. 5).

The idea of trust as encapsulated interest is first developed in Hardin (1991). He argues, quite in line with Coleman, that a trustor A trusts a trustee B if he believes that it is in B's interest to be trustworthy to A regarding a relevant matter X. By encapsulated interest he means that trustor A can see that trustee B knows that he will only be able to maximize his own interest if he takes A's interests into account: 'I trust you because your interest encapsulates mine, which is to say that you have an interest in fulfilling my trust' (Hardin, 2002, p. 3). By breaking the trust and thus damaging A's interests, B would harm himself.

Hardin (1991) examines how encapsulated interests come about and finds that they are mainly sustained by ongoing beneficial relationships or, more precisely, that actors will not break trust in a relationship and harm the other party if this jeopardizes the relationship and thus the longer-term benefits attached to it. This can be reinforced if the encapsulation of interests and the resultant trust are mutual (Hardin, 2002). Hardin refutes the so-called 'backward-induction argument' (Luce and Raiffa, 1957), which entails that an actor who should rationally be untrustworthy at the end of a relationship – when his interest no longer encapsulates that of his partner – cannot logically be assumed to be trustworthy at the beginning of a relationship (see below). He thinks that the backward-induction argument is flawed because actors may strategically act on 'as-if trust' (Hardin, 1993). This means that they act on trust although they do not trust yet, thereby setting in motion an encapsulation of interests that makes the other actor trustworthy. Actors may also demonstrate their trustworthiness strategically through credible commitments. Such strategies are designed to circumvent the detrimental effects of strict rationality as well as the problem that trust cannot be willed – and thus they may fail, but are rationally worth taking the chance (Hardin, 1991, 1993). I will discuss this point in detail in Chapter 4.

The argument typical of rational choice approaches – that trust springs from perceived trustworthiness p in the eyes of the trustor – is strongly reinforced by Hardin's (1993) concept of the 'street-level epistemology' of trust. Accordingly, a primary concern needs to be how trustors acquire and process the knowledge that they have about a potential trustee's understanding that his own interests in a certain matter depend on the trustor's interests. Hardin discusses two main epistemological routes for the street-level trustor, one applicable to 'thick relationships' (p. 510) and the other one applicable to more casual relationships or encounters where an 'instinctive Bayesianism' (p. 507) lets the actor learn to trust. Kramer's (1996) notion of the 'intuitive auditor' expresses a similar idea.

In sum, Hardin's concept of trust entails that trust is rationally accounted for when the trustor perceives that the trustee realizes that his own interest encapsulates the interest of the trustor, who learns to trust by drawing on his relevant past experience with the trustee, or with relevant other people, and by making and continuously updating an estimate for the trustee's trustworthiness. All in all, Hardin's contribution can be seen as a more precise and elaborate version of Coleman's approach, which explains trust primarily by the trustor's perception of the trustee's awareness of encapsulated interest. Increasingly, though, Hardin, like Elster, addresses the limits of rationality and investigates, for example, theoretical problems of indeterminacy in social interaction (Hardin, 2003). Trust, I surmise, relates to practical problems of indeterminacy.

Finally, Piotr Sztompka presents a sociological theory of trust which is eclectic but, at heart, rooted in the rational choice tradition. Like Coleman, but claiming that the metaphor of the bet occurred to him independently, Sztompka (1999) defines trust as 'a bet about the future contingent actions of others' (p. 25). Actors are seen as exerting choice in the commitments they make and in the probability and scale of risks they take. At the end of complex estimates and calculations, it is possible to evaluate how prudent or imprudent the placing of trust is, although in all rational choice concepts of trust, including Sztompka's, there is a risk involved in acting on trust due to the fact that the trustee must have a choice and might exploit the trust.

Sztompka discusses varieties of trust. He makes a useful distinction between primary and secondary targets of trust, the former being other actors whose contingent actions trust relates to and the latter being actors who may provide testimonies of the primary targets' trustworthiness. Another distinction is according to the expectations involved in the act of trusting. Instrumental trust essentially concerns the trustee's competence and past performance. This is the classic rational choice variant of trust, but, similar to Elster, Sztompka also recognizes two other varieties: axiological trust relates to the trustee's predisposition to follow normative rules, and fiduciary trust is a belief in the other's honouring of obligations irrespective of self-interests. At any rate, though, trustors will be intendedly rational and aim to reduce the risk of misplaced trust by taking the other's predispositions and motivations into account.

Hence, the decision to trust rests, above all, on an evaluation of the relationship with potential trustees (or a network of them). Thus Sztompka maps out the foundations of trust. Like Hardin, he is mainly interested in the relational trust dimension, meaning the calculative processing of available information about potential trustees. Where possible, estimates of trustworthiness are continuous, drawing on the 'meta-cue' for trust: the assumption of consistent trustworthiness (p. 97). Sztompka recognizes the trustor's 'trusting impulse' and the 'trust culture' in a society as foundations of trust which may be 'significant' or 'powerful' but are seen as only 'skewing' and 'supplementing' rational calculation. They do not supersede self-interested rationality. According to Sztompka, trust is a bet about the future contingent actions of others, which is placed rationally by a trustor whose complex reflections and calculations on the trustee's trustworthiness inform his decision to make a prudent, but still risky, commitment in a process that is also mediated by personal and cultural predispositions. In contrast to Elster and Hardin, who recognize limitations but favour the rational choice paradigm after all, Sztompka seeks to distance himself from orthodox rational choice theory, but his modified version remains somewhat unclear as to the status of the personal and cultural dimensions as constraints outside of rationality.

The rational choice perspectives on trust reviewed above are indicative of a fundamental paradigm as well as some variations therein and extensions to it. The paradigm explains trust as a rational result of a self-interested actor's perceptions of another actor's trustworthiness. Those perceptions are unanimously seen as imperfect estimates of (a probability of) trustworthiness, which makes acting on trust risky for the actor. Variations within this paradigm concern questions such as what kind of information the actor needs to consider, whether trust is a cognitive or behavioural category and how serious the conceptual limitations of the paradigm are. The last point gives rise to certain conceptual extensions: while irrationality or non-rationality are recognized as a possibility by all proponents, only some of them attempt to bring this into the model using constructs such as norms, culture and predisposition.

Rational choice theory is a social theory perspective based on an economic logic (Becker, 1976). In trust research, it is sometimes hard to tell when the line between rational choice and economics is crossed. It is fair to say, though, that rational choice conceptualizations of trust have provided an underpinning for trust research in economics where, apparently, models are more important than concepts. The next section reviews how trust has been addressed in economic theory-oriented research. Broadly speaking, this work turns trust from reasonable to calculative action, leading to useful new insights but amplifying the inherent paradoxes in understanding trust as being rational or primarily based on reason.

2.3 TRUST IN ECONOMIC THEORIES

It is striking that the common conceptual starting point for research on trust in economics is first and foremost a wariness, if not paranoia, of opportunism. To be sure, many studies are aimed at showing the positive effects of trust, but the underlying models are conservative in the sense that they emphasize the pervasiveness of opportunism, the risk of exploitation and the costs of safeguards against the detrimental actions of others. The focus is on averting negative outcomes (Lindenberg, 2000). By comparison, genuinely positive outcomes such as more effective communication or coordination are rarely at the heart of economic theories of trust. The key idea remains that trust is reasonable when the trustee is trustworthy, which in this context simply means unlikely to act opportunistically. Note that self-interest seeking as such, being the norm and expected of all, does not necessarily make a trustee untrustworthy. Rather, particular pay-off constellations determine who is 'trustworthy' from whose point of view in a given situation. However, sometimes trustworthiness also enters into economic models as a variable representing the opposite of self-interest seeking, thus effectively questioning or, at least, relaxing some basic assumptions underlying economic models.

Jeffrey Bradach and Robert Eccles (1989), for example, define trust as 'a type of expectation that alleviates the fear that one's exchange partner will act opportunistically' (p. 104). In other words, a trustworthy actor will not take advantage of arising opportunities and changing conditions (Ring and Van de Ven, 1992; Barney and Hansen, 1994; Nooteboom, 2002). The fact that an actor may gain an advantage without the other one even becoming aware of it is, of course, a large part of the uncertainty that remains after a trustor has estimated p and acted on it (see above). However, it is entirely rational – within the rationalist paradigm – for a trustee to exploit this uncertainty and be opportunistic.

Oliver Williamson (1985) adopts this behavioural assumption of opportunism and famously describes it as 'self-interest seeking with guile' (p. 47), pointing out that the utility maximizer is 'a more devious creature than the usual self-interest seeking assumption reveals' (Williamson, 1975, p. 255). Strictly, this should mean that no actor can ever be assumed to be trustworthy, as Peter Smith Ring (1997) and others have noted critically. Actor A may perceive that B's interest encapsulates his own, but he cannot be absolutely sure about it, whilst he can be sure that if it did not, B would exploit his trust guilefully.

Williamson (1985) recognizes two weaker forms of self-interest orientation: simple self-interest seeking (without guile) and obedience (without real interests), which, however, he deems unsuitable assumptions for an economic theory. Elsewhere he states: 'It is not necessary that all agents be regarded as opportunistic in identical degree. It suffices that those who are less opportunistic than others are difficult to ascertain ex ante and that, even among the less opportunistic, most have their price' (Williamson, 1979, p. 234).

Williamson (1993) criticizes Coleman's (1990) concept of trust, arguing that the trustor in this framework places himself at the risk of the trustee on the basis of a Bayesian risk and benefit calculation and not on some non-calculative basis. Hence, to speak of 'trust' actually obfuscates the true mechanism at work: 'calculativeness'. Richard Craswell (1993) points out, though, that Williamson preaches to the converted as Coleman and other proponents of the rational choice approach use the label 'trust' to refer to situations that constitute a subclass of those involving risk.

Thus, economists and rational choice theorists appear to fundamentally agree on calculativeness as the main mechanism in explaining behaviour. When trust is supposed to have a non-calculative meaning, it applies only to close personal relationships – and even in these it is usually hard to abstain from calculativeness. Thus Williamson (1993) hopes 'trust will hereafter be reserved for noncalculative personal relations' (p. 484). Far-sighted opportunism is a privileged behavioural assumption for economic theory. The issue of trust is explained away.

Despite this very clear positioning on the conceptual use of 'trust' in Williamson (1993; and again in Williamson, 1996), he has not managed to keep scholars from bringing trust into transaction cost economics, the economic theory of institutions attributed in its origins to Ronald Coase (1937) and John Commons (1934) and most prominently developed by Williamson himself since the 1970s. The central argument of transaction cost economics is that economic activities will take the form of governance that minimizes the costs of planning, adapting and monitoring transactions.

According to Williamson (1985) transaction costs occur both in advance of the transaction from drafting, negotiating and safeguarding agreements and after the transaction from having to deal with maladaptations and misalignments, running governance structures and bonding. Actors will choose the form of governance that best economizes on these costs, assuming that the production costs of the items to be transferred are given. Note that Williamson's version of transaction cost economics implies managerial choice (Chiles and McMackin, 1996) and it therefore adopts methodological individualism in contrast to the evolutionary approaches of new institutional economics (see Nelson and Winter, 1982; Hill, 1990). Market, hierarchy and hybrid represent the discrete structural alternatives available for organizing transactions, and transaction costs determine which form of governance is used (Williamson, 1991).

Transaction costs are the result of certain behavioural assumptions: *bounded rationality* entails that the context in which transactions take place is characterized by a higher or lower degree of *uncertainty* which the actor wishes to minimize (Williamson, 1975). The assumption of self-interest is particularly strong in Williamson's framework, presuming guile and referred to as *opportunism*. For a given type of transaction, the extent to which the actors involved have to make *specific investments* that result in sunk costs, lock-in effects and small numbers problems influences the vulnerability to opportunism and the (costly) precautions intended to avert it.

For present purposes the threat of opportunism is particularly interesting because one of the most common claims in the trust literature is that trust reduces transaction costs since '[i]n many ways, opportunism is the opposite of trust' (Barney and Hansen, 1994, p. 176). Presumably, when an actor perceives his transaction partner to be trustworthy, then he can economize on costly safeguards against opportunism. Numerous authors have adopted this idea (Bigley and Pearce, 1998) and I cannot possibly review or mention them all here. For example, Edward Lorenz (1988) concludes: 'A considerable amount of expense may go into fashioning safeguards designed to minimize the risks of being a victim of opportunistic behaviour. These expenses could be avoided if there were mutual trust' (p. 202). Larry Cummings and Philip Bromiley (1996) state: 'The core of our argument is that trust reduces transactions costs in and between organizations. Optimal expenditures on control, monitoring and other kinds of transactions costs are a function of opportunism. Opportunism, in turn, depends on and influences the level of trustworthy behavior in an organization' (p. 303).

The same reasoning underlies Ranjay Gulati's (1995) observation in the context of interfirm alliances, where '[t]he possibility of opportunistic behavior generates the most salient transaction costs' (p. 87), which may be reduced by the trust engendered by previous experience with an alliance partner. Jeffrey Dyer (2000) not only argues conceptually that for many reasons trust is more effective than legal contracts in minimizing transaction costs, he actually tests the argument empirically in the automotive industry and finds strong support. Bart Nooteboom (1996) criticizes Williamson's theory for making trust an irrelevant category and presents a framework that includes both trust and opportunism noting that '[t]ransaction on the basis of trust … economizes on the specification and monitoring of contracts and material incentives for cooperation' (p. 989).

The most systematic treatment to date of how trust may be integrated with 'relative ease' into transaction cost economics has been offered by Todd Chiles and John McMackin (1996, p. 96). They argue that trust is a 'social-context variable' that can be conceptualized as a parameter which raises the switchover level from one form of governance to another (market to hierarchy). Note, though, that this requires the relaxation of the behavioural assumptions of the original theory, especially a deviation from the opportunism postulate 'in order to bring greater realism into the model' (p. 75). In other words, the assumption of the rational utility maximizer is relaxed. Chiles and McMackin regard rational economics as

Transaction Costs

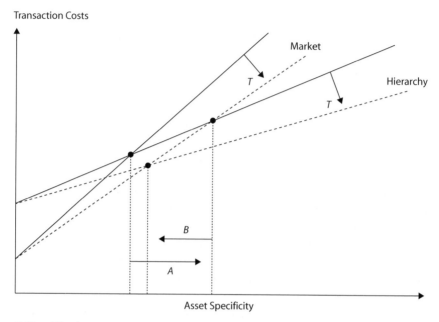

Asset Specificity

T 'Trust Effect'
A Effect discussed by Chiles and McMackin (1996)
B Effect *not* discussed by Chiles and McMackin (1996)

Source: Based on Williamson (1991), Chiles and McMackin (1996).

Figure 2.2   Effect of Trust on Transaction Costs

only one of three lenses showing the conditions that generate trust, the other two being non-calculative social norms and social embeddedness. Accordingly, they propose that 'trust's role in constraining opportunistic behavior allows parties to adopt less elaborate safeguards, thereby economizing on transaction costs and, in turn, altering the choice of governance structure' (p. 88) and, specifically, enabling the use of the market mechanism at levels of asset specificity that can be higher with trust than without (see Figure 2.2).

Chiles and McMackin exclude the hybrid form in their version of the diagram and look at market and hierarchy only, which makes the analysis incomplete. A more serious problem, though, is that no effect of trust on transaction costs within hierarchies is shown. If the same effect as for the market is assumed, then the hierarchy gradient should be reduced by trust, which lowers the switchover level from market to hierarchy and may actually cancel out the effect shown by Chiles and McMackin. The overall effect is therefore indeterminate, but the main idea applies: in any governance form, trust lowers the gradient representing the rise in transaction costs as a function of asset specificity.

Yet another conceptual problem surfaces regarding the other behavioural assumption: bounded rationality. An actor's knowledge of another's trustworthiness has to be imperfect and the other's awareness that this is the case actually creates his potential to be opportunistic. As Mark Granovetter (1985) observes, placing trust gives an 'enhanced opportunity for malfeasance' (p. 491). Any efforts to reduce this uncertainty will cause transaction costs, possibly in the same order as direct controls against opportunism. Therefore, following the economic logic, only the trust that costs less than safeguards will reduce transaction costs overall.

Many authors writing about trust from a, mostly modified, transaction cost perspective have noticed that Williamson (1975) used to be more open to the idea of trust and remarked for example that 'trust is important and businessmen rely on it much more than is commonly realised' (p. 108). He also thought that the governance of transactions reflects the transaction 'atmosphere', including trust. He concurs with Kenneth Arrow (1973) on the general importance of trust for economic organization but notes that 'operationalizing trust has proved inordinately difficult' (Williamson, 1985, pp. 405–06).

By now, several attempts have been made to operationalize trust and the concept of trust in 'relaxed' transaction cost economics can be summarized as follows: an actor who trusts perceives the trustee as not opportunistic and can thus economize on transaction costs when acting on trust in transactions with the trustee, although the transaction risk will not be eliminated by trust. This approach, once again, emphasizes that trust and the actions resulting from it, such as the choice of governance, are determined by how trustworthy the trustor perceives the trustee to be. The framework of transaction cost economics itself, however, hardly answers the question of how actors recognize trustworthiness and how they deal with the remaining uncertainty and vulnerability that neither trust nor governance mechanisms can fully remove.

Principal–agent theory – also known as agency theory – is not among those theories that are used most prominently and explicitly in trust research, perhaps because orthodox principal–agent theory predicts the absence and unsustainability of trust (Sheppard and Sherman, 1998). However, its basic construction very clearly models the problem of trust, and the ideas and instruments of principal–agent theory are frequently referred to in passing by many authors beyond the small stream of trust research rooted in this theory (see Shapiro, 1987; Ripperger, 1998; Whitener et al., 1998; Ensminger, 2001). The theory addresses the problems associated with situations in which one actor known as the principal hires another actor (the agent) to perform a task for him in return for a reward (Jensen and Meckling, 1976). The reward may be either a function of the task performance or a fixed compensation for the effort required from the agent (Ross, 1973). The principal's gain is a function of the effort that the agent puts into his performance. The effort actually made by the agent should be honest and dutiful, reflecting the reward offered by the principal (Huemer, 1998).

The theory demonstrates that what seems to be an ideal exchange in principle is in fact fraught with uncertainty and vulnerability from the principal's point of view, because the agent's goals and his attitude towards risk differ from those of the principal. The principal has 'good reason to believe that the agent will not always act in the best interest of the principal' (Jensen and Meckling, 1976, p. 308). As a rational, self-interested actor the agent seeks to minimize his effort if his reward is not outcome-based (Hendry, 2002). Shirking reduces the principal's gain while the agent still receives the reward as long as the principal is unable to ascertain that the agent's deliberate underperformance is the cause for the reduced gain (Eisenhardt, 1989). Given this basic situation, the issue of trust should be obvious: when a principal hires an agent to perform a task, the principal has to trust that the agent will not act in an opportunistic way that would make the principal worse off than if he had not hired the agent. Thus, the principal is a trustor and the agent is a trustee (Shapiro, 1987).

Principal–agent theory offers a number of distinctive constructs that capture the 'principal's problem' (Ross, 1973): hidden information (adverse selection), hidden action (moral hazard) and hidden intention (hold-up) represent the main sources of uncertainty and vulnerability for the principal (Arrow, 1985; Eisenhardt, 1989). The principal incurs agency costs consisting of the difference between the principal's gain when the agent puts in the proper effort and the (reduced) gain from the agent's actual effort. Moreover, agency costs comprise the costs arising from the initiatives that the principal undertakes to ensure the agent's proper effort. The agent also incurs agency costs in the process of signalling his capabilities, intentions and credible commitments to the principal.

Principal–agent theory thus seeks to explain the existence of exchange relationships and the way they are organized through a trade-off between agency benefits and agency costs. The theory also seeks to identify more normatively how principal–agent relationships should be constructed to make them attractive. If the principal is effectively a trustor, this question can be reframed as one of trust and trustworthiness: what makes an agent appear trustworthy to the principal so that he will place his trust in him by hiring him?

The standard solution offered by agency theorists is akin to Hardin's notion of encapsulated interest and the basic idea in rationalist trust theories that an actor will be trustworthy if it is in his own interest to be so (James, 2002). Hence, trust should be facilitated by using outcome-based, instead of effort-based, compensation. To give a classic example from the literature: if a manager (agent) owns equity of the company he manages, this will align his interests with those of the owners (principal) and the agent should have an incentive to maximize his effort (Jensen and Meckling, 1976; Eisenhardt, 1989). The principal can therefore reduce or abandon his screening and monitoring activities in this case.

The problem with such solutions is that, if they actually worked, the notion of trust would be superfluous because the principal would know with certainty that the agent will be trustworthy (James, 2002). As Gary Miller (2001) complains, principal–agent theory's perfect solution to the principal–agent problem eliminates the need for trust by the principal. If the theory were to take the assumption of bounded rationality seriously, however, principals and agents would never be able to devise a 'perfect' relationship with no surprises and possibilities for opportunism (Shapiro, 1987). For instance, John Hendry (2002) identifies some of 'the principal's other problems' and argues that, even when agents are completely honest and dutiful, the principal's own incompetence should give rise to agency costs. Consequently, uncertainty and vulnerability are present in all agency relationships and this makes them a matter of trust: the principal will only place trust and hire the agent if he perceives that the agent is likely to be trustworthy, although the threat of exploitation can never be completely eliminated.

Principal–agent research on trust sometimes also suggests that what makes principal–agent relationships efficient is not the trustworthiness induced by incentives but the (cost-free) trust between a principal and an agent as a given precondition for the relationship (Ensminger, 2001; Mills and Ungson, 2003). Trust in this sense becomes a solution to – rather than

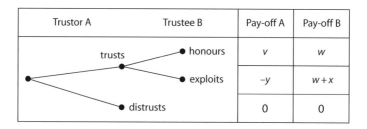

Figure 2.3 The Trust Game

offs. The designation of variables is borrowed from James (2002) with some modifications.

As in the classic prisoner's dilemma, the moves of trustor A and trustee B are considered at the same time, because A will base his choice on the likely choice of B, although the question for B whether or not to honour A's trust only arises if A has in fact chosen to trust. Moreover, the trust game is one-sided to the effect that the trustor cannot increase his pay-off by not trusting, while the trustee can receive an extra pay-off from exploiting the trust. The trustor A gains $v > 0$ if B honours the trust, and he loses $y > 0$ if B exploits his trust. On the other hand, the trustee B gains $w > 0$ if he honours the trust and $w + x$ if he exploits the trust, $x > 0$ representing the extra pay-off from breaking A's trust. Obviously, assuming that both actors know that they both know the pay-off structure (Dasgupta, 1988) and given that $w + x > w$, the trustee B has no incentive to honour A's trust and A should therefore refrain from placing it, which, however, means zero gain for both. As in the classic prisoner's dilemma, the more desirable outcome of A trusting and B honouring the trust (with $v, w > 0$) is not realized. Game theorists have suggested a range of modifications to the trust game (and other variations of the prisoner's dilemma), the most common of which will be reviewed briefly in this section. The suggested modifications always change the incentives in such a way that it will not be rational for B to exploit A's trust (Kelley and Thibaut, 1978; Bacharach and Gambetta, 2001; James, 2002).

The first 'solution' suggested is simply that $x < 0$ rather than $x > 0$, which would change the trustee B's preference from exploiting to honouring trust, because now $w > w + x$. The question is: why is $x < 0$ for B without any interference from A or a third party? A possible and common explanation is that B may feel guilty about having broken a private or

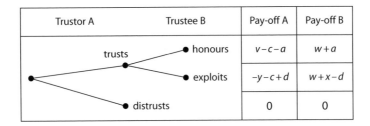

Figure 2.4 The Trust Game with Contractual Penalty and Incentives

internalized social norm (Deutsch, 1973; Dasgupta, 1988). Another explanation turns on the evolutionary argument that in any population a strategy of trustworthiness may be genetically reinforced and affect the trustee's preferences even when his cheating is unlikely to be detected and punished in the exchange at hand (Frank, 1987). One problem with these solutions could be that everybody has a price (Williamson, 1979). Once the positive incentives outweigh the internalized or inherited scruples, B will cheat: 'If the incentives are "right", even a trustworthy person can be relied upon to be untrustworthy' (Dasgupta, 1988, p. 54). Uncertainty and vulnerability remain and a prudent actor should thus strictly decide not to trust.

The second category of 'solutions' offered to the dilemma of the trust game suggests that A and B write a binding contract that modifies their incentives in such a way that the trust–honour sequence is preferred by both of them (Dasgupta, 1988; Lindenberg, 2000; James, 2002). The contract could define a penalty $d > 0$ on B if he is found to exploit A's trust. In another contract, A could offer B an additional incentive of $a > 0$ for honouring the trust. In both types of contract, A needs to monitor B and will incur an additional cost of $c > 0$. The contract will therefore induce B to be trustworthy if $d > x$ or $a > x$. And it should be in A's interest to write the contract with the penalty d or the incentive a as long as $v > c$ or $v > c + a$ respectively – the monitoring costs c (and the incentive a) do not overcompensate for his gain. Figure 2.4 summarizes the pay-off modifications for a contract between A and B that contains both penalty and incentive provisions (d, a). In this case, B will honour the trust if $a + d > x$. And under these conditions A will place his trust in B if $v - c - a > 0$.

Given the right values for a, c and d, as well as reliable information on x and the other variables, the contract should bring about the trust–honour sequence because this will be in both actors' self-interest. However, several serious limitations still remain. For example, there may be additional costs for enforcing the penalty d that have to be considered as they may consume, even exceed, the value of d. If B realizes this, the penalty may be ineffective. A third party might be called upon to enforce the penalty (Deutsch, 1973). Again, this will at least change A's calculations, who in addition now has a problem of trust in relation to the third party and their trustworthiness in enforcing the penalty (Shapiro, 1987; Dasgupta, 1988). Moreover, for A the use of a contract always reduces his potential gain and is therefore only second best to a non-contractual trust relationship. As long as A faces the possibility of incurring a loss from B's exploitation, prudence should lead him to distrust B as A should only trust B if he knows with certainty that B's pay-offs make him trustworthy and that B is a rational actor. In reality that certainty is not available to A, though.

The trustor may also decide to trust B on the basis of an implicit contract, that is effectively a social norm of honouring trust which can be enforced indirectly by some kind of social sanction such as ostracism or public blaming (James, 2002). In this case, A also has to monitor B incurring the cost of c. Moreover, when B exploits the trust, A has to expend an effort $e > 0$ in order to enforce the sanction which will reduce B's pay-off by $f > 0$. If $f > x$, then B's preference should change to honouring trust. However, B should also be able to see that it is not really in A's rational interest to spend e on enforcing a sanction and thereby increase his losses $(-y - c - e)$, although some experiments show that such 'altruistic punishment' actually occurs (see, for example, Fehr and Gächter, 2002). It follows that this proposed solution cannot be effective in an isolated interaction between A and B. It could be effective, however, if the sanction labels B as an untrustworthy actor and if such a label will make it less likely for B to be able to make profitable exchanges later with A or with other actors who also recognize the label (Kreps, 1990).

This leads on to the most common and powerful 'solution' to the trust game and other variants of the prisoner's dilemma: the 'shadow of the future' (Axelrod, 1984), which is the actors' awareness of the possibility that future interactions will occur and will be influenced by the current interaction (Pruitt and Kimmel, 1977; Granovetter, 1985; Gibbons, 2001). Assuming the basic structure of the game as in Figure 2.3, the trustor A might be able to communicate to B that if his trust is honoured, he will be prepared to trust him again in the future, but if his trust is exploited, then he will not trust him again (Dasgupta, 1988). If B believes this, then he should see that it is more beneficial to him to have a series of n interactions with A and an overall pay-off of nw rather than a single interaction with a pay-off of $w + x$ as long as $nw > w + x$. For example, if $w > x$, then even two trustful interactions will be better than a single exploitative one. (For simplicity's sake, future pay-offs will not be discounted here; see Axelrod, 1981.)

Critics of this solution argue, however, that the trustee will have an incentive to cheat on the final interaction to increase his pay-off to $nw + x$. As A can see this, he will not trust him in this final interaction. This, however, makes the penultimate interaction effectively the final interaction and the same logic applies: B has an incentive to exploit A's trust who will consequently not trust him. This is the notorious backward-induction argument already referred to briefly above: A will have to consider the first interaction as if it were the last and therefore he cannot rationally trust B (Luce and Raiffa, 1957; Axelrod, 1984; Dasgupta, 1988). According to Hardin and others, the backward-induction argument represents a very narrow view of the actor's rationale, though. For example, the trustor A may not mind being exploited in the last of a finite series of interactions if the loss y incurred in the last round does not eliminate the gains v from the previous rounds, that is if $(n - 1)v > y$. He may also keep placing his trust in B if B does not cheat all the time: if p is the probability of B honouring A's trust, then A should keep placing his trust in B as long as $p/(1 - p) > y/v$. From B's point of view this means that he can maximize his overall gain by honouring A's trust with a probability of $p = y/(v + y)$. This level of p, however, reduces A's gain to zero, meaning that he might as well distrust B.

Arguably the best condition for a trustful series of exchanges is when the interaction is supposed to be repeated indefinitely until the first exploitation of trust by B occurs (Axelrod, 1981) because if $n \rightarrow \infty$, then $nw > w + x$ and $(n - 1)v > y$. Consequently, A will always place trust and B will always honour it. Truly indefinite interactions are rare in reality, but it can be shown that it suffices if the probability q that there will be another interaction after the current one is high enough, that is from A's point of view when $q > x/(w + x)$. It is a precondition for these dynamic solutions, though, that the actors can actually monitor and recognize each other. In practice, interactions may be rather anonymous so that it is not always possible to develop or rely on a 'reputation' (Dasgupta, 1988). David Good (1988), however, maintains that 'rarely is it the case that exchanges requiring trust are ahistorical single instances' (p. 33).

It is not possible to devise normatively the one best strategy for actors in a trust game from the game's set-up as such. The prudent trustor A cannot completely eliminate his uncertainty and vulnerability from trusting B and should therefore choose to distrust so that B's actions will at least not make him worse off. If he trusts nevertheless, then A accepts more or less deliberately the uncertainty and vulnerability attendant upon doing so. Consequently, his trust cannot be explained by B's incentives to be trustworthy. The indeterminacy of abstract game theory has puzzled researchers because in practice the trust game seems to be played successfully (see, for example, Dawes, 1980; Axelrod, 1984; Yamagishi, 2001; James, 2002). In other words, it is found empirically that actors deviate from the strictly rational distrusting Nash equilibrium and, in doing so, realize beneficial exchanges.

Much game-theoretical research on trust has therefore moved from theory to experiment in order to better understand the phenomenon of trust in the prisoner's dilemma. I shall review two of the most prominent programmes of study here (see also Chapter 6). First of all, Morton Deutsch (1973) in his early experiments on trust in the 1950s relaxes the assumption that all actors are utility maximizers and introduces three different motivational orientations instead. In the cooperative orientation, the actor considers his own as well as the other's welfare. In the individualistic orientation, the actor is only concerned about his own welfare and unconcerned about the other's (homo oeconomicus). In the competitive orientation, the actor wants to do better than the other.

Deutsch finds strong evidence for the view that a cooperative orientation brings about behaviour equivalent to the desirable trust–honour sequence, while a competitive orientation induces the opposite. For the individualistic orientation, the outcome depends on the conditions under which the game is played: when subjects can communicate a commitment to cooperation and when they know the other's decision, then the equivalent of a trust–honour sequence is more likely to occur than when such possibilities are not given. These results demonstrate that, given certain motivational orientations and game conditions, the trust game need not be a dilemma with an unfavourable outcome.

Further experiments by Deutsch and his colleagues support the hypothesized impact of communication, motivational orientation, incentives, influence over the other's outcome, third parties and personality predispositions (see the collection of various studies in Deutsch, 1973). Actors who are willing to trust are also more likely to honour trust themselves.

Finally, Deutsch does not observe the generally positive effect of repeating the game as suggested above. Instead, where actors' motivations are competitive or individualistic, repetition produces more distrust! Game theorists might argue that the mediating variables identified by Deutsch and others could all be factored into the actors' pay-off matrices. In other words, although different motivational orientations may not be a matter of rationality, once they are known actors can make rational use of them. The experiments show that this is what happens, but only to some extent.

Second, another study that has had an extraordinary influence on trust research is a competition designed and run by Robert Axelrod (1984). He devised a prisoner's dilemma-type game and invited game theorists from a range of disciplines to submit programmed strategies. The winner would be the strategy with the highest overall pay-off, having played against all other strategies in a computer-simulated tournament. The remarkable and by now well-known result is that a rather simple strategy called tit-for-tat prevailed: cooperate in the first round and then do whatever the other has done in the previous round.

As Axelrod notes, apart from apparently being the most effective and also ecologically robust strategy, tit-for-tat is a rather nice strategy in the sense that the actor always starts by cooperating and keeps on cooperating as long as the other cooperates. It is at the same time provocable and willing to forgive defection if the other returns to cooperative behaviour. Tit-for-tat indicates that actors can rationally resolve the dilemma of the trust game by being not only trustful and trustworthy but also appropriately responsive to the other's past behaviour.

Axelrod does not overlook the fact that, despite the overall success of tit-for-tat, this strategy can lose quite badly against some exploitative strategies in the tournament. The success of tit-for-tat depends on the proportion of other 'nice' actors in the population and Axelrod manages to show that even a relatively small, but just about large enough, cluster of 'nice' cooperative strategies in a population, if able to interact with each other, can induce cooperation in the whole population. In sum, he claims to have found the mechanism by which cooperation emerges and evolves 'among egoists' (Axelrod, 1981). Over time, with experience and with a generally cooperative predisposition, the dilemma can be resolved and the trust game can reach a stable trust–honour pattern.

Returning to theoretical research, Martin Hollis (1998) considers in an intriguing thought experiment all the solutions discussed in this section, and a few more besides, but concludes that they are all ultimately indeterminate, just shifting and not eliminating the actors' mutual uncertainty and vulnerability. The only feasible solution that Hollis can think of in the end is a form of generalized reciprocity where rationality moves from the first person singular to the first person plural. Actors will place and honour trust if they look at the trust game and ask, 'What is good for *us*?' rather than 'What is good for *me*?' Clearly, given the game in Figure 2.3, the collective outcome for *us* is better in the trust–honour sequence than in the other possibilities (unless $v < x - y$).

Hollis' solution is far from a simple replacement of the *me*-rationality by an *us*-rationality – substituting collectivism for egoism and thus one extreme assumption for another. Rather, he argues that the individual actor wants to be and needs to be a member of a community who finds fulfilment in his contributions to the welfare of that community as long as the community does not deny him his individual identity and freedom. This kind of collective identity-based motivation to trust and be trustworthy is also recognized as a possibility by other researchers and even by Hardin (1991), who hints at an interpretation of encapsulated interest as including the idea that generalized trust 'may be little more than an encapsulation of the self-interest of all or most of us' (p. 206). However, the problem for the trustor facing a trust game still remains that, even when he adopts an *us*-rationality and places his trusts in a spirit of generalized reciprocity, the actions of the trustee cannot be certain to him. Trust remains fraught with uncertainty and vulnerability. If it were not, one might not want to call it trust any longer (James, 2002) as 'the problem of trust would not arise if it was common knowledge that we were all trustworthy' (Dasgupta, 1988, p. 53).

The far from exhaustive overview of the game-theoretical perspective on trust in this section demonstrates the heuristic value that this approach has for formulating key issues of trust more precisely. Game theory has also been open enough to allow researchers to try out their various 'solutions' to trust dilemmas. Given the diversity within this paradigm, it is hard to suggest a single game-theoretical view of trust. Nevertheless, the following summary should capture the essence of the concept of trust underlying most game-theoretical work in the trust literature: an actor rationally trusts and cooperates with another actor if he perceives the pay-offs from their interactions as positive for himself and constituted, or modified, in such a way that the other's dominant strategy will be sufficiently cooperative, even though the trustor's assessment of the 'game' is boundedly rational and, hence, his uncertainty and vulnerability is increased by trusting.

Before moving on, I would like to reflect on the fact that upon closer inspection most game-theoretical work supposedly about 'trust' is really about 'cooperation', equating the two terms quite liberally. It has been argued, however, that not all cooperation requires that the actors trust each other and that not all actors who trust each other cooperate necessarily (Kee and Knox, 1970; Gambetta, 1988d; Good, 1988; Hardin, 2001). Game theory is not designed to make such distinctions, because the unit of analysis is the actor's choice of action. This means that in the idea of trust as cooperation the trustee's perceived trustworthiness, the trustor's expectations and the trustor's trusting action coincide (Dasgupta, 1988). If game theory is consistent in this way, then 'trust' is indeed a redundant category as the phenomenon studied is calculative cooperation (Williamson, 1993). However, trust comes back into game-theoretical research as an independent exogenous parameter that explains why cooperation occurs when the theory predicts that it should not (James, 2002). Moreover, game theorists have started to separate trust from cooperation in experimental designs, proposing that this is critical for building trust relations and finding that cooperation leads to trust, not the other way round (Yamagishi et al., 2005).

Finally, the idea that the trustor's main problem is to recognize trustworthiness on the part of the trustee is also taken up by trust research that builds on signalling theory (Spence, 1974). Michael Bacharach and Diego Gambetta (2001) aim to identify the general properties of reliable signals of trustworthiness and their use of signalling theory can certainly offer an interesting 'solution' to the trust game (see also Beckert, 2005). Two preconditions need to be fulfilled. First, the population of potential trustees must be divisible into one type of trustee B_h who will be trustworthy when trusted by A, and another type B_e who will exploit trust (Dasgupta, 1988). In terms of the trust game, this simply means that for the trust–exploit sequence B_h has a pay-off of $w - u < w$, while B_e's pay-off is $w + x > w$ (Figure 2.5). When A encounters a potential trustee, his trust problem will easily be solved if he can distinguish between the two types before placing his trust. A's initial problem of assessing the game's pay-off structure is turned into a problem of discriminating between B_h and B_e. If this is not possible for him, then game-theoretical prudence would advise him to distrust in order to avoid a loss of y.

This is where the second precondition comes in. If the trustor A is able to receive a signal from potential trustees, then this signal may enable him to discriminate between B_h and B_e. Partha Dasgupta (1988) shows that

sibility that '[i]f people *just* trust each other, even when there is a possibility of being exploited, they may still feel it is in their interest to do so, but why that is true is an interesting and unresolved avenue of study for economists' (pp. 304–05, emphasis in original).

2.4 THE RATIONALITY OF EMOTIONS

A common weakness of the rational choice perspectives and economic theories discussed above is that their understanding of rationality in trust relies heavily on calculative cognition and prediction. Is this why they run into paradoxes and dilemmas? In contrast, many trust researchers agree with David Lewis and Andrew Weigert (1985) who find that 'trust succeeds where rational prediction alone would fail' (p. 969) and that '[t]rust in everyday life is a mix of feeling and rational thinking' (p. 972). Accordingly, trust should be conceptualized as having a rational and an emotional dimension. Emotional trust in this view rests on strong positive affect for the object of trust and is analytically distinct from rational reasoning about why the trustee will be trustworthy. Seeing that the cognitive approach tends to lead to indeterminacy, perhaps actual manifestations of trust can often be explained by positive affect for the trustee, even though behaviour motivated purely by affect (or purely by cognition) would not be classified as trust by Lewis and Weigert.

Daniel McAllister (1995) adopts Lewis and Weigert's concept in a study on interpersonal cooperation in organizations and conceptualizes 'cognition-based trust' and 'affect-based trust' as distinct forms of trust, the latter stemming from 'emotional bonds between individuals' and 'genuine care and concern for the welfare of partners' (p. 26). Although distinct, the two forms of trust are closely related and McAllister hypothesizes (and finds support for the view) that actors who have high levels of cognition-based trust in a trustee will also have high levels of affect-based trust in him.

'Emotional trust' in the measurement scale developed by Cynthia Johnson-George and Walter Swap (1982) refers mainly to the extent to which a trustor is willing to be open to the trustee and does not fear emotional harm from the trustee. The actual question here is whether or not the trustee is believed to have positive affect for the trustor. This is also the idea underlying McAllister's (1995) measures of affect-based trust, although he assumes affect to be mutual. Both Johnson-George and Swap's and McAllister's measures do not capture primarily the trustor's affect as a basis for trust but the trustor's perception of the trustee's affect towards him as a fairly cognitive basis for the trustor's trust. However, 'I trust him because he likes me and cares about my welfare' is not what Lewis and Weigert have in mind. Their notion of emotional trust entails: 'I trust him because I like him'. The difference is important.

Accordingly, Karen Jones (1996) conceptualizes trust 'in terms of a distinctive, and affectively loaded, way of seeing the one trusted' (p. 4). The twist of her definition is that positive affect becomes an interpretative lens that interferes with the trustor's cold cognitive assessment of the other's trustworthiness: 'The harms they might cause through failure of goodwill are not in view because the possibility that their will is other than good is not in view' (p. 12). Once the affective element in trust is taken into account the trustor can never be fully rational or justified in a cognitive sense when predicting that a potential trustee will be trustworthy or untrustworthy. Interestingly, Jones claims nevertheless that it is justified to take heed of one's emotions in trust. Drawing on Robert Frank (1988), she claims that 'emotions and other affective states often do represent the world in the way it is' (Jones, 1996, p. 24). The people we like are those who care about us and who will therefore not exploit our trust.

The above arguments explain at last why the issue of emotionality in trust is discussed here in a chapter on trust and reason: if it is rational for a trustor to place trust on the basis of positive affect for the trustee, then the underlying theory of emotions and affect embraces an idea of rationality far beyond the mainstream notion of calculativeness in economics. For one, this means an opening up of the concept of rationality to include non-calculative forms, rules of thumb and intuition. It implies that positive affect can induce trust and resolve a cooperative dilemma. Negative affect, via distrust, may keep the actor out of trouble. However, positive affect might equally induce an actor to trust and regret it later. Therefore, a closer look at the rationality of emotions is warranted.

In a remarkable book on this subject, Ronald de Sousa (1987) argues that what we commonly mean by rationality (cognitive reasoning) would not be possible without emotion. Facing a reality that appears at one extreme completely indeterminate ('everything is possible') and totally deterministic ('everything is already decided') at the other, emotions both clear and cloud the actor's vision and make it possible to define and attend to problems by means of rationality. In turn, the actor can apply rationality to his emotions. Although he may not be able to control his feelings, he can judge whether they are reasonable or appropriate, but such judgement is of course not detached from the emotional state in which it is made. And then again rational thinking uncovers and reinforces emotions and makes them available as excuses and justifications. All of this renders questions such as whether emotions are rational ultimately meaningless (Fineman, 1996) as emotion and reason constitute a duality.

In a notional trust game the trustor will perceive the potential trustee both affectively and cognitively. As affect and cognition influence each other, it will be hard to tell whether trust in any particular instance is 'emotional trust' or 'cognitive trust' as indeed it has to be seen as a combination of both (Lewis and Weigert, 1985). If the concept of rationality is extended in this way, we have to accept that liking or being liked by the trustee might be a good reason to trust, or at least no worse than an ostensibly more rational cognitive reason such as encapsulated interest.

In sum, a trustor's perception of a trustee's trustworthiness always has both affective and cognitive elements, and therefore positive affect towards the trustee or from the trustee, or both, is an equally reasonable basis for trust as cognitive reasons, while at the same time trust always implies uncertainty and vulnerability. Affective trust, although an inevitable conceptual extension to purely cognitive notions of trust (Williams, 2001), is only part of a possible explanation for why 'people just trust each other' (James, 2002, pp. 304–05), because positive affect removes neither the awareness nor the threat of possible exploitation completely. In other words, a perception of trustworthiness may be grounded in cognition and affect, but the trust it begets and the resulting trustful acts are risky and it remains to be explained how the actor deals with the uncertainty and vulnerability.

2.5 INDICATORS OF TRUSTWORTHINESS

The key assumption behind all the approaches reviewed so far is that people look for good reasons to trust. Their search may be more or less cognitive and/or affective, more or less calculative and framed in terms of probability, utility or heuristics such as the reliable signals described in abstract terms by Bacharach and Gambetta (2001). In more concrete and empirical terms, Diego Gambetta and Heather Hamill (2005) analyse how taxi drivers in New York and Belfast judge the trustworthiness of their customers. The same real-life trust game was already studied by James

Henslin (1968) who found in a classic ethnographic study that taxi drivers use a number of criteria including sex, age, ethnicity, neighbourhood and the person's degree of sobriety in order to discriminate between trust-worthy and untrustworthy passengers. Henslin's account of the taxi drivers matches very well the image of a self-interested actor who does not place his trust lightly, but who cannot distrust all potential passengers either and who must increase his uncertainty and vulnerability whenever he picks up a new fare. Interestingly, the taxi drivers can rarely draw on a history of previous exchanges or the prospect of future encounters with individual passengers. Nevertheless, they seem to be able to recognize trustworthiness quite effectively and some 'instinctive Bayesianism' (Hardin, 1993) could be at work here, too. Although they do not even acknowledge or mention Henslin's famous study, Gambetta and Hamill (2005) are able to replicate and update his insights while grounding them more firmly in signalling theory (see above).

Both the classic taxi driver study by Henslin and the recent one by Gambetta and Hamill ultimately aim to uncover 'indicators' (Zucker, 1986, p. 60) of trustworthiness and this is what much of the trust literature tries to achieve, too, albeit often without such deep empirical grounding, but mainly based instead on theoretical considerations. One of the most popular sets of generalized indicators has already been mentioned at the beginning of this chapter: Roger Mayer et al. (1995) identify ability, benevolence and integrity as three interrelated indicators of perceived trustworthiness. The model incorporates and integrates many previous insights such as Bernard Barber's (1983) distinction between fiduciary obligation and technically competent performance, which gave rise to the widely recognized idea that the trustee's ability and intention need to be considered. Proponents of different models sometimes debate, for example, whether ability lies inside or outside the concept of trustworthiness, whether benevolence and integrity are separate concerns and both relevant, whether there are additional indicators such as predictability, how the indicators are related to each other and how they should be weighted, and so on. At any rate, there are numerous lists of trustworthiness indicators. For example, Harrison McKnight et al. (1998) include benevolence, competence, honesty and predictability in their own model.

Moreover, across the literature, researchers define terms differently and use different terms to mean the same thing. If we strain for shared meaning (Bigley and Pearce, 1998), though, I would concur that the models are 'not so different after all' (Rousseau et al., 1998) and say that

the literature suggests an overall image of the trustworthy actor as someone who is *able* and *willing* and *consistent* in not exploiting the trustor's
vulnerability (Möllering et al., 2004).

Attempts at modelling indicators of perceived trustworthiness were
soon followed by studies aiming to operationalize, measure and validate
the indicators mostly in the form of Likert-type scales (for example
Butler, 1991; Mayer and Davis, 1999). While this is certainly a logical
step, certain issues need to be raised that call into question the strong
emphasis on the idea that trusting is reasonable if and when it is based
on perceived trustworthiness.

First, a very fundamental problem with the focus on indicators of trustworthiness as predictors of trust is that focusing on 'trustworthiness' could
actually render the concept of 'trust' superfluous if 'trust' were to denote
little or nothing more than a 'perception of trustworthiness'. For instance,
Jeffrey Dyer and Wujin Chu (2003) study the effect of perceived trustworthiness on transaction costs and performance and they have no real
need to refer to trust at all. If, however, trust is more than perceived
trustworthiness, as many authors claim, then indicators of trustworthiness
explain anything but trust. Put differently, such indicators may tell us
what kind of information trustors use, but not how they use it, unless we
assume some kind of rational calculative mechanism which, once again,
would reduce 'trust' to a form of mechanistic decision-making under risk
that does not require a separate category either (Williamson, 1993).

Second, indicators of trustworthiness suggest that it is rather easy for
trustors to assess others and decide whether to trust or not. However, the
typical and even conceptually required situation for trustors is that they
lack information and that their sources are unreliable and/or inconclusive.
Recall that without uncertainty and vulnerability on the part of the trustor,
the concept of trust is practically meaningless (James, 2002). With indicators of trustworthiness, however, we only look at what the trustor perceives to know and not at how the trustor deals with uncertainty and ignorance. In technical terms, the variance explained by indicators is rather
insipid compared to the variance that is not explained by them. True,
people trust in part because they perceive others as trustworthy, but they
also trust in spite of their uncertainty about others' trustworthiness. What
explains the latter?

Third, a further complication arises from the fact that trustors often
perceive conflicting signals, some of which speak for and some against
trustworthiness. Hence, at least, we also need to identify indicators of un-

trustworthiness. This raises a number of further issues, though, such as whether distrust represents the absence of trust, the opposite of trust on a continuum or even a distinct concept in a separate dimension (Sitkin and Roth, 1993; Lewicki et al., 1998; Lindenberg, 2000). This has important implications for modelling the relationships between indicators and outcomes. Rational choice and economic theories often suggest that trustworthiness as a basis for trust means an absence of opportunistic incentives or motivations (untrustworthiness). They hardly consider the positive indicators identified by Mayer et al. (1995), who in turn pay little attention to negative indicators.

An overall model would also need to clarify if and how the indicators interact with each other. Countless possibilities are conceivable in this respect: from no effect at all to complex complementary, substitutional or other joint effects. It should become clear that an even bigger problem than gaining information in the form of indicators of trustworthiness and untrustworthiness in the first place is how to process them in order to arrive at a state of expectation that enables 'reasonable' action. What do you do when you know that you know relatively little and what you know is inconclusive? In such a situation, trust is an alternative solution to the strategy of looking for ever more information and probabilities.

Fourth, indicators of trustworthiness suggest a very static view of trust. In contrast, it is of course possible and plausible that trustors update their perceptions of trustworthiness continuously, that they learn about others over time and thereby gain a more and more reliable assessment, and so on (Hardin, 1993). It is definitely important to adopt a dynamic view of trust, and Chapter 4 will be devoted in large part to this issue. It will be argued that is not enough to assume that in practice the indicators of trustworthiness used by a trustor will simply become more sophisticated and may even change over time, if it cannot be explained at the same time how the process starts initially in the face of little conclusive information and if it is assumed that the model in use will approximate a perfect model of perceived trustworthiness ultimately. The key consideration, once again, is that trust goes beyond the available good reasons that indicators of trustworthiness help to identify.

Lastly, by focussing on indicators of trustworthiness it is assumed that trustors are passive, calculative processors of those indicators and, hence, variance in trust is explained predominantly through the trustee. Yet, if trust is an expectation that forms in the mind of the trustor, this is where the emphasis should be placed. We therefore need to pay more attention (again) to factors affecting the trustor such as his predisposition in terms of personality and motivation (Wrightsman, 1966; Rotter, 1967; Deutsch, 1973). We must acknowledge that the uniform assumption of homo oeconomicus could be misleading and take the duality of rationality and emotion seriously (Lewis and Weigert 1985; de Sousa, 1987). We should also note temporal effects and the trustor's past experiences (Zand, 1972; Lewicki and Bunker, 1996).

Above all, the trustor (and the trustee) need to be seen as embedded in systems and structures consisting of social relationships, rules and resources that can have strong constraining and/or empowering influences (see Chapter 3). Mayer et al. (1995), McKnight et al. (1998) and others have already moved some way in this direction, but the key idea in their models remains that perceived trustworthiness is the (reasonable) basis for trust, even if some other factors may also play a role. In contrast, the next two chapters will focus on alternative perspectives as I aim to show how trust goes beyond reason and may be explained in terms outside our normal understanding of individual-based, self-interested, utility-maximizing rationality.

While Martin Hollis (1998) desperately wanted to see the triumph of reason at the end of his investigations into trust, I do not want to see reason defeated, but I propose that by focusing on reason only – and in particular by reducing it to questions of utility – we will miss the truly intriguing aspects of trust that may actually further our understanding of social life.

3

TRUST AND ROUTINE

3.1 TAKEN-FOR-GRANTEDNESS

Every day, we trust countless others without being able or required to perform any detailed reasoning about whether or not this is justified. Routinely, we are in a position of vulnerability towards others, expecting no harm from them or even presuming their benevolence and solidarity – and this often applies to others about whom we know very little, too. How is this possible? About a century ago, Georg Simmel ([1908] 1950) observed: 'The traditions and institutions, the power of public opinion and the definition of the position which inescapably stamps the individual, have become so solid and reliable that one has to know only certain external facts about the other person in order to have the confidence required for the common action. The question is no longer some foundation of personal qualities on which (at least in principle) a modification of behavior within the relation might be based: motivation and regulation of this behavior have become so objectified that confidence no longer needs any properly personal knowledge' (p. 319).

Beyond Simmel's concerns with the discontinuities of modernity and the increasing 'objectification' of culture, this quotation conveys an approach to explaining trust that emphasizes taken-for-grantedness. Instead of making difficult rational choices in an increasingly complex, dynamic and incomprehensible world, trustors draw on the things that are given and relatively stable. They seek to act and see others interacting with them in a normal and appropriate way. They very often trust if and when and because trust is taken-for-granted since 'it may be literally unthinkable to act otherwise' (Zucker, 1986, p. 58) in the particular, yet familiar, situation they find themselves in. The same applies, of course, to much of the distrust in the world where the choice to trust is not even considered because expectations 'automatically' turn negative. We are referring here to situations where literally, or at least from the point of view of the trustor, 'nobody would ever do this' or 'everybody would always do that', in this case, trust. And we can also think of cases where the taken-for-grantedness is strongly associated with identity and role acceptance where 'such a person' will only do this or that, irrespective of utility considerations, because their very social existence is defined by it.

I refer to *routine* in the title of this chapter and the book in order to suggest a very broad notion of trust that captures the idea of taken-for-grantedness. When trust is a matter of routine, it can still be reasonable, but the main point is that the routine is performed without questioning its underlying assumptions, without assessing alternatives and without giving justifications every time. It is a procedure or programme that people follow regularly and habitually (Misztal, 1996), a recurrent action pattern (Nelson and Winter, 1982; Feldman and Pentland, 2003; Becker, 2005; Becker et al., 2005). This suggests an unsettling and provocative image of trust, as it implies a certain blindness and passivity. What if the routine produces undesirable results? Where do routines come from and is it possible to adapt and improve them (Feldman, 2000)? Such concerns are legitimate – just as most routines are legitimate – and they will come into focus soon enough. First, however, it is worthwhile to recognize how prevalent and indeed 'useful' taken-for-grantedness is as a basis of action, even though it always carries an element of 'until further notice'. Without routines, we would not even have the capacity to attend to non-routine issues, which applies to issues of trust, too (March and Simon, 1958). Faced with pervasive uncertainty, routines can enable action (Becker and Knudsen, 2005).

When John Child and I studied the trust of Hong Kong based managers in the staff of operations located in mainland China, we knew that a major concern of external investors in mainland China is that they do not know what they can take for granted in the Chinese business context. They lack the routines that enable them to build or maintain trust. And China lacks much of the institutional stability for such routines to become established. Accordingly, we found that managers with higher contextual confidence also had stronger trust in local staff (Child and Möllering,

2003). We also found that trust was higher when managers had successfully transferred routine practices to the local operations. Agency clearly
must not be overlooked with regard to routines (Feldman and Pentland,
2003), but the possibility of agency is dependent on the stability, familiarity and continuity carried by routines in the sense of regular action
patterns and rules (Becker, 2005). I think that most of us will be able to
relate to these ideas from our own experience: it is in unstable, unfamiliar, discontinuous situations that we realize how much we normally take
for granted by following routines, especially when we trust. In a way,
what we (can) take for granted marks our identity and we would not be
able to maintain it and exercise agency if we ever had to question everything at once.

In this chapter, I will refer to a number of connected sociological theories that explain the meaning and significance of taken-for-grantedness:
phenomenology, ethnomethodology, neoinstitutionalism and more recent
work building on them. I will not discuss in detail the important research
on organizational routines undertaken in evolutionary economics and related areas of organization theory (Nelson and Winter, 1982; Cohen et al.,
1996; Feldman and Pentland, 2003; for a literature review, see Becker,
2004, for recent contributions see Becker et al., 2005). Instead, I will refer to institution and institutionalization as concepts that capture the
common ground and core ideas behind trust as a matter of routine at the
societal level beyond individuals and organizations. Many ideas and de-
bates on routines in the narrower sense are applicable to my discussion of
the routine-like character of institutions as bases for trust, though.

Since Zucker (1986), if not earlier, the notion that trust can be based
on institutions has been widely accepted in the literature. However, apart
from a few basic considerations offered by Lynne Zucker herself, studies
on 'institutional-based trust' have not incorporated carefully the underlying theory. I therefore aim to go beyond the common-sense notion that
institutions matter for trust and I propose strong conceptual support for
this idea by applying fundamental concepts such as 'natural attitude' and
'institutional isomorphism' to the problem of trust. Previous research has
left many holes in the theoretical foundations of the important and widely
recognized idea that trust between actors can be based on institutions,
because it rarely offers precise concepts of such institutions and the relationships of actors towards them. In management and organization studies, in particular, the focus has been on individual cognition or interpersonal social-psychological processes, merely acknowledging some influ-

ence of the 'environment' or 'context' without further theorization (see, for example, the contributions in Kramer and Tyler, 1996).

Sociological studies of trust, on the other hand, have tended to focus on the level of systems and institutions, attributing an almost marginal role to the trusting and trusted actors (Misztal, 1996). However, actors interpret and question institutions and do not merely reproduce them passively. The same applies to routines (Feldman and Pentland, 2003). Therefore, if a theoretically sound case can be made for why institutions can be a source of trust between actors, it also needs to be recognized that institutions become an object of trust for the trustors who exercise agency in relying on them (or not). A closer examination of this issue is another aim of this chapter. Clearly, without trust in institutions those institutions cannot be the source of 'institutional-based trust' in other actors. Again, this problem has long been recognized, for example by Shapiro (1987), but a systematic treatment of what makes institutions trustworthy and how actors interpret and (thereby) come to trust institutions is lacking.

Hence, this chapter first discusses trust in the light of the phenomenological roots of neoinstitutionalist theories, in particular Alfred Schütz's concept of the natural attitude and Garfinkelian constitutive expectancies, and moves on via Zucker to neoinstitutionalist organization theory. Next, the rather uncommon idea of trust as institutional isomorphism is discussed in detail and with reference to constructs such as rules, roles and (in a narrower sense) routines. This leads to an investigation of trust based on institutions, highlighting the idea that when institutions serve as a source of trust between actors those institutions become objects of trust, too. The background to these considerations is that, because of its phenomenological roots, this neoinstitutionalist approach to trust does not deny agency (which would eliminate the relevance of trust). Rather, a more processual and interpretative perspective of embedded agency suggests itself and will be presented in later chapters.

3.2   TRUST AS A FORM OF NATURAL ATTITUDE

In this section, I will give a first explanation for how institutions can be sources of trust, emphasizing the taken-for-grantedness implied in institutions. I will discuss whether manifestations of trust depend on how much an actor can take for granted in interactions with others. I will draw on theoretical perspectives grouped liberally under the label of sociological neoinstitutionalism (although several authors that I cite would not normally be called neoinstitutionalists). According to Ronald Jepperson (1991), 'institutions are socially constructed, routine-reproduced (ceteris paribus), program or rule systems. They operate as relative fixtures of constraining environments and are accompanied by taken-for-granted accounts. This description accords with metaphors repeatedly invoked in discussions – metaphors of frameworks or rules. These imageries capture simultaneous contextual empowerment and constraint, and taken-for-grantedness' (p. 149).

If we want to argue that taken-for-grantedness in particular enables trust, then such a neoinstitutionalist approach needs to recall its roots in phenomenology and, specifically, Schütz's concept of natural attitude. In this regard, Zucker (1986) is a rare but prominent example of a study of trust grounded firmly in neoinstitutionalist theory and, more importantly, explicitly in those phenomenological insights that make sociological neoinstitutionalism distinct from other kinds of institutional analysis. In Zucker's definition 'trust is a set of expectations shared by all those involved in an exchange' including both 'broad social rules' and 'legitimately activated processes' (p. 54). When actors involved in an exchange share a set of expectations constituted in social rules and legitimate processes, they can trust each other with regard to the fulfilment and maintenance of those expectations. By the same token, actors can only trust those others with whom they share a particular set of expectations. Either way, trust hinges on the actors' natural ability to have a world in common with others and rely on it. Zucker thus adopts a Garfinkelian perspective on trust which, in turn, is based on the phenomenological work of Schütz, whose writings also strongly influenced Berger and Luckmann (1966).

One central idea in Alfred Schütz's theoretical writings is that Husserl's transcendental, essentialist phenomenological method of *epoché* should be inverted, giving an existentialist phenomenology whereby the actor's 'natural attitude' towards the world becomes the starting point for the analysis of social reality rather than being seen as the major obstacle for such analysis (Giddens, 1993; Holstein and Gubrium, 1994): 'The object we shall be studying therefore is the human being who is looking at the world from within the natural attitude. Born into a social world, he comes upon his fellow men and takes their existence for granted without question, just as he takes for granted the existence of the natural objects he encounters' (Schütz, 1967, p. 98).

This natural attitude (sometimes also translated as 'attitude of daily life' or a similar expression) captures the observation that actors normally do not doubt the reality of their everyday world. This enables them to have what Husserl and other phenomenologists call a 'lifeworld' (*Lebenswelt*), meaning a fairly stable subjective reality in which individuals experience and conduct their daily affairs pragmatically and without questioning this reality. While Husserl wants to overcome this unquestioning attitude philosophically, Schütz reconstructs it as a precondition for social reality and sociological understanding. Moreover, as part of the natural attitude, actors assume that other people's view of reality is not too different from their own. The accomplishment of 'reciprocal perspectives' (Schütz, 1970b, p. 184) is that the everyday world is largely a 'world known in common with others' or a 'common-sense world' (Garfinkel, 1963).

Schütz investigates the processes whereby actors achieve intersubjectivity with others. An important assumption is that all consciousness is intentional, in the sense that actors in their stream of experience cannot observe events and acts without – not only automatically and inseparably but also tacitly and pragmatically – attaching meaning to them (Berger and Luckmann, 1966; Giddens, 1993). According to Schütz (1967, 1970a), they draw on 'stocks of knowledge at hand' and 'interpretative schemes' which enable them to typify their experiences. However, actors are capable of 'attentional modification' and have different 'relevance structures', meaning that some events and their typifications are taken-for-granted in the background while other matters are problematic and attract immediate attention in the stream of experience. Nevertheless, in the natural attitude, actors will seek to interact on the basis of (idealized) 'congruence of relevance' and 'interchangeability of standpoints', also described as 'reciprocal perspectives' (Schütz, 1970a, 1970b; see also Garfinkel, 1963; Heritage, 1987).

Schütz (1967) reveals that a precondition for social interaction is taken-for-grantedness, which he defines as 'that particular level of experience which presents itself as not in need of further analysis' (p. 74). However, it is clear from his writings that he does not take the natural attitude as such for granted. Instead, he is also concerned with how actors retain the facility to interpret part of their lifeworlds with an attitude of doubt or curiosity (Garfinkel, 1963; Holstein and Gubrium, 1994). The *epoché* of the natural attitude presents actors as rather skilful in handling the duality of familiarity and unfamiliarity in their stream of experiences (Schütz, 1970a; Endreß, 2001; see also Chapter 4).

Harold Garfinkel (1963) draws on and interprets Schütz's concept of the natural attitude when he states that '[t]he attitude of daily life furnishes a person's perceived environment its definition as an environment of social realities known in common' and that it 'is constitutive of the institutionalized common understandings of the practical everyday organization and workings of the society as seen "from within"'. The constitutive features of basic rules of a game serve Garfinkel as a heuristic for understanding stable social interaction: in particular, basic rules are constituted by three 'constitutive expectancies' (p. 190) by which players expect (a) the rules to frame a set of required alternative moves and outcomes, (b) the rules to be binding on all other players and (c) the other players to equally expect (a) and (b). Crucially, Garfinkel concludes that 'basic rules frame the set of possible events of play that observed behavior can signify' and 'provide a behavior's sense as an action' (p. 195), that is they literally define what can happen and has happened.

Garfinkel (1963, 1967) therefore sets out in his (in)famous breaching experiments to manipulate social interactions in such a way that the infringement of basic rules causes surprise, confusion, anomie and other kinds of strong irritation in the subjects of the experiments, thereby aiming to reveal the fundamental social structures that are ordinarily, routinely and tacitly referred to and reproduced in everyday life. He shows how actors quite actively 'normalize' and redefine events that fall outside of basic rules in order to maintain 'the game', in other words the perceived normality and stability of the social context (see also McKnight et al., 1998). They do so despite their awareness of a subjective character to the basic rules besides the known-in-common objective character. Actors have a 'private life', according to Garfinkel, but from a sociological perspective it is most interesting how they succeed in having a public world known in common with others, which is so pervasive that quite drastic breaches are required to reveal it.

What makes Garfinkel's interpretation of the natural attitude particularly interesting for this study is that it includes a concept of 'trust' (mostly set in inverted commas by him) which I regard as fundamental to the natural-attitude view of trust: 'To say that one person "trusts" another means that the person seeks to act in such a fashion as to produce through his action or to respect as conditions of play actual events that accord with normative orders of events depicted in the basic rules of play' and 'the player takes for granted the basic rules of the game as a definition of his situation, and that means of course as a definition of his relationships to others' (Garfinkel, 1963, pp. 193–94). This means, on the one hand, that people trust each other if their interactions are governed by the three constitutive expectancies listed above. If this is the case, then trust can be regarded more generally as 'a condition for "grasping" the events of daily life' (p. 190).

Moreover, though, compliance with basic rules and constitutive expectancies also means reliance on them. Trust in the natural attitude means interacting with others on the basis that everyone knows and accepts basic rules for the interaction. Garfinkel calls for a sociological method that recognizes both local specificity (ethno) and systematic procedures (methodology) in achieving social relations (Heritage, 1987; Giddens, 1993; Scott, 2001). It should be noted that Garfinkel's ethnomethodology implies that there is no *universal* set of basic rules for social interaction but that the *specific* basic rules in a given context are often highly institutionalized.

Around the same time as Garfinkel and equally drawing on Schützian phenomenology, Peter Berger and Thomas Luckmann (1966) propose at the heart of their seminal social-constructionist theory the components of the process whereby actors construct 'society as objective reality'. Berger and Luckmann seek to explain how basic rules are established and maintained over countless interactions independent of their origins and across more than one generation of interactors via 'institutionalization' and 'legitimation'. First, institutions are understood basically as 'a reciprocal typification of habitualized actions by types of actors' (p. 54). For institutionalization to take place the following is necessary: actors repeat an action to the extent that it becomes a habit of those actors. The habit is *externalized*, i.e. separated from the time and place of action and thus typified as a type of action that a certain type of actor will regularly engage in. When typifications become reciprocal in that they are shared by and available to most actors in the relevant group or community, then they are *objectivated* in the sense of a Durkheimian social fact and part of the taken-for-granted social reality. According to Berger and Luckmann, full institutionalization requires a third element: the *internalization* of social reality by the actors, whereby it is 'retrojected into consciousness' so that actors conform to generalized, reciprocal typifications (for example 'roles') in their own behaviour.

Berger and Luckmann (1966) describe institutionalization as 'an ongoing dialectical process' (p. 129), which they emphatically summarize as follows: '*Society is a human product. Society is an objective reality.*

Man is a social product' (p. 61, emphasis in original). Actors make society and are made by society. In Garfinkelian terms, they create and maintain the basic rules by which they as actors are constituted and governed. However, since actors cannot be involved in the making of all institutions but are supposed to internalize them anyway, Berger and Luckmann (1966) discuss the concept of legitimation as the second-order objectivation of meaning whereby a cognitive justification is added to established institutions in order to ensure, for example, that an institution can be passed on from one context or generation to the next and that competing institutional requirements can be reconciled. This is an interesting concept because it implies that the 'objective reality' of society is still open to interpretation and modification.

In a similar vein, Lynne Zucker (1977; see also Zucker, 1983, 1987) notes that institutionalization can be seen as a *process* of defining social reality or as a *property* of an act as socially more or less taken for granted. For example, institutionalizing a ban on child labour is a process (re)producing social definitions of childhood and labour. And it depends on time and place to what degree such a ban has the property of being taken for granted. Thus Zucker emphasizes on the one hand that objective reality or social facts may persist even when they are not internalized and on the other hand that the degree of institutionalization can vary from high to low (Jepperson, 1991). Highly institutionalized acts have ready-made accounts, meaning that they are easily legitimated, while less institutionalized acts are not so taken-for-granted and therefore will not influence the behaviour of others as strongly.

Zucker (1977) hypothesizes and finds experimental support for a positive relationship between the degree of institutionalization and 'cultural persistence', meaning the transmission, maintenance and resistance to change of cultural understandings. For example, framing an interaction as taking place in an organizational context – used as an example of high institutionalization – activates certain institutionalized basic rules about acting in such a context. The mere fact of being in an organizational context triggers certain taken-for-granted expectations, for example, about respect towards authority (Zucker, 1987). This research thus supports the phenomenological concept of the natural attitude by showing that in highly institutionalized contexts an actor is 'motivated to comply because otherwise his actions and those of others in the system cannot be understood' (Zucker, 1977, p. 726). At the same time, Zucker points out that many acts take place in contexts of low institutionalization, which has to

worthy just because of external pressure is not seen as a durable basis for social interaction (except in rationalist accounts). The idea of trust as coercive institutional isomorphism may still apply, though, if the external pressure is predominantly latent but gives 'structural assurance' (McKnight et al., 1998, p. 479).

The second mechanism of institutional isomorphism identified by DiMaggio and Powell (1983) is mimicry ('mimetic processes', p. 151) or 'modelling' (Galaskiewicz and Wasserman, 1989). An actor imitates, implicitly or explicitly, the behaviour of another. This mechanism applies especially in contexts of high uncertainty and ambiguity where legitimacy can be obtained by doing as everybody else or a recognized referent does. The act as such is detached from its utility and reduced to the question of 'appropriateness' (March and Olsen, 1989). Considering trust according to this logic, actors who do not know if it is prudent to place or honour trust will do whatever (relevant) others would normally do in this situation.

Third, normative isomorphism entails the general principle that socialization instils particular cognitive bases and legitimations in the actors subject to them (DiMaggio and Powell, 1983). This mechanism comes closest to the idea of a natural attitude and the view that institutions frame how actors can grasp their lifeworld and relate to it in their actions. Role expectations are learned and fulfilled because they go hand in hand with the actor's self-image or identity and 'what such a person must do'. Once actors have internalized norms and accepted roles associated with a part of their lifeworld, they enact those roles mostly implicitly but at times also explicitly. This produces isomorphism in the sense that all actors who play the same institutionalized role will do so in a standard, recognized, legitimate way. Trust as normative isomorphism would thus mean that actors who have been socialized to place or honour trust in certain types of situation will conform to this expectation, because otherwise they would be going against their own nature or against the objective reality of society (Zucker, 1986). This view of isomorphic, unquestioned trust can explain, for example, manifestations of trust that cannot be explained by calculativeness.

In summary, DiMaggio and Powell's three mechanisms of institutional isomorphism offer explanations for trust that represent a genuine alternative to rationalist accounts, since external pressure, modelling and socialization influence action independently of its conceivable utility to the actor. Nevertheless, there is some rationality in the idea of trust as institutional isomorphism, because legitimacy is considered a good reason for acting in a way that avoids sanctions, imitates generalized others or conforms to role expectations. However, the motivation to trust comes from the context of the action rather than from the specific trustee. The trustor relies on institutions instead of perceived trustworthiness: trust stems from the actors' isomorphism with institutionalized cognitions and actions and is thus due to external pressures to conform, the imitation of others in the face of uncertainty, or internalized norms and roles. This theoretical approach is further supported by Richard Scott's (2001) analytic framework, which consists of 'three pillars of institutions' and confirms the mechanisms suggested by DiMaggio and Powell, although Scott's three pillars do not match exactly their three mechanisms of institutional isomorphism. Despite the differences, when interpreting Scott's framework with a view to the concept of trust, compliance with institutions likewise emerges as a motivation for trust that is (to a greater or lesser extent) based on taken-for-grantedness and independent of utility.

3.4 RULES, ROLES AND ROUTINES

Although there is currently no established neoinstitutionalist school of trust research and the above sections only identify a few concepts that it might entail, the trust literature contains many relevant references to rules, roles and routines as bases for trust. Some of this literature will be reviewed briefly in this section in order to show that arguments building on notions of natural attitude and institutional isomorphism are not uncommon. I will not discuss those contributions that see rules, roles and routines primarily as carriers of cost or utility that can be factored into rational calculations – my reason being that it is often argued that these trust bases have to remain latent and can only support trust if they serve as background assumptions and as safeguards that are preferably not activated (Luhmann, 1979).

Contracts, for example, define the specific rules for the relationship between the contracting parties within the general rules of contract law. While Macaulay (1963) or Beale and Dugdale (1975) claim that contracts are generally a sign of distrust and that many businessmen prefer not to have them, Niklas Luhmann (1979) recognizes that 'legal arrangements which lend special assurance to particular expectations, and make them sanctionable ... lessen the risk of conferring trust' (p. 34). However, he makes it equally clear that 'trust cannot be reduced to trust in the law and in the sanctions which the law makes possible' (p. 35) and that in trust relationships 'calculation should remain latent, evolving in its generalizing fashion covertly, purely as a reassuring consideration' (p. 36).

Recently, Rosalinde Klein Woolthuis, Bas Hillebrand and Bart Nooteboom (2005) have also pointed out that the relationship between trust and formal contract depends very much in practice on when, why and how contracts are used. They show that trust and contract can be both complements and substitutes. Deepak Malhotra and Keith Murnighan (2002) distinguish binding and non-binding contracts and find that they have different effects on building and maintaining trust. It is clear, however, that whenever contractual mechanisms are used, the parties involved intend to agree on rules for their relationship and make reference to generalized sets of rules as embodied in contract law and trade customs. As Christel Lane (1998) remarks 'law and other social institutions are viewed as mechanisms to coordinate expectations which make the risk of trust more bearable' (p. 13). In a similar vein, James Hagen and Soon-kyoo Choe (1998) point out in their study on trust in Japanese interfirm relations that 'the institutionalized industry practices that we call "institutional sanctions," in the context of societal sanction, are key determinants of interfirm cooperation' (p. 598) and in their opinion also foster trust. Not the enforcement of sanctions but the assurance and orientation gained from their existence promotes trust.

The proposition that legal and other institutionalized regulations support trust between actors has received the most comprehensive treatment to date as one theme in the Cambridge Contracting Study involving a group of researchers at the University of Cambridge (see also Chapter 6). They 'examine how legal institutions influence actors' decisions to either readily trust their business partners or to be highly suspicious of them' (Lane and Bachmann, 1996, p. 368). They see contract law, trade associations, technical norms and standards, financial and educational systems, the role of the state and other elements of the institutional framework as important for trust-based interaction (Lane and Bachmann, 1996; Arrighetti et al., 1997; Lane, 1997; Deakin and Wilkinson, 1998). Reinhard Bachmann (1998) proposes that 'trust-based relationships and the generation of trust in economic relationships are highly dependent on the nature of the institutional environment in which they are embedded' (p. 299). The main concepts are borrowed from Luhmann's (1979, 1988) functionalist system-theoretical view of trust, in particular the notion of connectability, but they have much in common with the phenomenological roots of neoinstitutionalism (Lane, 1997), as the following key assumption reveals: 'Institutions are thus reconstructed as mechanisms to reduce risk and uncertainty for social actors whose first problem is not how to select profitable occasions for trust investment but, above all else, to establish shared meaning as a fundamental precondition of the possibility of social action' (Lane and Bachmann, 1996, p. 370).

If the main problem of trust, accordingly, is not opportunism but the ability to engage in meaningful interaction in the first place, then contract law, trade associations and technical standards are social institutions that embody systems of rules for interaction and thus a basis for trust, if rules are understood as cultural meaning systems (Lane, 1997). It should be noted that the scholars involved in the Cambridge Contracting Study seem to have a particular mechanism in mind when they say that rules are a basis for trust: put simply, following Luhmann, they imagine that rules reduce complexity to a level where the further reduction of complexity by trust becomes possible. Moreover, following Zucker, this theory allows that, once common expectations are institutionally given, the agents' self-interest can come into play. Institutional reduction thus precedes and prepares trust. I would be inclined to conclude that this notion is close to explaining trust away in the manner of rationalist theories, were it not for the phenomenological need for meaning that is provided by rules and, indeed, required to conceive of more or less trusting social interactions at all.

A similar logic applies to the idea that trust can be based on roles. For example, when Bernard Barber (1983, p. 9) identifies the 'expectation of technically competent role performance' as one key element of trust, he already presupposes institutionalized roles or what he calls 'shorthand ways of referring to complex patterns of expectations among actors' which make it possible to trust (or distrust) a role incumbent. The 'swift trust' in temporary systems described by Debra Meyerson, Karl Weick and Roderick Kramer (1996) is a special but highly illustrative example of how reliance on clearly defined roles makes trustful interactions possible even when these interactions are relatively isolated and transient as, for example, in project work: 'If people in temporary systems deal with one another more as roles than as individuals ... then expectations should be more stable, less capricious, more standardized, and defined more in terms of tasks and specialities than personalities' (p. 173).

That the notion of role-based trust applies not only to temporary but also to long-term interpersonal relations can be inferred from Shmuel

Eisenstadt and Luis Roniger's (1984) social anthropological study of institutionalized trust in patron–client relationships across a broad range of
societies, where taking the role of patron or client respectively implies
society-specific expectations of trust. However, Eisenstadt and Roniger
(1984) also emphasize the 'dialectics of trust and the social order' (p. 294),
meaning that while trust becomes institutionalized in patron and client
roles on the one hand, actors also seek to establish a 'pristine' trust on the
other, whereby they avoid and subvert institutions.

According to Berger and Luckmann (1966) – who claim that their
conception is very close to George Herbert Mead's (1934) definition of
role and is an expansion of his role theory in a broader frame that includes a theory of institutions – roles are types of actors in a context
where action is typified and available as common knowledge to a collec-
tivity of actors. Roles distance the actor from the action because, by enacting a type, the unique individual is only partially involved in the action. At the same time, the individual requires roles in order to become
socially active: 'By playing roles, the individual participates in a social
world. By internalizing these roles, the same world becomes subjectively
real to him' (Berger and Luckmann, 1966, p. 74). In return, roles are only
maintained by being enacted: 'The institution with its assemblage of
"programmed" actions, is like the unwritten libretto [script] of a drama.
The realization of the drama depends upon the reiterated performance of
prescribed roles by living actors' (p. 75).

Although the analogy of the drama might be a bit forced and even
misleading, it is often used in the literature and surfaces, for example, in
Meyer and Rowan's view of isomorphism as dramatic enactment (see
above). The notion that actors need roles while not being totally defined
by them also features in Erving Goffman's (1959) famous study on 'the
presentation of self in everyday life', and particularly in his description of
the actors' use of 'front', 'impression management' and other skills in
achieving coherent social interaction including the handling of discrepant
roles. James Henslin (1968) hits a similar note in his taxi driver study:
'When an actor has offered a definition of himself and the audience is
willing to interact with the actor on the basis of that definition, we are
saying trust exists' (p. 54). Thus roles carry the taken-for-granted expectations on which trust can be based.

The concept of role is also central to Adam Seligman's (1997) social-
philosophical analysis of trust, but in his framework reliance on role expectations merely gives 'confidence', whereas the problem of 'trust' only

arises in the face of role negotiability: 'Trust is something that enters into social relations when there is role negotiability, in what may be termed the "open spaces" of roles and role expectations' (pp. 24–25). Seligman claims that pervasive role negotiability is a defining aspect of modernity and stems from the proliferation of roles, ensuing dissonances and gaps in (no longer) taken-for-granted definitions of roles. While Seligman's account thus points to the limits of the institutional approach, the unconditionality that to him characterizes trust may not be too different from the Schützian natural attitude, where actors play an active part in interpreting their lifeworlds, normalizing events and socially constructing reality. At least Seligman supports the view that role expectations are a basis for confidence. If we assume further that all roles may in principle be negotiable but cannot be negotiated all at once, then Seligman's 'confidence' and 'trust' have to go hand in hand, requiring a kind of Garfinkelian constitutive expectancy that at any given moment in time most role expectations will not be negotiated. After all, even Garfinkel's experiments would not have 'worked' (in the sense of producing meaningful findings) if he and his students had breached all rules and roles at once, which would be difficult to imagine anyway.

Finally, routines (in a narrower sense) will be introduced here as a third heuristic alongside rules and roles in order to lend the notion of trust based on institutions greater plasticity. Routines are regularly and habitually performed programmes of action or procedures. They may or may not be supported by corresponding (systems of) rules and/or roles, and they represent institutions in as much as they are typified, objectivated and legitimated, not senseless repetitions, although their sense is mostly tacit and taken-for-granted whilst they are performed (Scott, 2001). As with rules and roles, 'the reality of everyday life maintains itself by being embodied in routines' (Berger and Luckmann, 1966, p. 149). Similarly, Anthony Giddens (1984) points out: 'Routine is integral both to the continuity of the personality of the agent, as he or she moves along the paths of daily activities, and to the institutions of society, which are such only through their continued reproduction' (p. 60).

As the last quotation suggests, by drawing on the work of Erikson and Goffman, Giddens (1984) argues that 'routinization' sustains and is sustained by 'ontological security', the basic trust of the actor within and towards the 'habitual, taken-for-granted character of the vast bulk of the activities of day-to-day social life' (p. 376; see also Giddens, 1990). More specifically, routines can be a basis for trust because they mean predictability to the actors involved, who take for granted that a known sequence of actions and (presumably desirable) outcomes will unfold again, in which their own vulnerability should be minimal or, at least, not greater than in the past (Misztal, 1996).

Chris Grey and Christina Garsten (2001) confirm the trust-enhancing potential of routines at the organizational level when they state that 'bureaucratic organizations have been extremely effective in producing trust' (p. 244) in the sense that classic bureaucratic structures confer predictability, but these authors also point out convincingly that the advent of 'post-bureaucratic organization' (Heckscher and Donelleon, 1994) implies a need for organizational flexibility. This flexibility, however, could undermine the bases of trust, which can only be replaced partially by corporate culture within the organization and by transorganizational professionalization (Oliver, 1997). Predictability and stability have also been at the centre of attention in research on organizational routines (Becker, 2004) while the possibility of seeing them also as a 'source of continuous change' has become a popular refinement of the traditional view (Feldman, 2000).

It should be noted that, in contrast to rationalist theories in which predictability is an indicator of individual trustworthiness, the neoinstitutionalist view stresses a non-calculative view of routines as unquestioned (though 'questionable') procedures. The placing and honouring of trust itself is seen as part of the routine. For example, most parents will not fret every morning when their child leaves for school, because entrusting the child to the care of bus drivers, teachers and others is part of a daily routine. However, this brings up a higher-order problem of trust again: trust in the reliability of the routine in continuously producing the same (range of) outcomes and more importantly trust in the motivation and ability of the actors involved not to deviate from the programme of action – for whatever reason. Agency cannot be explained away (Feldman and Pentland, 2003).

In sum, rules, roles and routines are bases for trust in so far as they represent taken-for-granted expectations that give meaning to, but cannot guarantee, their fulfilment in action. However, this explanation has to be incomplete, because a neoinstitutionalist view affords both the trustor and the trustee a non-passive role in challenging, changing and cheating the institutions, albeit not all of them all at once and all the time. This notion of agency (DiMaggio, 1988; Beckert, 1999) will be addressed in the next chapter, but first I should perhaps pursue the simpler issue that a trustor who trusts on the basis of institutions needs to have trust in those institutions, given that they cannot be assumed to be infallible and immutable.

3.5 TRUST IN INSTITUTIONS

Lynne Zucker's (1986) 'institutional-based trust' is conceptually interesting and, according to her, empirically vital because it implies that a trustor can trust a trustee without establishing 'process-based trust' in a personal relationship. However, as Jörg Sydow (1998) argues, this makes institutions an object of trust, too, and not only a source. An analytical distinction therefore has to be drawn between the influence that institutions have on the trustor–trustee relationship on the one hand and the trust that actors have in the institutions on the other. This latter notion of trust in the system, in particular at the societal level, has been the main area of interest in a significant part of the trust literature, notably political science-orientated work, such as Barber (1983), Dunn (1988), Coleman (1990), Fukuyama (1995), Putnam (1995), Sztompka (1999) and Warren (1999), and those studies analysing trust items in large-scale surveys like the General Social Survey in the United States (for example Paxton, 1999; Glaeser et al., 2000). Niklas Luhmann's (1979) assertion that 'the old theme of political trust … has virtually disappeared from contemporary political theory' (p. 54) no longer applies.

In this regard it is interesting to note that Barbara Misztal (1996) presumes that the concern for trust in the social sciences has been – from the classics to the present day – above all else a search for the bases of social order, that is a dependable social system. The requirement of 'trust in the system' is already evident for Hobbes' Leviathan just as much as for Locke's social contract (see for example Dunn, 1988). What this means for modernity and beyond the question of government has been expressed by Georg Simmel ([1907] 1990), who in his discussion of the transition from material money to credit money notes that 'the feeling of personal security that the possession of money gives is perhaps the most concentrated and pointed form and manifestation of confidence in the socio-political organization and order' (p. 179).

Niklas Luhmann (1979) introduces his concept of 'system trust' by reflecting on money, too, and supposes that an actor 'who trusts in the stability of the value of money … basically assumes that a system is functioning and places his trust in that function, not in people' (p. 50). According to Luhmann, system trust builds up through continual, affirmative experiences with the system. It grows and persists precisely because it is impersonal, diffuse and rests on generalization and indifference. However, he recognizes that such systems are difficult to control as 'the person trusting realizes his dependence on the functioning of a highly complex system which he cannot see through, although it is, in itself, capable of being seen through', so that in effect the individual actor 'has to continue trusting as though under compulsion to do so' (p. 50).

Interestingly, Luhmann suggests that abstract systems should have in-built controls which can be maintained by experts. Actors do not need to trust in an impenetrable system as a whole but 'only' in the functioning of controls. In stark contrast to Susan Shapiro (1987), Luhmann does not see an infinite regress of controlling the controls and thus the danger of a spiral of distrust. Moreover, according to Luhmann, system trust also rests on the actor's assumption that everybody else trusts the system, too. While the assurances of experts and others thus give a 'certainty-equivalent', system trust overall means confidence in an unavoidable, disinterested and abstract entity (Luhmann, 1988).

Luhmann does not address a point implicit in his trust concept which I regard as crucial, namely that trust is essentially not so much a choice between one course of action (trusting) and the other (distrusting), but between either accepting a given level of assurance or looking for further controls and safeguards. System trust (and also personal trust) fails or cannot even be said to exist when this state of suspending doubt is not reached. The 'inflationary spiral of escalating trust relationships and the paradox that the more we control the institution of trust, the more dissatisfied we will be with its offerings' attested by Shapiro (1987) for modern societies, where 'the guardians of trust are themselves trustees' (p. 652), are only set in motion if the response to a need for trust is always the installation of more controls, instead of being satisfied at some point that the system apparently 'works'.

That Shapiro's (1987) bleak view could sometimes be justified is demonstrated by Peter Walgenbach (2001), who finds in a sample of German companies that 'the adoption of the ISO 9000 standards and the certification of the quality system did not, as was intended, result in trust in interorganizational relationships. On the contrary, it produced distrust in the ISO 9000 certification' (p. 696). Overall, this supports the view that institutions cannot be effective bases for trust if they are not trusted themselves. If and when they are trusted, though, this fosters trust at the interpersonal or interorganizational level, as John Child and I were able to show in our survey of Hong Kong managers' trust in Chinese operations (Child and Möllering, 2003). We found that Hong Kong managers' confidence in China's legal system, in the reliability of officials and in the availability of competent human resources influences their trust in local staff positively.

As Seligman (1997) and Lane (1998) have noticed, the ideas of Anthony Giddens and Niklas Luhmann on impersonal trust are very similar and the former has certainly borrowed from the latter, although their frameworks are by no means identical. In particular, Giddens (1990) captures more lucidly than Luhmann how actors can have trust in abstract systems or institutions. He describes the 'access points' where the actor experiences the system by interacting with other actors, typically experts who represent the system. If institutionalization in the terminology of Giddens means 'disembedding', i.e. 'the "lifting out" of social relations from local contexts of interaction and their restructuring across indefinite spans of time-space' (p. 21) and if '[a]ll disembedding mechanisms … depend upon trust' (p. 26), then 'reembedding', i.e. 'the reappropriation or recasting of disembedded social relations' (p. 79) which happens at the 'access points' of abstract systems, enables the constitution of trust in those systems. Put less technically, patients, for example, develop trust (or distrust) in the medical system to a large extent through their experiences with doctors and other medical professionals, such as nurses and midwives, who represent and 'embody' the institutions of medicine (see recently Brownlie and Howson, 2005; Lowe, 2005).

Referring to the example of medical professionals, Talcott Parsons (1978) notes that a 'competence gap' between professionals and laypersons 'must be bridged by something like what we call trust' (p. 46). He argues that this trust has to be based on a 'feeling' of solidarity within collective groups, which acquires a certain autonomy of its own once it is established. In other words, according to Parsons, as long as doctors and patients perceive a mutual moral obligation, it is not necessary that the patients increase their knowledge about the medical profession in order to close the competence gap, which would be neither feasible nor sensible anyhow. While Parson's account is probably debatable and certainly one-sided (see also Misztal, 1996), it matches Giddens' view in that solidarity between doctors and patients produces trust in the abstract system of medicine *indirectly* at the interaction level. Patients who experience solidarity from their own doctors will develop and maintain trust in the medical system as a whole on this basis.

However, as Luhmann pointed out, too, the object of system trust is indeed the system as such, but since it is impossible for individual actors to comprehend the system, they can only assure themselves of its proper functioning through the re-embedded performances of experts who refer to and represent a particular system. Giddens (1990) goes further than Luhmann (1979) and places a different emphasis, because he does not see the role of experts primarily in controlling the system but in bringing it to life. According to Giddens (1990), if trust in systems is 'faceless' and trust in persons involves 'facework', then systems obtain a 'face' at their 'access points', which sustains or transforms 'faceless commitments' (p. 88). This interplay of disembedding and re-embedding is not unproblematic, which Giddens demonstrates by describing, on the one hand, how carefully system representatives design their performances in order to quell doubts about the system's functioning while, on the other, actors pragmatically accept the system but also retain an attitude of scepticism. Again, trust seems to involve 'normalizing' (Garfinkel) or 'good faith' (Meyer and Rowan), that is a certain acceptance of ignorance and suspension of doubt, which is typical for the natural attitude but requires further examination. Neither Luhmann nor Giddens would be called neoinstitutionalists, but their concepts of trust in systems connect well with the idea of trust in institutions. Trust in an institution means confidence in the institution's reliable functioning, but this has to be based mainly on trust in visible controls or representative performances rather than on the internal workings of the institution as a whole.

Institutions can be seen as bases, carriers and objects of trust: trust between actors can be based on institutions, trust can be institutionalized, and institutions themselves can only be effective if they are trusted (see also Child and Möllering, 2003). While this is perfectly in line with sociological neoinstitutionalism, it has become apparent in the course of this chapter that this approach reveals, but does not fully explain, how actors achieve the natural attitude, the acceptance of normality, the assumption of good faith and similar notions that actually point towards the imperfection of institutions. Hence, a more elaborate development of this approach will also have to face the questions which currently plague neoinstitutionalism. For example, the power of institutional explanations hinges on the possibility of defining in empirical terms the reach and the boundaries of institutions. This leads DiMaggio and Powell (1983) to conceptualize the organizational field as 'those organizations that, in the aggregate, constitute a recognized area of institutional life' and, more generally, 'the totality of relevant actors' (p. 148). But how can actors who come from very different, possibly contradictory environments establish a new common context in which they trust each other?

A similar issue is captured by the discussions about the 'institutional entrepreneur' (DiMaggio, 1988) as an actor who plays an outstanding role in reflexively creating, preserving and changing specific institutions (see also Beckert, 1999). Can a corresponding role be conceived for a kind of trust entrepreneur who actively shapes context in a trust-enhancing manner? In other words, the image of 'routine trust' provokes questions such as: Where do trust routines come from? Who influences them? What is the role of those using them? And how do the consequences of trust routines feed back into their constitution? These questions suggest that it may be necessary to view trust in terms of a reflexive process. In the next chapter, I will adopt this perspective.

4

TRUST AND REFLEXIVITY

4.1 ADOPTING A PROCESS VIEW

In the previous two chapters, I discussed research that presents trust as a matter of reason or routine. In both cases, trust depends on the availability of 'given' factors, for example pay-off estimates or institutionalized rules. I also argued, though, that such factors cannot always be taken for granted and that trust would even become meaningless if they were. So let us go to the other extreme and ask whether trust is possible at all in situations when it may be needed most, that is in highly uncertain and unfamiliar circumstances.

Daniel Defoe's ([1719] 1994) *Robinson Crusoe* still captivates our imagination to the present day with a scenario that places the protagonist on an apparently uninhabited island. Life is risky, but trust is not an issue for him until he meets Friday (Craswell, 1993). At the first encounter, Robinson cannot really apply reason or routine as he would at home, because he knows nothing about trustworthiness, utility, rules, institutions and so on in this setting. Hence, it is difficult for him to decide on a trusting 'strategy', which is complicated further by the fact that Friday's own 'strategy' in response to discovering Robinson is uncertain, but crucial, too (Tsebelis, 1989). In other words, there is no game to start with or, at least, not one that gives a basis for trust; there is only the extreme prospect of killing or being killed, which is likely to be unrealistic, but too dangerous to be naively or heroically ignored in favour of a hope for cooperation and solidarity. What would be required is that, in a *process*

may be destroyed, if it develops at all, or undesirable trust may persist. If trust were not open-ended like this, then again we would be thinking in terms of an assumed certainty that makes the notion of trust superfluous. In the following sections, I will discuss how trust processes may be started 'blindly', how trust typically undergoes gradual growth and trans- formations, how it relates to reflexive familiarization and structuration, and how, in all of this, actors play an active role which is expressed most strongly in the concept of active trust.

4.2 THE FUNCTIONALITY OF 'BLIND' TRUST

Rational choice theories of trust in particular, but to some extent neoin- stitutionalist theories too, face the problem of inadequacy (Elster, 1989b) when they predict that under certain conditions actors will not trust, but then realize that empirically trust occurs nevertheless. From an observer's point of view, and perhaps equally from the actor's perspective, any trust that goes against, overlooks or ignores rational or institutional good rea- sons would have to be considered 'blind' trust. It will be argued later that all trust is partially blind, but here it should first be examined how and why a number of researchers argue that this 'blind trust' is actually quite functional although it may not be strictly rational or backed up by taken- for-granted accounts.

In other words, sometimes actors can serve their interests better by be- ing non-rational or even irrational rather than rational. For instance, with reference to why trustors are often slow to change their views and pre- conceptions, even if contrary information is available, David Good (1988) points out that '[t]o be non-rational in this way is a decidedly rational strategy for coping with limits in one's rationality' (p. 42). Even Oliver Williamson (1993), who rejects the usage of 'trust' for explaining ra- tional, calculative economic phenomena, acknowledges 'that it is some- times desirable to suppress calculativeness. If, however, the decision to suppress calculativeness is itself purposive and calculative, then the true absence of calculativeness is rare if not nonexistent' (p. 479). While these assertions raise the higher-order problem of how the actor can determine rationally whether it pays to be rational or not, it is generally recognized that apparently non-rational acts that trigger a process of trust building can be functional and, with hindsight, 'rational' or at least justifiable.

Moreover, it is a common idea that 'blind' action in the sense of unintentional or coincidental behaviour may trigger a process of desirable interactions that could not have been willingly produced as easily. For example, as already mentioned above, Axelrod (1984), who is interested in cooperation and repeatedly states that trust is not required for cooperation, nevertheless makes an interesting observation with regard to 'blind' trust when he says that cooperation between actors in a prisoner's dilemma-type situation is more likely, first, if there are actors who are simply nice in that they never defect first although the pay-off matrix tells them to do so. Second, cooperation can even emerge from actions that were not meant to be either cooperative or non-cooperative, but are interpreted and reciprocated as such by others, as in the case of 'live and let live' practices observed in trench warfare. Axelrod goes on to use examples of cooperation from biology to show that neither rationality, intent, friendship, trust or even communication are necessary, although each may be helpful, to set in motion a self-reinforcing process of cooperation on which trust may then grow (see above). Without examining Axelrod's evolutionary theory of cooperation in more detail, it is interesting to note for the purposes of this chapter how he describes non-rational 'blind' solutions as possible ways out of dilemmas.

Diego Gambetta (1988d) highlights that Axelrod's findings only make sense if we assume the presence of a basic disposition towards *conditional* trust. In other words, we need to explain why actors in reality are basically nice, provocable and also forgiving as captured by the tit-for-tat strategy that won Axelrod's tournament (see Chapter 2). The main point, however, is that actors are able to learn 'that it can be rewarding to behave *as if* we trusted even in unpromising situations' (Gambetta, 1988d, p. 228). This learning process enables trust-building processes to take place (see also Nooteboom, 2003).

Russell Hardin (1993) makes repeated reference to a very similar idea when he allows for strategic 'as-if trust' alongside rational trust based on encapsulated interest (see Chapter 2). Accordingly, imagine an actor who thinks that trust would be desirable but cannot rationally trust the potential trustee yet. This actor may *nevertheless* choose to feign trust with the aim of building up genuine trust. Hardin claims that 'as-if trust can be willed repeatedly so that one may slowly develop optimistic trust, just as Pascal said one may wilfully set about following religious practices in order to come to believe' (p. 515). In an earlier paper, Hardin uses similar reasoning to dismiss the backward induction argument in game theory (Luce and Raiffa, 1957): 'I can now wreck your backward induction by simply cooperating on our first encounter. You may now suppose that I am irrational, or you may reconsider your induction. Either way, you may now decide it is in your interest to reciprocate my cooperation, so that we both benefit far beyond what we would have got from continuous mutual defection' (Hardin, 1991, p. 188). In short, trust-like action might produce trust (see Chapter 5).

Hardin's idea of 'as-if trust' as a mental strategy that should produce genuine trust sits uneasily with his insistence on rational choice. In his street-level epistemology of trust he recognizes the possibility that blind, trust-like action may trigger at least some of the instances that cannot be explained by, but rather produce, an encapsulation of interest. Hardin envisages as-if trust being used when the trustor only has a vague notion that a trustful, cooperative relationship with the potential trustee could be beneficial. However, as already noted above, it is difficult to determine within a rational choice framework how much non-rationality will be rational for the actor in such an uncertain context. As-if trust therefore remains at least partly non-rational itself – the trustor *just does it*.

While authors like Axelrod, Gambetta and Hardin merely acknowledge the potential functionality of non-rational trust, Niklas Luhmann (1979) puts the functionality of trust as a mechanism for the reduction of social complexity at the heart of his concept of trust, arguing that any sense of 'rationality' in trust should only be considered in terms of its functionality for the trustor in dealing with complexity. Through trust, the trustor gains an 'inner certainty' that raises the 'tolerance of uncertainty in external relationships' (p. 26). Individual acts or decisions of trust, however, cannot be judged rational in themselves: 'Trust is not a means that can be chosen for particular ends, much less an end/means structure capable of being optimized. Nor is trust a prediction, the correctness of which could be measured when the predicted event occurs and after some experience reduced to a probability value. ... Trust is, however, something other than a reasonable assumption on which to decide correctly, and for this reason models for calculating correct decisions miss the point of the question of trust' (p. 88).

Luhmann surely recognizes the role that the trustor's considerations play, but he ultimately describes trust as 'blind' in the sense that it is only rational if it is functional for the system. Not the rational validity of expectations and generalizations as such but their availability in the first place is what makes trust functional: 'Without trust only very simple forms of human co-operation which can be transacted on the spot are possible' (p. 88). What for Axelrod and Hardin represents a possibility, like an exception that proves the rule, comes out as the rule in Luhmann's concept: trust can be functional and system-rational by not being rational in itself.

David Lewis and Andrew Weigert (1985) take their lead directly from Luhmann when they present rationality and trust as 'a functional alternative to rational prediction for the reduction of complexity. Indeed, trust succeeds where rational prediction alone would fail, because to trust is to live *as if* certain rationally possible futures will not occur' (p. 969). Luhmann says that, as far as the techniques of rational choice and optimization extend, trust is unnecessary, but conversely the need for trust reflects the limited effectiveness of those techniques. And Lewis and Weigert underscore this view: 'Trust begins where prediction ends' (p. 976). They do not eliminate rationality from their concept of trust, but combine rationality and emotionality, arguing that trust is a mix of feeling and rational thinking. Emotion and affect in themselves may not be rational, but they can rescue the actor from dilemmas and dysfunctional social paralysis, for better or worse (see also Chapter 2).

As a final reference to the common recognition in the literature of the functionality of 'blind' trust, Piotr Sztompka (1999) should be mentioned, if only because he draws on both Luhmann and Hardin when he concludes: 'It may be argued that under some circumstances extending trust a priori, without any grounds, as a pure "leap of faith", may be functional' (p. 109). This follows a discussion on the question of the functionality of trust in which Sztompka argues that trust is dysfunctional when it is placed in the untrustworthy, just as distrust towards the trustworthy is dysfunctional. On the one hand, this raises the important qualification, recognized also by Luhmann, Gambetta and Hardin, that trust is not always, and by definition, functional in terms of desirable or ethical outcomes. Not only are there potential errors due to the bounded rationality of the trustor and the principal freedom of the trustee; functionality also depends on what trust is used for and whose functionality is assessed (trustor, trustee, third parties, society).

On the other hand, Sztompka is forced to acknowledge that the conclusion cannot be that 'blind' trust is always dysfunctional, but that it may actually be extremely functional in a situation where sufficient evidence is not available. Such situations may not be uncommon, especially since Sztompka states earlier on, when discussing the foundations of trust, that 'grounds for trust are never conclusive nor foolproof' (p. 69). This does not fit well with the rational choice perspective that Sztompka favours. Even his Colemanian definition of trust as a 'bet' (p. 25) is supplemented, and in my view thereby qualified, when Sztompka states: 'Placing trust we behave "as if" we knew the future' (pp. 25–26). This statement is framed by quotations from Good (1988) and Luhmann (1979) which highlight the element of non-rationality in the trustor's expectations. The 'as if' could thus be a reference to Lewis and Weigert's notion of trust beyond the limits of rationality, but in Sztompka's application it might well connote a strategic decision by the trustor along the lines of Hardin's 'as-if trust'. At any rate, Sztompka acknowledges that trust may be more than a rational choice and that the non-rational, 'blind' part of trust may be functional (see also Chapter 5).

Overall, trust researchers recognize the possibility that a kind of 'blind' trust can emerge in the absence of reliable foundations for trust and that the functionality of trust, though never guaranteed, is in principle independent of how 'blind' trust is. The argument presented here emphasizes the potential irrelevance of rationality for the emergence of trust, but an equal line of thinking could be constructed regarding the possibility of trust to emerge 'blindly' in the absence of reliable institutions. Functionalist approaches would indeed argue that all that matters is that a trust-building process emerges *at all*. Actors may choose to 'just do it' and trust blindly in order to overcome rational or institutional vacuums and paradoxes. In the light of this, I now propose to discuss the common view that trust builds over time, which is related to the points just raised, because this view also suggests that it does not matter what induces the trust-building process, if only it gets started somehow in the first place.

4.3 EXPERIENCE AND THE 'PRINCIPLE OF GRADUALNESS'

Hardin (1993) clearly presents the strategy of as-if trust as a temporary solution which enables a process whereby the trustor can gradually cease to feign trust because genuine trust develops as the trustor uses his instinctive Bayesianism to update and refine his estimates of the others' trustworthiness over time, according to Hardin's 'street-level epistemology' of trust (see Chapter 2; see also Henslin, 1968; Gambetta and Hamill, 2005). This somewhat mechanistic, but only mildly rationalistic process is also referred to as 'learned trust' (Hardin, 2002) and captures the idea that trusting choices may be based on an extrapolation of past experience in an embedded context, rather than on concrete utility considerations in a specific situation (see also Buskens, 2002; Buskens and Raub, 2002). Charles Sabel's (1993) concept of 'studied trust' expresses a similar notion. Moreover, if trust is generally functional in that it reduces social complexity, it does not necessarily mean that trust has to reduce complexity immediately or completely. Instead a 'principle of gradualness' (Luhmann, 1979, p. 41) can be followed. Trust is generated and extended step by step, beginning with relatively small steps. This implies that trust building requires time and may be rather tentative (Barnes, 1981; Larson, 1992). In this section, I will discuss some of the classic, and some more recent, treatments of trust as a matter of gradual experience and learning from interactions.

In his seminal work on social exchange theory, Peter Blau (1964) makes several references to trust. For example, when discussing the distinction between economic exchange and social exchange, he notes that one of the properties of social exchange is the tendency to 'engender feelings of personal obligation, gratitude, and trust' (p. 94). Blau does not define trust and essentially takes the concept for granted. He only makes some tentative remarks that trust involves an inherently diffuse feeling that is different from the technical notion of contractual, enforceable obligation. The image of 'blurred' trust rather than 'blind' trust would seem to fit here. Indeed, he associates trust with unspecified obligations and open-ended reciprocity (Burt and Knez, 1996; Lane, 1998). Most importantly for the discussion here, though, Blau (1964) contributes the idea that trust evolves and expands gradually in parallel to social associations from minor initial transactions. In another source (Blau, 1968), he gives the following description of this process: 'Social exchange relations evolve in a slow process, starting with minor transactions in which little trust is required because little risk is involved and in which both partners can prove their trustworthiness, enabling them to expand their relation and engage in major transactions. Thus, the process of social exchange leads to the trust required for it in a self-governing fashion' (p. 454, quoted in Burt and Knez, 1996, p. 70).

All in all, Blau thus formulates a variant of what Luhmann (1979) later calls the 'principle of gradualness' for trust. A possible explanation for the mechanism identified by Blau is given by Dale Zand (1972), who presents a 'spiral reinforcement model of the dynamics of trust' (p. 233). This model is based on small group research and builds on earlier work

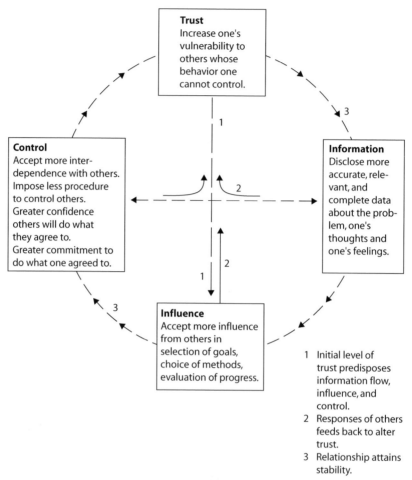

Source: Zand (1972, p. 231).

Figure 4.1   Spiral Reinforcement Model of Trust

by Gibb (1964). In order to show how trust leads to more trust and distrust to more distrust, Zand uses disclosure of information, acceptance of influence and exercise of control as constructs that have a feedback relationship with trust (see Figure 4.1). Accordingly, high initial trust will lead the actor A to disclose information, accept influence and reduce control, which the other actor B perceives as positive signs of trustworthiness that increase B's level of trust and induce similarly open behaviour. This reinforces

A's initial trust and thus leads to further trusting action, reinforcing B's trust and so forth. In the same way, a negative spiral of distrust can occur when the actors start out with low trust expectations, which they then reinforce by their own concealing, defensive and controlling interactions.

Sim Sitkin and Darryl Stickel (1996, drawing conceptually on Sitkin and Roth, 1993) investigate such 'dynamics of distrust' empirically as they emerged in conjunction with the introduction of quality management techniques in a research laboratory. The 'road to hell' that they describe came about when those techniques were interpreted as signs of distrust. In other words, expectations of trust or distrust and the resultant trusting or distrusting action would be a typical example of a self-fulfilling prophecy (Merton, 1949). Zand's model not only illustrates how trust or distrust builds up in a process of interaction, but also highlights the importance of the initial expectations and actions – the first move.

Niklas Luhmann (1979) introduces the 'principle of gradualness' as an example of 'the social conditions which make it easier to bring about relationships of trust' (p. 40) and offers a number of further interesting thoughts on the kinds of action that help to produce trust. Like Zand, who argues, for example, that information sharing by one actor reinforces his being perceived as trustworthy by others, Luhmann assumes that '[t]rust is founded on the motivation attributed to behaviour' (p. 41) and infers from this that actions which are predetermined cannot be significant expressions of an actor's trustworthiness. Rather, the actor must be seen as free to act and then use this freedom in a way that the other will interpret as trustful or trustworthy: 'Acting according to the norm is usually inconspicuous and weak in expression, and therefore is not a suitable base from which love and trust can be generated' (p. 42).

Luhmann describes intensely the necessary features of a trust-building process, only the most important of which can be summarized here. First of all the trustor must increase his vulnerability while the trustee must act against his own interests and forego the possibility of abusing the trust. This establishes the mutual commitment of the actors. However, the actors must also be able to understand that what has happened are deliberate displays of trust and not some ordinary or chance events. The process of building trust may then lead to persistent trust if the actors keep displaying what Luhmann calls 'supererogatory performance' (p. 43), that is action beyond duty or obligation. Such exchanges start with small stakes that are amplified over time unless one of the actors refuses tactfully to participate in the process early on.

As much as Luhmann's trust-building model has in common with the ideas of Blau and Zand, it is remarkable in its emphasis on deliberate imprudence and deviance on the part of the actors. This can be explained to some extent by Luhmann's assumption that trust building is a process of selection which actors engage in continuously in order to determine whom they trust and whom they distrust. Only *exceptional* experiences are valuable to the actor in selecting who can be trusted or not. This is an extreme view, though. Many authors say that simply positive experiences can be the basis for trust development, in particular when such experiences recur consistently.

This perspective of trust based on positive experience matches Lynne Zucker's concept of 'process-based trust' (mentioned in Chapter 3). Zucker (1986) states that process-based trust is 'tied to past or expected exchange such as in reputation or gift-exchange' and informed by 'a record of prior exchange, often obtained second-hand or by imputation from outcomes of prior exchange' (p. 60). Actors establish an exchange history analogous to the traditional giving of gifts and counter-gifts (Mauss, [1925] 1954; Blau, 1964), which involves a trust-inducing time lapse and a formation of mutual expectations of reciprocity. Zucker (1986) points out: 'These kinds of informal process-based mechanisms require extensive interaction over long periods of time and/or produce trust between a small number of individuals involved in a limited set of exchanges. Under most conditions they are highly specific to the individuals (or firms) engaged in the transaction and are governed by idiosyncratic understandings and rules' (p. 62).

The possibility of having direct exchange relationships with others is a condition for process-based trust which, according to Zucker, became increasingly difficult to fulfil in the United States during the 1800s due to immigration, internal migration, social segregation, geographically dispersed non-separable transactions and the instability of firms: when background expectations are not shared and/or exchange partners are variable or anonymous, the trust-building process between specific actors cannot easily be started or maintained.

Unlike, for example, Hardin or Luhmann, Zucker regards the possibility of actively developing process-based trust as extremely limited in modern societies. In her view, process-based trust seems rather to be typical of traditional societies, where exchange relationships emerge automatically among socially and geographically proximate actors. It is therefore a kind of local trust that is 'blind' in the sense of being rather unselective, while it is also an 'active' trust because it becomes established and con-tinuously verified through action. However, Zucker does not suggest that modern actors should aim to establish individually the background expec-tations and proximity which facilitate process-based trust production. In contrast, she observes that institution-based trust replaces process-based trust. Hence, her study describes process-based trust as one important mode of trust, but does not encourage actors to make the experimental 'first moves' discussed above towards others with whom they do not al-ready have a direct continuous exchange relationship.

Moving on to the literature on trust in work relationships, the notion that trust develops gradually and grows with mutual experience in rela-tionships over time is captured very instructively in the model by Roy Lewicki and Barbara Bunker (1995, 1996). Building on concepts by Boon and Holmes (1991) and Shapiro et al. (1992), they describe three types of trust that serve to illustrate the stages of trust development over time. They argue that in the first stage of a new relationship 'calculus-based trust' is required. It rests on calculative reasoning about the other's incen-tives to maintain the relationship and the deterrents preventing him from breaking trust. Where calculus-based trust proves to be valid, the actors may get to know each other better and understand each other's needs, preferences and priorities more generally so that, in the second stage, 'knowledge-based trust' develops, which 'is grounded in the other's pre-dictability – knowing the other sufficiently well so that the other's be-havior is anticipatable' (Lewicki and Bunker, 1996, p. 121).

Interestingly, Lewicki and Bunker point out that not all relationships develop knowledge-based trust on top of calculus-based trust: some rela-tionships will stabilize just on a calculus level, though many relationships do reach knowledge-based trust because the getting-to-know-each-other is almost inevitable. A few relationships may even evolve after some more time to the stage of 'identification-based trust', where the 'parties effectively understand and appreciate the other's wants' and 'each can effectively act for the other' (p. 122). Although calculus and knowledge are still present as bases for trust, identification with the other's desires and intentions becomes the perceptual paradigm for the actors.

Lewicki and Bunker illustrate that trust does not simply grow stronger over time but the 'frame' in which the actors consider trust changes as trust develops, so that the issues faced at an early stage should be very different from those in a long-established, identification-based trust rela-tionship. This is a view that would also be supported, for example, by

Luhmann (1979): 'Once mutual trust has been safely established, it would be blatantly tactless – if not a quite disastrous lapse – if one of the participants wanted to return to the learning stage and to use the cautious strategies which were sensible at that early juncture' (pp. 44–45). In sum, process models suggest that the 'blind', cautious first moves in the trust-building process may not only be functional in the short run, but also be replaced gradually by more thoroughly understanding and committed moves as the content of trust itself evolves along with the relationship.

John Child (1998) adopts Lewicki and Bunker's model in combination with McAllister's (1995) distinction between cognition-based and affect-based trust, and proposes a model of trust evolution, from calculation to prediction to bonding, which mirrors development phases of strategic alliances and joint ventures, from formation through implementation to evolution (see also Child, 2001). He draws on extensive qualitative case-study material to illustrate his model distinguishing between a 'low-trust option' and a 'high-trust option', which foreign investors may use in joint ventures with Chinese partners and which have an impact on the ensuing trust-building processes. Child agrees that to 'begin gradually' (Smitka, 1994, p. 98; see also Larson, 1992) may be sound advice but, interestingly, he also notes that the high-trust option promises a firmer basis than the low-trust option for establishing cooperation in China since it is 'more in tune with underlying Chinese cultural preferences' (Child, 1998, p. 269). Starting with too little trust due to short term economic considerations, partners may never get the trust-building process going, especially in China. This refers us back to the functionality of blind trust discussed earlier in this chapter. It also points to the role of active trust development, which I will look at more closely at the end of this chapter (see also Child and Möllering, 2003).

Other authors studying interorganizational relationships adopt a process view of gradual trust building, too. For example, Ranjay Gulati (1995) studies how mutual experience can engender trust among partners and how prior ties between firms lead to more trusting governance in the future, because contractual choices in alliances 'also depend on the trust that emerges between organizations over time through repeated ties' (p. 108). Gulati's work on repeated alliances supplements the work of Peter Smith Ring and Andrew Van de Ven, who study the preconditions and effects of repeated interactions in interorganizational relationships more generally.

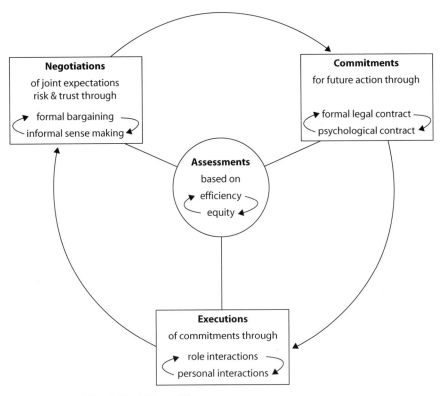

Source: Ring and Van de Ven (1994, p. 97).

Figure 4.2 Process Framework of the Development of Cooperative IORs

As already mentioned, Ring and Van de Ven (1992) argue that trust emerges as a consequence of interactions over time. In another article, the same authors propose that 'informal psychological contracts increasingly compensate or substitute for formal contractual safeguards as reliance on trust among parties increases over time' (Ring and Van de Ven, 1994, p. 105). Note that trust is only one of many elements in their process framework of the development of cooperative interorganizational relationships (Figure 4.2). The model comprises the three consecutive stages of negotiations, commitments and executions, which are supplemented by continuous assessments of the balance of efficiency and equity in the relationship. Accordingly, negotiations enable the development of joint ex-

pectations followed, ideally, by the commitments stage, in which obligations and rules are agreed upon. These commitments are then executed
through interactions between the parties and, completing the cycle, the
executions feed back into further negotiations, in which joint expectations
are stabilized and/or updated.

According to Ring and Van de Ven, formality and informality need to
be balanced at each stage, and the continuous assessment of efficiency
and equity also influences the further development of the relationship. The
authors point out that relationships will undergo a repetitive sequence of
the practically overlapping but analytically distinct stages proposed in
their framework.

Regarding the process view of trust, three aspects of this framework
are important to note. First, trust matters from the beginning but is supposed to be rather weak initially and expected to build up gradually. It is
an input and an output of relationship development. Second, the framework emphasizes the need for the parties involved to get to know each
other through mutual experiences as they go through the cycles. While
utility considerations and formal rules clearly play their role, too, the fate
of a relationship depends mainly on the reflexive process of developing
trust and joint expectations over time. Third, the framework suggests, on
the one hand, that relationships will become more stable and robust, the
more often they successfully complete the negotiation–commitment–exe-
cution cycle, not least because of the trust that is built up; on the other
hand, when key persons involved in the interorganizational relationship
are replaced or when assessments turn negative, trust may be lost, expectations may no longer match and there is always the possibility of dis-
solving the interorganizational relationship.

The possibility of the dissolution of trust relationships deserves special conceptual consideration in process models such as that of Zand, Lewicki and Bunker or Ring and Van de Ven. For, one the one hand, many
authors point out that there is a self-reinforcing mechanism at work in the
sense that trust grows, even spirals, into ever stronger, deeper more resil-
ient forms (see also Ring, 1997) once the trust-building process itself has
been established. One might apply the notion of path dependency here
(David, 1985; Arthur, 1994; Mahoney, 2000), even up to the point where
actors are seen as becoming locked into trust relationships. As long as
such relationships are desirable this may be seen as unproblematic, but
when the lock-in means that failing trust relationships, in which trust
has been destroyed or the interaction outcomes are no longer satisfactory,

cannot be exited, then this may have effects that are highly problematic on a small or even larger scale.

Horst Kern (1998), for example, attributes an innovation crisis in German industry partly to a surfeit of trust which, allegedly, has paralysed German interfirm networks vis-à-vis competitors in the global race for radical innovation. While Kern's analysis may be debatable, it does raise the empirical question of whether a trust-building process regularly faces the risk of lock-in or whether the actors remain masters of the process, which comes closer to the vision of 'path creation' developed by Raghu Garud and Peter Karnøe (2001). There is no simple answer and while examples of inescapable trust lock-ins can be found (for example Gambetta, 1988c on the Mafia), the agency-based idea of 'active trust' discussed below certainly carries much plausibility, too.

Bart Nooteboom (1996) recognizes the risk of path dependency in connection with trust. Together with his colleagues, he has studied trust in terms of a process for a long time (Nooteboom et al., 1997; Nooteboom, 2002; Nooteboom and Six, 2003; Klein Woolthuis et al., 2005). While in Nooteboom (1996) he focuses mainly on how interacting parties learn about each other's opportunism and adapt governance mechanisms accordingly, his later work on the process of trust draws on Zucker (1986), Lewicki and Bunker (1996) and others to formulate more positively how trust builds up and becomes more than a suspected lack of opportunism. Nooteboom has also developed a learning perspective of trust, which reinforces his position that, within limits, trust can go beyond calculative self-interest and can be learned in the sense of building empathy and identification (Nooteboom, 2003), namely by reference to emotional elements of trust that other authors have highlighted, too (notably Lewis and Weigert, 1985; see also Chapter 2 and above).

Among the most rigorous and inspiring works on the trust process in this context is Frédérique Six's study of the dynamics of trust and trouble in two Dutch firms, a professional services firm and an engineering consultancy, based on in-depth fieldwork (Six, 2005). Although her analytical efforts are ultimately directed at quantification and hypothesis testing, she offers rich insights into trust as an interactive process in which both sides learn about each other's trustworthiness. Interestingly, she finds that the occurrence of 'trouble' is not necessarily detrimental to trust building but can promote trust because it is in instances of trouble that the trustworthiness of the other is revealed. The experience of successfully and constructively resolving trouble strengthens the basis of trust. Lars Huemer's (1998) fieldwork on business relationships in Sweden shows likewise that the trust process in reality includes difficult phases in which the parties involved are challenged to maintain and restore trust even when there are severe tensions in the relationship (see also Chapter 7).

Although there are important differences between the process concepts of trust proposed by different authors discussed in this section and although it may be debatable whether the stages and phases of trust development will follow exactly the patterns suggested, an overall conclusion common to all of these contributions can be drawn: actors do not need to trust each other fully right from the beginning of a relationship, because they can engage experimentally in a kind of as-if trust which may gradually produce genuine trust. While such a process may simply emerge, the more interesting possibility is that actors may actively produce mutual experiences with the aim of testing whether a trust relationship is feasible, but without being able to know in advance the associated benefits and risks. For example, Karen Cook and her colleagues study 'trust building via risk taking' and find that it is an effective strategy in principle, but one that is also culturally variable (Cook et al., 2005b). It follows again that an essential feature of trust and its development must be the actor's ability to 'just do it' and overcome, at least momentarily, the irreducible uncertainty and vulnerability involved in social exchanges.

4.4 FAMILIARITY, UNFAMILIARITY, FAMILIARIZATION

In this section, I will explore another approach to the question of how trust is possible when there seems to be no basis for it and the actors involved are required to learn and gain experience. This time, the original problem is expressed in terms of familiarity and unfamiliarity, and trust building is understood as a matter of familiarization. Gulati (1995) asks in the title of the article cited above 'Does familiarity breed trust?' and concludes that it does, meaning by 'familiarity' favourable previous ties between actors. This presumed connection between familiarity and trust can be applied more widely if we adopt the general meaning of familiarity as an actor's close acquaintance with something – not only with persons but also with artefacts, concepts or emotions previously encountered in the stream of experience and explicitly or implicitly recognizable by the actor again. According to Luhmann (1979) 'trust is only possible within a familiar world' (p. 20) and, in line with the neoinstitutional approach, the presence of many familiar elements in an interaction context positively influences the actor's ability to confer or deny trust (Luhmann, 1988; Sztompka, 1999).

The concept of familiarity recalls the discussion on trust and routines in Chapter 3, because familiarity essentially represents taken-for-grantedness and the 'natural attitude' that actors have towards their lifeworld. However, the main points of interest here are how actors deal with and overcome unfamiliarity and how they may be able to develop trust (gradually) in contexts of low familiarity through a process of familiarization. To this effect, I present in this section some more conceptual groundwork by Schütz (1970a), Berger and Luckmann (1966) and Luhmann (1979, 1988) as well as Seligman's (1997) thesis that familiarity as a condition for trust has been eroded in modernity while the need for trust has increased.

Familiarity in Alfred Schütz's terms (1970a) 'demarcates, for the particular subject in his concretely particular life-situation, that sector of the world which does from that which does not need further investigation' (p. 61). Objects regarded as familiar are 'beyond question' and thus 'taken for granted'. Familiarity requires the natural attitude as it 'presupposes the idealizations of the "and so forth and so on" and the "I can do it again"' (p. 58). Another way of interpreting familiarity, according to Schütz, is that it expresses 'the likelihood of referring new experiences, in respect of their types, to the habitual stock of already acquired knowledge … by means of a passive synthesis of recognition' (pp. 58–59). In other words, even a new object can be sufficiently familiar to the actor if it can be recognized as typical.

This indicates, however, that familiarity implies the unfamiliar, too, at least in two respects. First, 'the now unquestioned world … is merely unquestioned until further notice' (p. 61), meaning that all that the actor is subjectively familiar with could in principle be questioned. Second, unfamiliarity is not just something that actors can choose to direct their attention towards and question if and when they please, but rather something that actors cannot avoid because 'unfamiliar experience imposes itself upon us by its very unfamiliarity' (p. 28) and becomes thematic and topical whether the actor likes it or not, especially in processes of social interaction.

Schütz does not see the actor as locked into the natural attitude but as able to respond constructively to 'imposed relevance' when prompted to in the stream of experience. If trust builds on familiarity, then the good news from Schütz is that unfamiliarity need not automatically mean distrust as long as the actor uses his capacity of familiarization to increase his familiarity when necessary.

Peter Berger and Thomas Luckmann (1966), in close correspondence with Schützian ideas, refer to familiarity in order to show how the 'social stock of knowledge differentiates reality' (p. 43) in the sense that it gives actors detailed knowledge of the sector of everyday life that they frequently deal with and only general and imprecise knowledge of remoter sectors. This also implies that the actor has more extensive access to routines and typifications in his highly familiar sectors than in less familiar or unfamiliar sectors, explaining why familiarity in the sense of rich and specific knowledge of the workings of everyday life should be conductive to institutional trust. Moreover: 'As long as my knowledge works satisfactorily, I am generally ready to suspend doubts about it' (p. 44).

However, the familiarity of everyday life 'appears as a zone of lucidity behind which there is a background of darkness' (p. 44), in other words, the unfamiliar, because the actor cannot know everything there is to know. Interestingly, Berger and Luckmann on the one hand present this darkness as bothersome, but on the other hand suggest that, thanks to familiarity and relevance structures, the actor does not need to know everything, even if he could, because much of reality is simply irrelevant. The authors do not discuss, though, the 'imposed relevance' that Schütz talks about. Imposed relevance challenges actors to question familiar knowledge or to venture into the unfamiliar darkness. It describes moments when actors cease to suspend doubts. Thus actors in Berger and Luckmann's view appear to be rather passively dependent on the 'social stock of knowledge' and 'what everybody knows'. Active familiarization is not envisaged.

In contrast and more like Schütz, Luhmann (1988) sees an intimate connection between the familiar and the unfamiliar, because the underlying distinction can re-enter its own space in what I would label a process of familiarization: 'We can live within a familiar world because we can, using symbols, reintroduce the unfamiliar into the familiar' (p. 95). However, 'we know in a familiar way about the unfamiliar' (p. 95), which means that Schütz's 'imposed relevance' of the unfamiliar can only be dealt with in familiar terms. Thus, familiarization shifts the boundaries of familiarity *from within*. Unfamiliarity only renders trust impossible when the actor fails to engage in familiarization.

Trust in this sense relies on both familiarity and familiarization. Hence, trust requires familiarity, but the two concepts must not be confused (Luhmann, 1988). Rather, according to Luhmann (1979), they should be seen as 'complementary ways of absorbing complexity and are linked to one another, in the same way as past and future are linked' (p. 20). In familiarity, past experiences are condensed and their continuity assumed, which makes future-oriented trust possible: 'But rather than just being an inference from the past, trust goes beyond the information it receives and risks defining the future. The complexity of the future world is reduced by the act of trust. In trusting, one engages in action as though there were only certain possibilities in the future' (p. 20).

This can be interpreted to mean, on the one hand, that familiarization is a kind of hindsight that can strengthen the familiarity base for trust. However, on the other hand, I would claim that familiarization is very much future-oriented, too, so that trust in general and active trust in particular may be described as the familiarization with the future: trust 'risks defining the future' as Luhmann puts it in the above quotation. Clearly, in trust as familiarity with the future there is less taken-for-grantedness than in familiarity with the past. The trustor needs to accept that the as-if on which his expectations are based preserves the contingency implied by all trust: the trustee's principal freedom to break trust. Luhmann also observes that the need for trust 'is now decreasingly met by familiarity' (p. 20) and that there is an 'increasing diversification and particularization of familiarities and unfamiliarities' (Luhmann, 1988, p. 105). He concludes that this needs to be compensated for by system trust (see Chapter 3), but I would argue that, at the actor level, familiarization and active trust should have the same effect, albeit more local and restricted, especially as 'it may be possible to build up trust on the micro-level and protect systems against loss of confidence on the macro-level' (p. 104).

Finally, Adam Seligman (1997) develops an elaborate argument on the relationships between trust, familiarity and the conditions of modernity which connects in many places with Luhmann's work but gives a very different perspective altogether. He states that familiarity commonly means the actor's ability to impute the values that condition the actions of another actor and thus enables the first actor to have expectations towards the second (Seligman, 1997, p. 69). This is a Durkheimian idea, somewhat narrowly focused on values, but not in contradiction to the phenomenological concepts presented above. However, a state of expectation that is based on the imputed conditionality of the other's acts would not be called 'trust' by Seligman. Instead, he emphasizes throughout his book the 'unconditionality' of trust as its essential feature, be-

also cope with the need to trust in abstract systems and with the particular risks of modernity through strategies that imply an active engagement. In sum, active trust is trust that needs to be worked on continuously by the actors involved through mutual openness and intensive communication; it reflects contingency and change in an ongoing process of reflexive constitution.

As Jens Beckert (2002) points out, Giddens sees active trust as functioning along with routine and habit. Without a certain level of ontological security (Giddens, 1979) and basic trust (Erikson, 1965), actors are hardly able to engage in active trust (see Chapter 3). Nevertheless, Giddens' emphasis on 'deliberative commitments of the actors' (Beckert, 2002, p. 264) draws our attention to the active and creative role of actors in building trust and also in shaping the conditions for trust-building processes.

John Child and I have attempted to show that this active trust development happens in reality and can be effective in strengthening the trust basis in relationships between Hong Kong managers and the staff of their mainland Chinese operations (Child and Möllering, 2003). Assuming that trust is not merely 'given' to trustors but created by them as well, we hypothesize and find support for the positive influence that successful efforts at establishing personal rapport, recruiting local personnel and transferring standardized practices have on the trust of Hong Kong managers in local staff. In other words, whether these managers have trust in their Chinese colleagues and partners depends not only on economic incentives and the larger institutional context, but also on active trust-building measures and commitments from the managers themselves.

Interestingly, somewhat less academic publications on trust naturally talk about what people, especially managers, can do to promote trust (Shea, 1987; Shaw, 1997; Reynolds, 1997; Shurtleff, 1998). As the evidence in these texts is mostly anecdotal or cursory, it is a theoretical challenge for scholarly work on trust to devise a comprehensive framework for understanding active trust.

Returning to Giddens, his conceptualization of trust does not contradict his theory of structuration (Giddens, 1979, 1984) but he does not draw specifically on this theoretical framework when he discusses trust. That it might be quite instructive to do so is demonstrated by Jörg Sydow (1998), who conceptualizes trust in terms of a modality in the duality and recursiveness of structure and (inter)action. The constitution of trust, according to Sydow's structuration perspective on trust building (see also Sydow

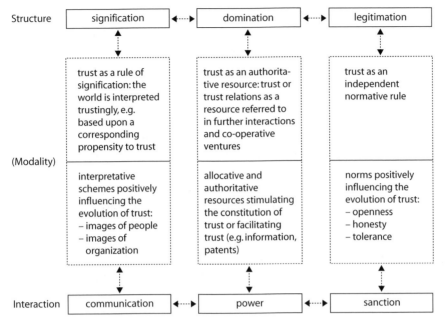

Source: Sydow (1998, p. 40).

Figure 4.3   Duality and Recursiveness in the Constitution of Trust

and Windeler, 2003; Sydow, 2006), involves the development of interpretative schemes, resources and norms to which the actor refers in trustful and trustworthy interaction, thereby (re)producing the social structure
of signification, domination and legitimation in which the phenomenon of
trust is constituted and to which further action will refer (see Figure 4.3).
When speaking of trust in structuration-theoretical terms, we therefore
have in mind a phenomenon that comes into being through the insepara-
bility and recursiveness of social structure and action in the three dimensions of the social identified by Giddens.

Sydow (1998) applies his structuration-theoretical trust concept to networks and collaborations between insurance brokers and analyses the
process of trust constitution by drawing on 47 semi-structured interviews.
Thus he can illustrate how insurers may develop through their social practices a rule of signification, that is a common understanding that trust is
desirable because it increases communication efficiency and effectiveness
in the insurance industry. By referring to this rule, the insurance brokers

also reproduce it. Similarly, insurance brokers may use their trust relationships as resources for action and, in turn, they may also deliberately invest resources to build such relationships. Finally, the dimension of legitimation entails practices that refer to and support the normative element of trust: for example, accepted rules among insurance brokers about honouring trust overall and displaying openness, honesty and integrity in order to build trust.

The arrows in Figure 4.3 highlight, once again, that the three dimensions and the levels of structure and interaction are recursively related to each other. Such a view implies, of course, a processual perspective whereby trust only materializes in reflexive social practices which, over time, mostly reproduce trust but may always change it as well, either intentionally or unintentionally. This 'structuration theory of trust', sketched only in its basic outlines here, can accommodate all the ideas presented in this chapter so far, specifically the possibility of trust emerging blindly in social interaction, the process of building up trust gradually, the role of both familiarity and familiarization from the actor's point of view, and the importance of the actor's continuous reflexive practices of social (re)production from the system's perspective.

While the structuration framework is effective in describing the constitution of trust and leaves room for the crucial 'unconditionality' (Seligman, 1997) of trust, it cannot explain clearly how this latter aspect is handled within trust. In other words, additional concepts are required to understand how actors can live with the fact that the ongoing process of structuration itself is open-ended – *despite* or rather *because of* the actor's agency, which represents the irreducible social contingency without which trust would be neither required nor possible but which the trustor treats *as if* it were resolved. Giddens (1990, 1991) himself highlights in connection with the concept of trust a kind of 'suspension of reflexivity' akin to the suspension of doubt within the natural attitude. Active trust in particular is always a kind of trust-in-the-making which requires the trustor to go down an essentially unknowable path. This suspension needs to be looked at more closely in the next chapter.

In this chapter, it has become clear that trust is a matter of reflexivity in that it often needs to develop gradually in processes which, once they get started, may be partly self-reinforcing but require active agency, too. While I have shown that there is a wealth of fundamental work in this area, more adequate theories still need to be found or created in order to develop this process view of trust further. As just discussed, structuration theory is a good candidate, but there are certainly other candidates, too. After all, understanding the world in process terms has a long tradition going back to the metaphysics of Heraclitus (c. 550–480 BC), who famously pointed out that 'all things flow'. A little more recently, an elaborate and impressive process theory was developed by the philosopher and mathematician Alfred North Whitehead ([1929] 1978). Although many social scientists are not aware of his work and would probably find it fairly impenetrable anyway, there has been at least one attempt made to adopt it for the study of trust. Mark Dibben (2000) uses Whitehead's concepts to address fundamental philosophical issues and, remarkably, to study empirically the role of trust in entrepreneurial ventures. Thankfully, a little closer to home at least from my own academic background, there is a growing body of literature on process theory and how it may be applied in organization studies (Van de Ven and Poole, 1995, 2005; Langley, 1999; Poole et al., 2000; Tsoukas and Chia, 2002). This is a highly promising but, to my knowledge, currently unexplored area for trust research, and I will return to this in later chapters when considering methodological issues and future avenues of research. It will be interesting to see whether in process research there is a place for the concept of suspension (the leap of faith) which I discuss next.

5

THE LEAP OF FAITH

5.1 THE MISSING ELEMENT: SUSPENSION

Our understanding of trust is already enhanced significantly if we recognize that all three perspectives introduced in the previous chapters highlight important aspects of the phenomenon we are interested in. Trust is indeed a matter of reason, routine or reflexivity depending on how we look at it. When we look at empirical manifestations of trust, though, we must acknowledge that our analytical distinctions are somewhat artificial and simplistic, even if helpful for systemizing the literature (Lane, 1998), because the three 'mechanisms' usually play together. Research focusing on only one of them, for example on cognition, taken-for-grantedness or communication loops, is bound to miss important influences from, and interactions with, other mechanisms that cannot easily be held under *ceteris paribus* conditions. Trust research needs to be broad, applying multiple perspectives in order to form a picture of the enormous elephant called trust, as in the classic Indian fable.

So far, in this book, continuing the fable analogy, I have brought together three of the most important 'blind men' who attempt to describe trust. My central argument, however, relates to the fact that they are indeed blind, because they tend to confound reason, routine or reflexivity as bases for trust with the process of reaching the state of trust as such. In trying to explain trust by looking at one or more mechanisms, they cannot see that the essence of trust, by definition, cannot be captured fully by those mechanisms. Put differently, by subsuming trust as a form of ra-

in expected ill will, and an increase in trust presumes that roles in temporary systems are clear' (p. 173). When people deal with each other more
as roles than as individuals, they can trust routinely. In other words, the
natural attitude in temporary teams may be to comply with the usual roles
and routines. Nevertheless, this can only be an incomplete and probably
misleading explanation, too, because there is no certainty for the trustor that
everybody on the team knows the roles and routines and is competent and
willing to perform them. If this certainty existed, trust would be obsolete.
Since it cannot exist and since there is always role negotiability (Seligman, 1997), trust refers to role expectations but requires more than that.

Third, swift trust may develop almost instantaneously but there is still
a reflexive process to be observed. As Meyerson et al. show, the team
members tend not to commit themselves too much in the beginning and
remain more cautious than they appear. They follow the 'principle of
gradualness' (Luhmann, 1979) and the main difference to other situations
could be that, by the nature of the project, the intensity of interaction
between team members is very great from the start so that, even within
hours of working together, trust builds up reflexively and the stakes can
be raised relatively quickly. Frequent communication is required on projects and this may facilitate the maintenance of trust even when there are
changes in the project. Team members are thus able to work on trust as
envisaged by Giddens (1994b). The first encounters that set the reflexive
trust-building process in motion remain crucial, though, and Meyerson et
al. (1996) observe that 'people have to wade in on trust rather than wait
while experience gradually shows who can be trusted and with what'
(p. 170). Swift trust is therefore a very active trust. This said, there is no
guarantee that a self-reinforcing spiral of trust development will emerge
from initial interactions. Meyerson and her colleagues remind us that
many temporary work groups fail to develop swift trust and quite a number of projects go wrong, especially in the early stages, when a cooperative
team can turn into a competitive one, jeopardizing its chances of success.
Once again, although it is instructive to consider the processual element
even in swift trust, the problem of uncertainty and vulnerability on the
part of the actors involved is not explained away, but rather emphasized,
when we consider situations in which people on a team just have to get
on with it pragmatically.

Even if swift trust is only a cursory example intended as an illustration
of the argument so far, it seems fair to note that we regularly arrive at the
point where reason, routine and/or reflexivity are mechanisms that pro-

vide a basis for trust but do not explain how irreducible uncertainty and vulnerability are dealt with in trust. By focusing on the bases for trust only, we run the risk of explaining away trust itself or, at least, of explaining anything but trust.

As I have already claimed elsewhere (Möllering, 2001), I believe that Georg Simmel identified the missing element in the concept of trust about a century ago, but we lost sight of it again even though his original ideas had a strong influence on some important contributions to the trust literature (notably Frankel, 1977; Luhmann, 1979; Lewis and Weigert, 1985; Giddens, 1990; Misztal, 1996; Lane, 1998). Simmel ([1907] 1990) notes that trust needs to be 'as strong as, or stronger than, rational proof or personal observation' for social relationships to endure, and he gives examples of one kind of trust which 'is only a weak form of inductive knowledge' (p. 179). The examples are the farmer's belief that his crops will grow and the trader's belief that his goods will be desired. The important detail here is that Simmel does not regard mere weak inductive knowledge as proper trust (Giddens, 1991). Within trust there is a 'further element of socio-psychological quasi-religious faith' (Simmel, 1990, p. 179).

In the same source, Simmel expresses that he finds this element 'hard to describe' and thinks of it as 'a state of mind which has nothing to do with knowledge, which is both less and more than knowledge'. He expresses this element of faith as 'the feeling that there exists between our idea of a being and the being itself a definite connection and unity, a certain consistency in our conception of it, an assurance and lack of resistance in the surrender of the Ego to this conception, which may rest upon particular reasons, but is not explained by them'.

In another source, Simmel (1950, p. 318) describes trust as 'an antecedent or subsequent form of knowledge' that is 'intermediate between knowledge and ignorance about a man'. Complete knowledge or ignorance would eliminate the need for or possibility of trust. He explains that there is a type of trust that stands outside the categories of knowledge and ignorance. Accordingly, trust combines weak inductive knowledge with some mysterious, unaccountable faith: 'On the other hand, even in the social forms of confidence, no matter how exactly and intellectually grounded they may appear to be, there may yet be some additional affective, even mystical, "faith" of man in man'. Anthony Giddens (1990) recognizes that Simmel believes that trust differs from weak inductive knowledge and he strongly supports the view that trust 'presumes a leap to commitment, a quality of "faith" which is irreducible' (Giddens, 1991, p. 19).

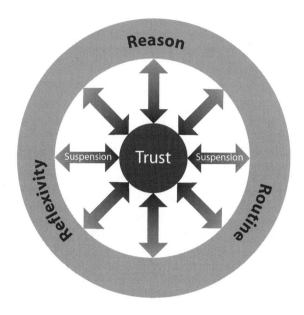

Figure 5.1   The Trust Wheel – An Integrative Framework

In the remainder of this chapter, I will analyse the meaning of the 'leap of faith' as the essential feature of trust. A rather extreme and, for most of us, highly disconcerting notion of the leap of faith appears in Søren Kierkegaard's work, in particular when he discusses Abraham's decision to sacrifice his son Isaac by God's will (Kierkegaard, [1843] 1985, see also below). However, sociologists such as Anthony Giddens (1991), Adam Seligman (1997) and Piotr Sztompka (1999) refer to the leap of faith in less existentialist terms and it has even found its way into organization theory (for example Bradach and Eccles, 1989; Zaheer et al., 1998). Although the image of the leap of faith is a very fortunate one since it connotes agency without suggesting perfect control or certainty, I prefer to speak of 'suspension' as the process that enables actors to deal with irreducible uncertainty and vulnerability. Suspension is the essence of trust, because trust as a state of positive expectation of others can only be reached when reason, routine and reflexivity are combined with suspension.

At this point, suspension is only a vague notion and in the following sections I will suggest a number of ways to give more concrete meaning to it. However, an integrative framework illustrating how suspension connects trust and the bases for trust can already be introduced here (Figure 5.1). In this visualization, trust is the hub of a wheel surrounded by reason, routine and reflexivity in the rim. Suspension is depicted as the spokes that connect hub and rim.

I should be clear immediately that the 'Trust Wheel' is no more than a simple heuristic. However, even this simple visual expresses a number of abstract ideas that might inspire further theorizing. For example, trust corresponds via suspension with reason, routine and reflexivity as bases for trust. This means also that trust is not identical to nor directly connected with these trust bases. And, without suspension, the bases for trust cannot lead to trust. The Trust Wheel implies feedback mechanisms, suggesting that, when trust is reached, this will have an effect on the trust bases, too. There is learning. Moreover, reason, routine and reflexivity are connected and may interact. They may also vary in the degree of influence that they have on trust, and they could reinforce each other or compensate for each other.

These are merely tentative propositions emerging from the framework and the concept of trust suggested so far. It can be summarized as follows: trust is an ongoing process of building on reason, routine and reflexivity, suspending irreducible social vulnerability and uncertainty *as if* they were favourably resolved, and maintaining thereby a state of favourable expectation towards the actions and intentions of more or less specific others.

It is clear that suspension is at the heart of this concept and that the wheel will fall apart unless we get a better notion of this 'mystical' (Simmel) element. I suggest three ways of coming to terms with suspension. First, I will return to the idea that trust implies an 'as-if attitude'. I will show that 'as if' is a rather common expression in the literature on trust which, however, is generally taken far too lightly. Is trust essentially a form of fiction if it is reached on an as-if basis? Second, the term 'bracketing' is common in phenomenology and it expresses a kind of temporary blending out. Perhaps in trust uncertainty and vulnerability are bracketed, but how is this achieved? Third, trust might be a matter of willpower and, more specifically, William James' notion of the will to believe could be instructive. The leap of faith is evident here but where does the will come from? In the last part of this chapter, I will review empirical work to date that gives evidence of suspension in practice. Can we observe leaps of faith in real life? How important are they? This section also prepares the ground for the following chapters on studying and experiencing trust.

5.2 AS IF: TRUST AS FICTION

In Chapter 4, I have already discussed the idea suggested by several authors that actors might pretend to trust in order to start building trust. This 'as-if trust' (Hardin, 1993) is not considered to be proper trust. For example, Meyerson et al. (1996) clarify that their 'swift trust' is 'not a sort of pseudo-trust or "trustoid" behavior' (p. 192) as might be suspected. In this section, however, I will focus on another idea already suggested to some extent in Chapter 4: *all* trust requires a kind of as-if attitude on the part of trustors towards the social reality they face. David Lewis and Andrew Weigert (1985) express this most clearly when they state that 'to trust is to live *as if* certain rationally possible futures will not occur' (p. 969, emphasis in original) and that 'to trust is to act as if the uncertain future actions of others were indeed certain' (p. 971). Another example is Piotr Sztompka's (1999) remark that '[p]lacing trust we behave "as if" we knew the future' (pp. 25–26), which refers to Niklas Luhmann's (1979) statement that to show trust is 'to behave as though the future were certain' (p. 10). The power, but also the fragility, of the 'as if' must not be underestimated. Trust does not rest on objective certainty but on 'illusion' (p. 32). It rests on the fiction of a reality in which social uncertainty and vulnerability are unproblematic. And this fiction of trust needs to be achieved and sustained psychologically by the individual, even though it is also a 'socially constructed fiction of trust' (Beckert, 2005, p. 19) produced intersubjectively through interaction with others and through institutionalized practices.

How do actors create the fiction that enables them to trust? As a first attempt in answering this question, consider the concept of 'overdrawn information' (*überzogene Information*) introduced by Luhmann (1979, p. 32). When actors overdraw information they make inferences beyond what the underlying information can actually support. In the face of a deficit of information, they deliberately overinterpret whatever information is available to 'serve as a springboard into uncertainty' (p. 33). Simmel (1950) mentions that for the individual actor trust is 'a hypothesis *certain enough* to serve as a basis for practical conduct' (p. 318, emphasis added). This implies that it is possible to arrive at the state of trust from an imperfect informational basis, if and when actors are able to make the leap from that basis.

We are reminded of the search for indicators of trustworthiness discussed in Chapter 2, the signals perceived by taxi drivers (Henslin, 1968;

Gambetta and Hamill, 2005) and Zucker's (1986) 'characteristic-based trust'. However, while 'overdrawn information' is a plausible idea that confirms the need for at least some kind of basis for trust ('the leap of trust cannot be made from nowhere nor from anywhere', Möllering, 2001, p. 414), we still need to be able to specify the conditions under which actors come to not only accept but also go beyond a given level of information and construct a fiction of reality that allows them to trust.

Jens Beckert (2005) has recently reminded us that the trustee plays a very important part in creating the trustor's fiction. Through his performance the trustee offers 'a definition of himself' (Henslin, 1968, p. 54) as well as a definition of the situation (Wenzel, 2001) and does so with empathy for the trustor's needs, 'creating the impression of trustworthiness' (Beckert, 2005, p. 19). Such an approach is more easily said than done and goes beyond the mechanistic signalling games suggested by Michael Bacharach and Diego Gambetta (2001; see also Chapter 2). The trustee's performative acts require impression management (Goffman, 1959), self-confidence and ontological security (Erikson, 1965) and an active engagement in social relations (Giddens, 1994b): 'Whoever wants to win trust must take part in social life and be in a position to build the expectations of others into his own self-presentation' (Luhmann, 1979, p. 62).

Steven Maguire, Nelson Phillips and Cynthia Hardy have studied how, in the relationships between pharmaceutical companies and HIV/AIDS community organizations in Canada, identification-based trust could be generated over time through the discursive construction of new categories of identity or through changes in existing ones. Starting out from a highly antagonistic set-up, the parties involved essentially had to partly redefine themselves and construct a new fiction that would enable them to trust each other. The original myth of 'patients to be protected from pharmaceutical companies' first deteriorated into 'activists in conflict with pill-pushing profiteers' but then turned into 'advocates collaborating with compassionate and consultative partners' (Maguire et al., 2001, pp. 295–99). This process required discursive interaction and performances over many years.

To give just one other example, Nicole Gillespie and Leon Mann (2004) show that in R&D teams the team members' trust in their leaders depends significantly on leadership practices. Leaders 'earn' trust through performative action, for example consultative instead of top-down decision-making, by which they signal to team members their openness and respect (on trust and leadership, see also Dirks and Ferrin, 2002).

In sum, somewhat paradoxically, trustors rely to a great extent on trustees when constructing an image of those trustees as worthy of trust or not. Nevertheless, the fiction co-produced by trustor and trustee remains a fiction, potentially a dangerous 'fake', and it is ultimately still up to the trustor to suspend uncertainty and vulnerability. The trustee's performative acts and a high level of familiarity with the situation merely assist the trustor in making the leap of faith.

Another, slightly evasive approach to explaining the maintenance of an as-if attitude for trust could return to the kind of theories introduced in Chapter 3. There we saw that the 'natural attitude' enables actors to have 'lifeworlds' as a stable fiction of reality, as it were. We saw that society and actors are socially constructed, that a kind of drama comes to life by being performed and that actors engage in normalizing to preserve their fiction as normality. They even put up façades and dwell in myths and ceremony. This sociological approach is supported by a broad range of psychological work, for example gestalt theory or research demonstrating the confirmation-seeking bias that individuals display especially when confronted by uncertainty and ambiguity (see Good, 1988). It makes trust relatively robust because a fiction of reality tends to be maintained and may even become 'real' in the sense of a social fact. In other words, all social life is 'fictional' and the fictions needed for trust are only one part of this. It is all the more important that we gain an understanding of the underlying processes as they occur at different levels, for instance at the level of abstract systems, such as the fiction of an effective medical system, or at the interpersonal level, where an actor infers from a number of cues a broad image of another as trustworthy or untrustworthy.

Moreover, we have to remain aware that actors are also the creators of the fictions they live in (McCloskey, 1994), which implies that uncertainty and vulnerability are not removed by creating fictions, but only suspended. Which fictions are maintained and which are changed or challenged is also at least partly a matter of interests, power and politics. This suggests yet another way of accounting for fictions and it also underlines the fact that fictions are indeed real in the sense that they have consequences, not only for trust. Günther Ortmann (2004) shows that countless daily activities and interactions rely on fictions and only become possible because people act *as if* they were possible.

Ortmann also points out convincingly that the 'as if' can have many different meanings. First, the 'as if' in the sense of the Schützian natural attitude refers to the action-enabling qualities of taken-for-grantedness and continuity. We have already seen how this can support trust. Second, 'as if' can also refer to the more performative 'taking something for something' or 'defining something as something'. With reference to trust, this comes close to Hardin's (1993) 'as-if trust', where trust and trustworthiness are produced by trust-like interaction. An actor becomes trustworthy because others treat him more or less deliberately as if he were trustworthy. They take him for a trustworthy person and thus they also define him as a trustworthy person, irrespective of the 'true' underlying facts. Note the 'almost compulsory power' that Simmel (1950, p. 348) attributes to trust. Third, the concept of 'as if' can also refer to the construction of unrealistic but nevertheless helpful idealizations. For example, the image of an 'ideal' institution, organization, person or practice as being trustful and trustworthy may never be realized fully in reality, but by actors behaving as if it were reality or, at least, as if the 'ideal' were seriously pursued, trust is facilitated. Ortmann's (2004) analysis of the different forms and effects of 'as if' is, of course, much more detailed and elaborate than the few ideas I have just mentioned. At any rate, to make progress on understanding the as-if element in trust, further research on the meaning of 'as if' appears to be particularly helpful.

5.3   BRACKETING: JUST DO IT

The above considerations focused mainly on the idea that a holistic fiction can be created from incomplete pieces of information by reference to the 'as if'. Actors are seen as able to trust if and when they manage to fill the gaps and make up missing pieces. This is certainly one instructive way of interpreting the leap of faith; however, I will suggest in this section that the more important approach holds that trust is possible because actors manage to live with the fact that there are gaps and missing pieces. The 'as if' here means that actors interact with each other as if ignorance, doubts and dangers that exist alongside knowledge, convictions and assurances are unproblematic and can be set aside, at least for the time being. The result is also a fiction of reality, but in this case it is the result of blending out issues that actors might be aware of but cannot penetrate or resolve fully. Specifically, they bracket out irreducible social vulnerability and uncertainty as if they were favourably resolved. This is the main underlying idea of suspension. The logic of the 'as if' in trust is specified further as a logic of 'despite', 'although' and 'nevertheless'.

Once again, Niklas Luhmann (1979) developed key initial ideas for this approach. Although, as we have just seen, he also talks about 'overdrawn information' as a basis for trust, he mainly sees trust as a mechanism of *reducing complexity* rather than inflating it. As Poggi (1979) notes, Luhmann argues that 'successful responses to the problem of complexity ... typically do not eliminate complexity, but rather reduce it: that is, make it "livable with" while in some sense preserving it' (p. x). Interestingly, Poggi also suggests that Luhmann could have used the Hegelian notion of *Aufhebung*: the dialectical principle of synthesis transcending thesis and antithesis, thereby simultaneously preserving and rescinding them (Hegel, [1807] 1973). And, indeed, Luhmann argues that trust involves 'a type of system-internal "suspension" (*Aufhebung*)' (Luhmann, 1979, p. 79). When actors achieve suspension they treat uncertainty and vulnerability as unproblematic, even if it could turn out that they are problematic. Luhmann (1979) describes trust as 'a movement towards *indifference*: by introducing trust, certain possibilities of development can be excluded from consideration. Certain dangers which cannot be removed but which should not disrupt action are neutralized' (p. 25, emphasis in original).

This comes very close to the phenomenological concept of bracketing to which Anthony Giddens, among others, refers prominently in defining trust as 'the vesting of confidence in persons or in abstract systems, made on the basis of a "leap into faith" which brackets ignorance or lack of information' (Giddens, 1991, p. 244). More generally, Giddens discusses trust initially as a matter of 'ontological security' (Giddens, 1979) in the sense of 'basic trust', drawing on particular aspects in the work of Erikson (1965) and Goffman (1963; see Giddens, 1984). Essentially, Giddens captures how individual actors require and ascertain through trust constancy in their self-identity, that is their own being-in-the-world generally and their social being in interactions and relationships with others in particular (Giddens, 1990, 1991). By reference to Garfinkel's breaching experiments, Giddens illustrates the significance of basic trust and links it conceptually to the natural attitude in sociological phenomenology. Like the natural attitude, basic trust presumes a suspension of doubt, but Giddens (1990) points out with Garfinkel the fragility of this state and the possibility of a 'suspension of trust' that threatens to bring back existential anxiety. The paramount importance of the suspension of doubt for the actor is thus emphasized.

In particular, Giddens (1990) argues that the suspension that enables trust has to be learned in infancy through the ambivalent experience of love from caretakers on the one hand and the caretakers' temporary absence on the other, whereby the infant develops the ability to reach a state of trust which 'brackets distance in time and space and so blocks off existential anxieties' (p. 97). This trust as a kind of skill learned in infancy remains essential as actors grow up to become adults. According to Giddens, the faith in the loving caretaker's return 'is the essence of that leap to commitment which basic trust – and all forms of trust thereafter – presumes' (p. 95). The infant's anxiety can be generalized to the problem of ignorance that actors face in any social encounters with others whose actions and intentions they cannot fully know or control (Giddens, 1991). Generally, trust presumes 'a leap to commitment, a quality of "faith" which is irreducible' (p. 19).

In Giddens (1990), the author does not go into further detail as to how exactly this solution is achieved, except to note that it is an 'extremely sophisticated methodology of practical consciousness' (p. 99), in other words not primarily a cognitive achievement, but a tacit, continuous monitoring of the normality of the situation. In Giddens (1991) this 'methodology' is described in more detail: 'Practical consciousness, together with the day-to-day routines reproduced by it, help bracket such anxieties not only, or even primarily, because of the social stability that they imply, but because of their constitutive role in organizing an "as if" environment in relation to existential issues' (p. 37).

As briefly mentioned earlier on, another source that may enhance our understanding of suspension is Kierkegaard ([1843] 1985), who presents a highly disturbing view of the leap of faith in his essay *Fear and Trembling*, where he refers to Abraham's 'teleological suspension of the ethical' (p. 83) when he is supposed to sacrifice his son Isaac by God's will. It is the extraordinariness of the situation faced by Abraham which reveals very strongly the essential meaning and quality of the leap of faith. Abraham cannot justify the sacrifice of Isaac to himself or anybody else on utilitarian grounds nor on any moral (or institutional) grounds. His faith is the absurd and unfounded belief that Isaac, if sacrificed, will be restored. He thus suspends 'the ethical' for an unknowable higher end (*telos*), which, however, does not make his decision ethical in a roundabout way. The act of killing Isaac – which Abraham is ultimately spared from carrying out – is not simply a proof of his belief in the existence of God but of his belief (without resignation) that the absurd or at least improbable will happen after all, due to forces above human expression and comprehension.

Even though the gravity and intensity of Abraham's leap of faith is extraordinary and untypical for most practical situations that we face, the incident illustrates how the suspension required for all trust overcomes the irreducible uncertainty and vulnerability of the trustor towards the trustee. As Seligman (1997) puts it elliptically, in trust between socially embedded people 'Kierkegaard's "leap of faith" become[s] oriented towards a mundane other' (p. 74). In the same way that Abraham could not have constructed a perfectly justified and acceptable argument for sacrificing Isaac, every trustor – by definition – lacks certainty about the consequences of his trust and can only reach the state of trust through a kind of faith which Simmel (1950) called the 'affective, even mystical, "faith" of man in man' (p. 318). Suspension itself is 'irreducible' (Giddens, 1991, p. 19). It may be identified and described, but not explained or justified. It is not the whole of trust, but the defining element.

Admittedly, especially after this reference to Kierkegaard, the idea that trust requires bracketing or, more generally, suspension may not be a very welcome one, as it might be taken to suggest that actors should heroically or foolishly ignore the perils of life in order to trust. Moreover, the underlying notion of 'just do it' (see also Möllering, 2005b) could be more disconcerting than actually encouraging. In response to this, it should be noted that, while on the one hand actors make more leaps of faith every day than they realize, and do so without experiencing existential angst, on the other hand they also face situations in which they find it impossible to suspend uncertainty and vulnerability or in which they can only take one very small leap of faith after the other (see also the final section of this chapter). By highlighting the essential role of suspension in trust, we merely clarify when it is justified to speak of trust and when it is not. It is a different question how big or small, difficult or easy the leap of faith actually is.

For example, I would challenge Saunders and Thornhill's (2004) conclusion that there is little support for the notion of the trust-enabling leap of faith when respondents can rationalize their feelings about trust and mistrust. First of all, as Luhmann (1979) puts it: 'Although the one who trusts is never at a loss for reasons and is quite capable of giving an account of why he shows trust in this or that case, the point of such reasons is really to uphold his self-respect and justify him socially' (p. 26). More importantly, though, this process of rationalization obscures the leaps of faith which the actors, including Saunders and Thornhill's respondents, still make if they genuinely trust. After all, a perfect rationale would make trust obsolete altogether. As I have pointed out elsewhere before, the concept of suspension implies the methodological challenge to grasp what constitutes the unknowable from the point of view of the trustor (Möllering, 2001). It may be necessary to discourage respondents from over-rationalization and to probe specifically for references to information that trustors consciously miss or dismiss as well as to the ways they generally deal with the Socratic conundrum of knowing that one knows nothing.

Further, despite the paramount importance attributed to trust generally, authors who argue that there are many interactions in which trust is not really necessary also have a point (see for example Cook et al., 2005a). Finally, suspension has a strong element of agency, implying that although many leaps of faith may not be made consciously, they are not made unwillingly either. On the contrary, without denying social embeddedness, it is hard to see how the 'leap' or the 'faith' necessary for trust as a state of expectation could be forced. We would speak of compliance, not trust, if suspension were not voluntary.

5.4 THE WILL TO BELIEVE

This brings us to Luhmann's (1979) remark that trust is an 'operation of the will' where 'the actor willingly surmounts this deficit of information' (p. 32). Trust goes beyond that which can be justified in any terms by the actor, but the actor exercises agency through his will to either suspend uncertainty and vulnerability or not. Luhmann's reference to 'will' in the context of trust and suspension inspires a closer a look at William James' essay on *The Will to Believe*, a pragmatist approach to the theme of faith which Jens Beckert (2005) has also identified as highly instructive for understanding trust. James ([1896] 1948) defends the actor's right to believe – in religious matters but also generally, for instance in social relations – even when there is no conclusive evidence. Such a belief would be called faith: 'we have the right to believe at our own risk any hypothesis that is live enough to tempt our will' (p. 107). Note that by introducing the condition that the hypothesis has to be 'live enough', James points out that actors should not be allowed to believe anything but that 'which appeals as a real possibility to him to whom it is proposed' (p. 89).

Implicitly, he thus refers back to his essay *The Sentiment of Rationality* (James, [1879] 1948) and major principles of his pragmatist philosophy. In this earlier source, he says that faith is 'synonymous with working hypothesis' (p. 25). The ability to have faith is distinctly human according to James and he defines faith as follows: 'Faith means belief in something concerning which doubt is still possible; and as the test of belief is willingness to act, one may say that faith is the readiness to act in a cause the prosperous issue of which is not certified to us in advance' (p. 22).

From the standpoint of James' pragmatism, faith requires the 'sentiment of rationality', in other words the actor's genuine but not conclusively justifiable conviction that what he believes is 'true' in the pragmatist sense of being useful, giving expectations and (thus) enabling action. This sentiment produces the 'will' to believe. Faith in these terms matches exactly that element in trust which – like a 'tranquilizer' (Beckert, 2005, p. 18) – allows the trustor to have favourable expectations towards the actions and intentions of others whose behaviour cannot be fully known or controlled.

At least two more points worth mentioning in the light of the discussion so far emerge from James' essays. First, an important aspect of the trust process presented in the previous chapter and again in this chapter has been that the development of trust depends on getting the process started somehow, after which there is a chance that it will be self-reinforcing. In this regard, faith would not only be instrumental in getting the process started but is itself a prime example of a self-fulfilling attitude, as James points out: 'There are, then, cases where a fact cannot come at all unless a preliminary faith exists in its coming. *And where faith in a fact can help create the fact*' (pp. 104–05, emphasis in original). Or, more graphically and directly related to trust: 'A social organism of any sort whatever, large or small, is what it is because each member proceeds to his own duty with a trust that the other members will simultaneously do theirs. Wherever a desired result is achieved by the co-operation of many independent persons, its existence as a fact is a pure consequence of the precursive faith in one another of those immediately concerned' (p. 104).

Second, interestingly enough, James also employs the image of a 'leap' with regard to faith. In *The Sentiment of Rationality* he uses the example of having to make a 'terrible leap' from a dangerous position while climbing on a mountain (p. 27). The mountaineer has no conclusive evidence of his ability to make the leap successfully, but his will produces the faith that will help him to achieve it. In Möllering (2001) I tried to illustrate my concept of trust in a similar way by reference to the analogy of jumping across a gorge, an image commonly associated with trust: 'trust can be imagined as the mental process of leaping – enabled by suspension – across the gorge of the unknowable from the land of interpretation to the land of expectation' (p. 412). I stretched the analogy further by pointing out that such leaps are not unique events in life, but required recurrently, and I even suggested thinking about preferred crossing places and 'suspension bridges'. This may be taking the analogy too far, but if we want to imagine what a conscious leap of faith feels like, the moment of jumping to cross a gap without being certain that one will make it unharmed is one of the best illustrations, and it does not even involve a trustee or much of a social context either.

A similar 'experience' of suspension is expressed in the image of the 'leap in the dark' and it is noticeable that William James' essay *The Will to Believe* closes with a quote from Fitz-James Stephen, who asserts: 'In all important transactions of life we have to take a leap in the dark' (James, 1948, p. 109). Overall, James clearly does not assume that actors take such leaps lightly or foolishly. Faith as a part of trust has to resonate with the actor's experience. It has to feel right, true, plausible and so on in spite of inconclusive evidence. It follows that trust rests on a kind of 'will to trust', but trust cannot be willed against the trustor's very personal and private sentiments. It is in this sense that Simmel's (1950) widely accepted remark that trust 'cannot be requested' (p. 348) needs to be understood, pointing out the irreducible agency on the part of the trustor who, just like the trustee, ultimately cannot be forced to make that leap and play his part in the trust–honour game. He may pretend to be trusting – raise a façade of trust – but genuine trust requires that he makes a leap of faith, which may be bigger or smaller, more or less difficult, but never completely taken for granted. A strong emphasis needs to be placed on the key role of actors' idiosyncratic interpretation and suspension of doubt in trust, because trust implies an 'as-if' attitude which is ultimately realized at the actor level, notwithstanding the fact that this important element of agency in trust is socially embedded and, to some extent, also socially constructed and locally variable (see Meyer and Jepperson, 2000).

5.5 EVIDENCE OF SUSPENSION

It has been my aim not only in this book but also in earlier articles (Möllering, 2001) to stimulate the re(dis)covery of the leap of faith as the essential element of trust in both theoretical and empirical research. In recent years, several empirical studies have taken this suggestion seriously and together they provide preliminary evidence of what suspension entails in practice (see also the case material presented in Chapter 7 below). It is striking that the notion of the leap of faith appears to resonate particularly well when trust is considered in the context of medical care. On the one hand, trust between doctors and patients has been a classical and extensively explored theme at least since Parsons ([1969] 1978; more recently in Lee-Treweek, 2002; Gilson, 2003; and see also Chapter 3), but in contrast the findings on trust reported for instance in *Social Science & Medicine* tend not to be picked up in other fields. As the following sections show, it might be instructive to look at them when it comes to understanding the empirical meaning of suspension.

By way of example, Mark Bernstein and his colleagues interviewed patients facing brain tumour surgery (Bernstein et al., 2004). The narrative remarks from patients that they report clearly document the presence of suspension. The patients recognize that trust does not mean objective certainty: 'You can be very confident in your doctor and there still can be an error. It just makes you feel comfortable going through the process if you have confidence in the doctor' (p. 210). Beckert's (2005) analogy of trust as a tranquilizer applies almost literally here. Bracketing is evident in the following quote from one of Bernstein et al.'s patients: 'And a slip of the scalpel ... you think of these things, but I ... have confidence in him and I'll just have to be, you know, I will just assume everything will go right' (p. 210). And other patients that they interviewed said that they do not worry about the risk of an error during surgery because they feel that this is something they cannot control – and therefore have to blend out. By achieving suspension, patients can be less terrified and undergo life-threatening brain surgery in a trustful, optimistic way.

In another study, Martin McKneally et al. (2004) analyse interviews with patients recovering from the elective surgical removal of their gallbladders. It should be noted that in contrast to the Bernstein et al. study, these patients were interviewed after the treatment, not before, and that the operation they underwent is far less frightening than brain surgery. When surgery is 'elective', it is done with the patient's prior consent, as opposed to emergency surgery on an unconscious patient after an accident for example. A key aspect emerging from McKneally et al.'s analysis is how 'doubts and fear were set aside, but not eliminated, using various mechanisms to manage them' (p. 53). A minority of patients (six out of 33) approached the decision to undergo operative treatment with an unquestioning attitude, a form of trust without reservation, requiring no objective proof and displaying a 'let's do it' approach.

Most patients, however, had to 'put aside' serious misgivings or doubts, although without completely eliminating them. The authors describe how patients accumulated information about their disease, treatments and medical institutions, but they could not manage their fear and doubts purely by reason. Patients 'made a leap to trust rather than simply building a bridge of reasoned arguments across the chasm of doubt and fear' (p. 55). In preparation for the decision 'not to worry', they started to focus on positive aspects rather than risks, but for some it was also a kind of resignation to the fact that they had 'no choice' (p. 54).

Overall, McKneally et al. found that 'ways of leaping were as diverse as the patients themselves. Some patients gained confidence to make the leap by becoming more informed about the surgical procedure and competence of professionals who would take care of them. Many were prodded to make the leap by increasingly intolerable symptoms, or by fear of the consequences of not acting. Patients were ultimately encouraged, that is, they were rendered courageous enough to leap, by the empathy, understanding, and confidence of the doctors and nurses who cared for them' (p. 55). The last point about the encouraging role of medical staff highlights the fact that although people have to make leaps of faith individually, they are not alone in this but embedded in social networks.

Julie Brownlie and Alexandra Howson (2005) have stressed this embeddedness argument recently in an empirical study that builds on my article on the Simmelian notion of trust (Möllering, 2001) and demonstrates the role of suspension in parental and professional talk about vaccination against measles, mumps and rubella. In what follows, I extract only a few of the most illuminating passages from Brownlie and Howson's (2005) rich article. Parents who have to decide whether to have their children vaccinated look for good reasons and proof but realize that they have gaps in their knowledge. They can even list, and then partly set aside, what they do not know. Their suspension can be routinized ('You just go and do it', p. 227), but in important situations, such as the vaccination decision, it can also be highly reflective and dynamic in the sense that they are able to bracket some uncertainties but not all – and not instantaneously nor all the time. There is a temporal aspect to suspension, as one parent put it: 'Probably I was hoping that your will, your resistance will wear down and you will just go ahead and say "oh lets just go and get it done, get it over and done with"' (p. 228).

As already mentioned, Brownlie and Howson (2005) emphasize that parents do not suspend in isolation: when suspension occurs, it occurs within relationships and networks' (p. 228). In particular, parents receive relevant information not only from health professionals but also from their families and friends as well as the media and authorities. They also draw on their own experiences as children (who were routinely immunized in the past, for example) and as parents (who have already had to make similar decisions before). Overall, leaps of faith are made possible by the 'relations of familiarity' that parents develop over time, not only with particular medical professionals but also within their larger social networks that extend as far as the political arenas of government and state. This view corresponds with the idea that individual leaps of trust refer to a fiction of reality that is produced individually, collectively and institutionally.

Embeddedness clearly plays a role in the empirical case that I presented in a recent article on the duality of trust and control (Möllering, 2005a). There, I refer to the deterioration of trust that a German publisher had in a very prominent author and politician. Their relationship was complex as it had dimensions of business, party politics and friendship and was embedded in overlapping economic, political and personal networks. However, what suspension means is ultimately recognizable at the level of the individual, for instance when the publisher stated: 'I know Oskar Lafontaine so well that I am sure he has his good reasons' or 'I have no doubt that Oskar Lafontaine has told me the truth' (p. 296). In both cases the publisher could not be perfectly certain but he was willing to bracket uncertainty and vulnerability. The example shows that suspension can have detrimental effects because in this case it turned out that the publisher lost a lucrative book deal because his trust was broken by Lafontaine.

In her work on the development of trust in small business cooperation in Tanzania, Malin Tillmar also frames trust as a combination of the trustor's subjective knowledge and a leap of faith (Tillmar, 2002; Tillmar and Lindkvist, 2005). The colourful case of the initiatives within a community in the remote Tanzanian town of Singida is, first of all, remarkable due to the unusual and, more importantly, highly difficult and unreliable institutional context. In the absence of effective jurisdiction and police, people refer to tribal rules and witchcraft as the basis of their exchanges. Modern business initiatives seem almost impossible in this context. Nevertheless, Tillmar observes cases of successful cooperative business ventures where the partners have been able to build up enough trust. In explaining how they were able to do so, Tillmar and Lindkvist (2005) note that there was 'a need to be creative and in a sense try to "invent" good enough reasons for trust' (p. 18), in other words to create a trust-enabling fiction of reality. In practice this meant overcoming distrust initially by finding reasons for why the others would not be untrustworthy. Accordingly, the researchers found that the Tanzanian business people they observed would try to avoid big leaps of faith and, instead, they would take much smaller 'steps of faith' in less risky kinds of cooperation.

The Tanzanian business people's reluctance to take larger leaps of faith is understandable given the general precariousness of their situation. It could be argued that what they achieved, nevertheless, was an 'as-if trust' of the kind Hardin (1993) talks about or a weak form of trust still in the early stages of a gradual trust-building process. At any rate, even the small 'steps of faith' seem to have had a very positive effect and they even spread within the community by imitation. Moreover, we simply have to accept that there are many situations in which people are unable to make a leap of faith and, therefore, they are unable to trust. Sometimes this is unproblematic and sometimes it seriously paralyses them in their social activity. I never meant to suggest that the leap of faith is easy and perhaps the motto 'just do it' suggests a misleading ease when the ensuing question 'do what?' is omitted (Möllering, 2005b). It is one thing to define the suspension of uncertainty and vulnerability as the essential element of trust; it is a completely different matter to suggest normatively that people should take leaps of faith or to try and specify when suspension is in order (Möllering, 2005a).

The ideas presented in this chapter support the essential role played by suspension in reaching trust as illustrated in the Trust Wheel (Figure 5.1 above), even if we only have a rough and preliminary notion of suspension so far. When clarifying the meaning of suspension further, probably the most important question to be answered will be what it is – *beyond* reason, routine and reflexivity as bases for trust – that enables the trustor to make a leap of faith? The quick answer is 'agency': the idea that, although there are deterministic forces, social actors always have room for idiosyncratic, contingent initiatives which, in this case, they may or may not use to make a leap of faith for the sake of reaching trust. However, precisely what agency means in the literature and how exactly it is constituted in reality varies greatly.

On the one hand we have Anthony Giddens' (1984) concept of the actor, which is certainly not an undersocialized concept but Giddens nevertheless sees the actor as individually knowledgeable and powerful. Accordingly, actors can also face the unknowable and engage in the 'active trust' Giddens (1994b) describes later (see also Chapter 4). On the other hand, Giddens' actor model was criticized early on especially by Hugh Willmott (1986), who points out that Giddens underestimates the role of unconscious sources of motivation, resulting in an untenable assumption of sovereignty.

Writing from a somewhat different theoretical angle, John Meyer also challenges the notion of agency as a 'natural' property of sovereign human beings (see for example Meyer and Jepperson, 2000). He argues that ideas such as 'free will' and 'independent choice' are not only socially constructed and attributed; they are also conditional upon continued legitimacy in the social arenas in which they are applied. In other words, agency can be withdrawn, thus making leaps of faith impossible. Alternatively, agency may be forced onto social beings, whereby they become obliged to take on unwanted responsibility for their actions. The latter suggests a kind of self-management à la Foucault, in this case the idea that actors seek to conform by making or avoiding leaps of faith, depending on what is legitimate in a particular situation. Seen somewhat more positively, when the uncertainty and vulnerability implied in all trust is partly borne by society at large, this may facilitate suspension. However, ultimately individuals suffer the consequences of their more or less embedded and legitimated acts, which means that trust is genuinely a question of agency and an idiosyncratic achievement that may be supported or hindered, but not replaced, by social structure or, for that matter, unconscious motivations (see also Chapter 8).

In conclusion, this is still only the beginning of a new direction in trust research that builds on existing perspectives while placing the concept of suspension at the heart of an overall concept of trust. In order to develop this direction further, we need more theorizing but, quite definitely, we also need more empirical work exploring these ideas. In the next two chapters I will therefore present and discuss, first, some important methodological considerations for studying trust (Chapter 6) and, second, an analysis of rich empirical case material that brings out the experience of trust using all the elements of the Trust Wheel (Chapter 7).

6

STUDYING TRUST

6.1 OVERVIEW OF EMPIRICAL APPROACHES

As is evident from the chapters so far, this book is aiming to review and develop mainly the theoretical and conceptual foundations for our understanding of trust. Nevertheless, I have already referred to many important empirical findings and illustrations, too. In this chapter, I will take a closer look at how trust has been studied empirically and what we can infer from different perspectives on trust for studying the phenomenon in the future. Paul Hirsch and Daniel Levin (1999) have introduced the rather colourful dialectic of 'umbrella advocates versus validity police' to describe how a field of research is typically torn between devising broadly coherent and rigorous theoretical frameworks on the one hand and on the other proving more narrowly the empirical validity and specific practical relevance of the constructs produced. At different points in time – and to some extent at different points in geographical and disciplinary space – we can observe that either the 'umbrella advocates' or the 'validity police' appear to have the upper hand, while ultimately both are required in order to keep the field productive. Moreover, many of us tend to switch happily between the two sides ourselves.

In so far as trust research represents a single field of research in the first place, as 'umbrella advocates' would be eager to claim, certain changes in emphasis on either theoretical or empirical work are also perceptible here. It is my own impression, for example, that the 1960s and 1970s were particularly fruitful with regard to exploratory studies that would generate, rather than answer, many of the conceptual problems of trust from empirical settings. Afterwards, from about 1980 to the second half of the 1990s, the conceptual output was particularly strong. Towards the end of the 1990s, however, there were explicit calls for empirical studies of trust and, since then, we have certainly seen a remarkable number of books and special issues devoted to reporting surveys, experiments and ethnographies that would apply and test theoretically derived concepts. The 'umbrella advocates' have not disappeared, though, for which a forthcoming *Handbook of Trust Research* edited by Reinhard Bachmann and Aks Zaheer (2006) might be taken as evidence.

Ultimately, what matters most is that theoretical and empirical work remain mutually enriching, and it is in this spirit that I seek to demonstrate in this chapter not only how much we can gain from the wealth of empirical studies carried out to date but also how the theoretical conclusions reached in the previous chapters hold implications for further studies out there 'in the field'. I will focus on the different approaches that have been used to study trust empirically. The actual findings of the studies are only a secondary concern in this chapter and I do not perform a meta analysis (as found, for example, in Geyskens et al., 1998; Dirks and Ferrin, 2001, 2002).

It takes more than one chapter to chart the landscape of empirical work on trust and probably a whole book to do justice to all the studies that deserve to be mentioned. I will merely propose a number of heuristics with indicative examples, to enable us to distinguish meaningfully between the highly diverse empirical investigations that have been undertaken (Figure 6.1). We can of course distinguish between studies from different social science disciplines and I am mindful that my own knowledge of empirical studies is biased towards research in organization and management studies. I try to show, however, that the heuristics I suggest are broadly applicable, irrespective of discipline.

One difficulty has to be acknowledged beforehand and constitutes the first heuristic: in quite a number of highly relevant and instructive studies, trust is not a *central* concern but only a *peripheral* item or an issue that the researchers stumble across relatively late in the analysis (for example, Sitkin and Stickel, 1996; Uzzi, 1997). This makes it even harder to provide a picture that is complete and parsimonious at the same time. Nevertheless, it is important to know whether a particular study focused on trust or not, because this tells us how far and how deep we can expect the study to be embedded in trust theory. By way of illustration, Peter

Heuristics	Categories
Centrality of Trust	– central – peripheral
Stage of Causal Chain	– preconditions – antecedents – manifestations – consequences
Level of Analysis	– micro – meso – macro
Aim of Investigation	– explorative – descriptive – predictive – normative
Viewpoint of Operationalization	– trustor – trustee – third party
Method of Fieldwork	– quantitative – qualitative – comparative

Figure 6.1   Heuristics for Categorizing Empirical Work on Trust

Lane and his colleagues (2001) test a model predicting the relationship between 'absorptive capacity' (Cohen and Levinthal, 1990), interfirm learning and performance in international joint ventures. Trust is ultimately only one out of their 17 variables and it is measured by a single five-point scale from 'low' to 'high'. While it is commendable that the researchers include a question on trust at all, we cannot expect far-reaching conclusions from such a shallow treatment of trust.

The second heuristic suggested here draws on a very common framework denoting the stages of the 'causal chain' underlying a studied phenomenon. This has been used more or less explicitly across the social sciences and also in trust research. The basis logic entails that certain *preconditions* need to be fulfilled for the phenomenon, in this case trust, to become relevant; that a number of *antecedents* jointly produce trust; that *manifestations* of trust as such can be observed; and that the *consequences* of trust can also be established (see, for example, Huemer, 1998). Each stage can be refined further, and we can distinguish between necessary and sufficient preconditions, between a vast number of more or less specific antecedents (including mediators and moderators, which play a somewhat different role), between a trusting attitude and trustful behaviour as different manifestations of trust, and between various consequences of trust ranging from individual security (Erikson, 1965) to the prosperity of nations (Fukuyama, 1995). Many researchers also recognize feedback loops, in particular the impact of the consequences of trust on trust antecedents over time (see also Chapter 4).

It is probably not surprising to find that, when we apply this heuristic, empirical studies of trust tend to be selective with regard to the stage(s) of the causal chain they focus on and/or the degree to which they analyse each stage. Hence, many studies are predominantly interested in the consequences of trust (see Sako, 1998; Dirks and Ferrin, 2001; McEvily and Marcus, 2005). They would treat trust as one of many antecedents to something else (for example, economic efficiency) and largely disregard the antecedents of trust itself. Other studies, especially those where trust is a central and not peripheral concern, seek to explain manifestations of trust (attitudes or behaviours) and therefore model how antecedents lead to trust while worrying less about the consequences of trust (see Inkpen and Currall, 1997; Mayer and Davis, 1999; Bijlsma and Van de Bunt, 2003). A different way of expressing this heuristic would be to look at what stage in the causal chain holds the main dependent variable and which independent variables are considered. Within each stage, the perspective can be more or less limited because, for example, the researchers may choose to include a smaller or larger subset of possible antecedents or they may look at either trusting attitude or trustful behaviour but not both.

I would be inclined to say that the more comprehensively a study treats the whole causal chain, the better it is – but there are of course not only practical but also sound conceptual, epistemological and methodological reasons for more restrictive studies. It depends on what you want to show and how you want to show it. At any rate, it should be helpful to establish the focus of any individual study in these terms in order to be clear what it is supposed to contribute and what it is not.

The third heuristic I propose to use is the well-established, but not necessarily unproblematic, distinction drawn in the social sciences between micro, meso and macro levels of analysis (Figure 6.1; see also Tyler and Kramer, 1996; Bachmann, 1998; Rousseau et al., 1998; Nooteboom, 2002). Trust can be studied empirically at the *micro* level of individuals and interpersonal relationships. It can also be studied at *meso* (intermediate) levels of association ranging from small groups, such as families, work groups or sports teams, to larger groups, such as clubs, clans or organizations, or to entire subsystems of societies, such as local communities, industrial sectors or professions. At the *macro* end of this scale we would find studies addressing, for example, trust at the level of broad institutional frameworks or entire economies and societies, perhaps even international or global systems.

Clearly, studies of trust between lovers, between fire fighters, between companies in a strategic alliance or between a population and its government raise very different questions because they focus on very different societal issues and levels which we need to be able to distinguish. At the same time, though, I think it is also important to recognize that, in most practical situations, more than one level matters and there are also possible interaction effects between the levels. This should be clear from the conceptual chapters in this book and many researchers are aware of this problem irrespective of their theoretical preferences. For example, James Coleman (1990) notes: 'It is useful to gain a sense of macro-level phenomena involving trust, for in these are found combined the three components of a system of action: the purposive actions of individual actors, deciding to place or withdraw trust or to break or keep trust; the micro-to-macro transition through which these actions combine to bring about behavior of the system; and the macro-to-micro transition through which some state of the system modifies the decisions of individual actors to place trust and to be trustworthy' (p. 175). In other words, we need multilevel and, notably, cross-level empirical analyses of trust.

In organization studies, this challenge has been addressed by research on interorganizational relationships (for example Currall and Judge, 1995; Zaheer et al., 1998; Inkpen and Currall, 2004). When organizations cooperate, interpersonal trust plays a very important role in enabling, sometimes even preventing, successful exchanges between organizations. However, there is also an interorganizational relationship which is more than the aggregate of interpersonal relationships. Hence, we find situations in which a manager trusts his opposite number in another company personally but does not trust the other company as a whole. In other cases, it is the trust that the manager has in the other company or even the institutionalized trust that has developed between the two companies which enables the manager to trust his opposite number as well (see also Chapter 7 below). While interpersonal trust is a recognized phenomenon, it is a more contentious issue whether a person can trust an organization or organizations each other (Zaheer et al., 1998; Blois, 1999; Nooteboom, 2002; Sydow, 2006). It is considered bad practice not to be clear about the level of measurement and, especially, to 'anthropomorphize the organization' (Zaheer et al., 1998, p. 142).

This takes us back to the issue of trust in institutions discussed in Chapter 3 and the literature examining if and how the trust that people have in institutions at the level of society is related to the trust that these people have in their immediate neighbours, friends or colleagues, or vice versa (see, for example, Stolle, 2001). While it makes sense to distinguish between trust at micro, meso and macro levels, it is important to note that in virtually all conceptualizations the individual as trustor or trustee plays a crucial role so that the micro level is rarely completely irrelevant in studies of trust. For example, it is individuals who complete the questionnaires even when the surveys are intended to establish the aggregate level of trust in a community or society (Glaeser et al., 2000). Overall, I think it is not only important to appreciate that empirical studies differ in the level of analysis that they focus on, but also to see that new and exciting questions arise when empirical work considers cross-level effects.

Furthermore, when we look at different studies of trust, we should also distinguish between the different aims that an investigation can follow. According to my fourth heuristic (Figure 6.1), empirical research can be explorative, descriptive, predictive or normative in its aims. *Explorative* studies essentially seek to discover new questions and new facets that have not yet been treated in previous work on trust. Naturally, to demand that the same studies give all the answers as well would be expecting too much in most cases. In the next category, *descriptive* studies of trust generally build on already established analytical frameworks and aim to present in rich detail, often in the form of case studies, how empirical reality corresponds to, or possibly contradicts, those frameworks. The value of such work lies in bringing abstract categories to life and in suggesting ways of elaborating on a framework. It is often seen as a disadvantage that findings from rich individual case studies may not be representative or generalizable, but this is not their aim in the first place and they can increase our understanding of trust nevertheless.

Hence, this category differs very much from the next one: empirical work on trust that seeks to be *predictive*. All studies that devise formal models of trust and seek to operationalize and verify them through statistical (or other) tests essentially aim to discover robust and generally applicable causal mechanisms between trust and certain trust-related variables or 'factors'. What they do in practice is usually to explain ex post the level and variance of trust in the population they study by a number of independent variables. Ultimately, though, they also claim more or less explicitly that their models are able to make predictions ex ante, presuming similar conditions. It is probably fair to say that in many trust-related disciplines the empirical literature is dominated by predictive studies of this kind. They are highly systematic, transparent and coherent, yet they are often simplistic, mechanistic and unoriginal also. They reduce the problem of trust to something that the methods can deal with and this entails the risk of losing many important aspects of the phenomenon, not least its inherent paradoxes and dynamics (Kramer, 1996). Nevertheless, once we understand that the aim of such investigations is to be predictive – and not explorative or descriptive – we can appreciate their contributions to trust research better.

Finally, some empirical studies strive mainly for *normative* insights and many studies include at least some normative implications or undertones. This means that the researchers use their empirical studies to come to conclusions that enable them to give advice to their audience, for example policy makers, group leaders or simply anyone with a practical interest in trust. Compared to the predictive studies just discussed, these studies do not simply aim to grasp empirical reality but also try to shape it by making a case for things that *should* be done or changes that *ought* to come about. For example, Mari Sako (1998) is one of many authors who recommend that in business relations the parties involved should put less emphasis on safeguards against opportunism and invest more into enhancers of trust. Sometimes empirical findings such as the success of 'tit-for-tat' in Axelrod's (1984) studies are also interpreted normatively beyond the merely explorative, descriptive or predictive intentions of the researcher (see also Chapter 2). Generally speaking, though, most authors stick to rather tentative and cautious formulations when discussing the normative implications of their studies. This contrasts with the legitimate expectations of a significant part of their audience who hope for sound 'solutions' to various issues of trust, not least in view of the 'crises of trust' regularly attested to in so many areas of private and public life (Barber, 1983; Misztal, 1996; Cook, 2001).

A further heuristic that I propose to include is called the 'viewpoint of operationalization' (Figure 6.1). Put simply, empirical studies differ in how much they focus on the trustor, the trustee or a third party in a given setting. When the *trustor* is the main concern, typical questions addressed would be what kind of personal traits, experiences, perceptions and emo-

ognized that we cannot automatically infer trust from cooperation and vice versa (Kee and Knox, 1970). More recent experiments have tried to account for this (Yamagishi et al., 2005).

As an aside, I find it interesting that, in many social science disciplines over the past 25 years, the value of experiments in laboratories and similar artificial environments (notably cyberspace) has been severely debated, even to the point where the publication of findings is practically banned, especially when the subjects of the experiments are the researchers' own students, because the results are seen as systematically unreliable. The online 'Notes for Contributors' to the journal *Human Relations* are a case in point: 'Studies based on laboratory experiments are normally unacceptable unless presented with confirmatory field data. Studies referring to simulation exercises involving students or others without experiential knowledge of the simulated context are particularly discouraged.' Such an explicit policy may be rare but it still represents a general scepticism towards the value of experiments in the social sciences.

On the other hand, Gregory Dobbins and his colleagues (1988) warn against 'throwing out the baby with the bath water'. Experiments may be appropriate as long as it is clear what they can reveal (basic cognitive processes in a controlled setting) and what not (complex social dynamics in real life). For example, Don Ferrin and Kurt Dirks (2003) use an experimental design to show that reward structures mediate interpersonal trust and that the effect is mediated by a number of other factors. The results are very clear and convincing but, presumably, much caution is required when applying the findings to more complex settings.

However, with the advent of behavioural economics as a 'new' discipline largely unaffected by previous methodological headaches in other disciplines, the field is currently flooded by experimental studies of cooperation, which are often misleadingly labelled 'trust research' and contribute incrementally to the elaboration of ever more specific game-theoretical problems (see Ostrom and Walker, 2003; and numerous publications in periodicals such as *Games and Economic Behavior* and *Journal of Economic Behavior & Organization*). For my own opinion on this, I can only refer to Chapter 2 again and acknowledge the heuristic value of game theory as well as the pivotal contributions of researchers such as Morton Deutsch and Robert Axelrod to the literature on trust, although I am afraid that behavioural economics, for all the important insights it has to offer, definitely misses most of the points I raise in Chapters 3 to 5 (see also Kramer, 1996).

What the second and third quantitative approach have in common according to my broad categorization is that they use surveys (questionnaires) to measure the extent to which respondents have a trusting attitude. The main difference between them is that, on the one hand, standardized surveys assess the respondents' disposition towards the trustworthiness of generalized others (for example, politicians) while, on the other hand, what I call target-related surveys ask respondents about their perception of fairly specific others (for example, your local mayor Mr. Jones). The standardized survey approach is common in psychological work on personality (Rotter, 1967; Wrightsman, 1966) and in political science research on social capital (Putnam, 1995; Paxton, 1999; Glaeser et al., 2000). For example, the General Social Survey in the United States contains the following standard item: 'Generally speaking, would you say that most people can be trusted or that you can't be too careful in dealing with people?'

Julian Rotter's (1967) Interpersonal Trust Scale (ITS) contains similar questions but there are more of them. It has 25 trust items formulated in the form pioneered by Rensis Likert (1932) where respondents are asked to indicate their level of agreement or disagreement with a set of relevant statements. All items together give an additive scale. The reliability and unidimensionality of the scale is usually tested by calculating a coefficient called Cronbach's alpha (Nunnally, 1978; Cortina, 1993). Examples of the items used by Rotter are: 'Parents usually can be relied upon to keep their promises' and 'Most elected public officials are really sincere in their campaign promises.'

Scales like the ITS and the GSS items have been used in at least two ways. First, by administering the survey to a representative sample of a given population, researchers obtain descriptive statistics for this population in the aggregate and are able to quantify the average predisposition and the variance within the population as a whole or according to subsets of the population defined by gender, ethnicity or income and so on. Changes over time can be traced if the survey is conducted repeatedly. Second, at the level of the individual, it is interesting to study how a person's general predisposition to trust acts as an antecedent to actual trusting behaviours or how it correlates with other attitudinal constructs and predispositions (for example happiness; see Rotter, 1980).

While the predisposition of the trustor is nowadays generally recognized as a significant influence on trust (Mayer et al., 1995; Costa, 2003; Ferres et al., 2004), the standardized survey approach may lack external validity as the attitude revealed in a survey situation may not predict actual manifestations of trust in specific everyday situations. Internal validity can be questioned, because the respondent's attitude may be a reflection of a range of individual factors such as personality, past experience, perceived qualities in others, or all of these. In other words, it is hard to infer from the survey answers why the respondents answer in the way they do, whether they would always answer in the same way and, if so, how they became the kind of person who answers in this way.

The target-related approach to measuring trust requires respondents to report how they perceive a specific other actor. The instruments applied are also predominantly compound Likert scales (for example, Johnson-George and Swap, 1982; Sako, 1992; Mohr and Spekman, 1994; Zaheer and Venkatraman, 1995). The main methodological difference to the standardized survey approach lies in the target-related phrasing of the statements. For instance, the first statement from Rotter's ITS quoted above would have to be rephrased assuming a specific actor B as the target to read: 'B usually can be relied upon to keep his promises.' The external and internal validity of this empirical approach is somewhat problematic, too. It needs to be understood that what is measured is a posed snapshot of A's subjective perception of B's trustworthiness at a single point in time, in the context of their specific relationship and guided by the researcher's particular questions. Even if such snapshots are taken at regular intervals and from different angles, the basic approach remains fairly static and detached.

The kinds of statements used in target-related surveys usually reflect the context of the relationship (for details of the following examples of trustworthiness scales, see Möllering et al., 2004). For example, Robert Larzelere and Ted Huston (1980) are interested in very close personal relationships and a typical statement for their dyadic trust scale would be, for example: 'My partner is perfectly honest and truthful with me.' Daniel McAllister (1995) measures perceptions between colleagues at work and so includes items like this: 'I can talk freely to this individual about difficulties I am having at work and know that (s)he will want to listen.' Larry Cummings and Philip Bromiley (1996) design their Organizational Trust Inventory to be used throughout organizations and therefore their items are phased in somewhat more general terms, for example: 'In our opinion, ___ is reliable.' Aks Zaheer and his colleagues (1998) study interorganizational relationships. They include items such as 'Supplier X has always been even-handed in its negotiations with us.'

Overall, though, while the phrasing of statements varies according to the context of the relationship (for example, romantic couple as opposed to industrial buyer–supplier relationship), the actual thematic content of items does not vary very much and would typically include appropriately worded references to ability, care, fairness, honesty, openness and reliability. As I said in Chapter 2, the literature suggests an overall image of the trustworthy actor as someone who is *able* and *willing* and *consistent* in not exploiting the trustor's vulnerability, and this image also informs the construction of scales for measurement, the result being that they differ more in style than in substance. In other words, it would not be too difficult to rephrase the Larzelere and Huston scale into a scale that could be used in a business context.

Having expressed the basic similarities between many trust measurement scales, it still needs to be acknowledged that there are very good reasons for why researchers keep constructing and validating new scales (for example Mayer and Davis, 1999; Gillespie, 2003; Tzafrir and Dolan, 2004; Mayer and Gavin, 2005). In particular, as long as there is no single, generally accepted and universally applicable definition of trust and its concomitant constructs, researchers will adapt their scales and methods to the specific conceptualization of trust that they favour or to the individual context that they study.

Moreover, in the absence of a 'definitive' scale, some researchers seek the challenge of improving on existing scales by replicating them and/or comparing them with refined, extended, shortened or otherwise modified versions. While it may be futile to dream of a 'perfect' trust scale, it is of course a basic requirement and particular challenge for all quantitative studies to demonstrate convincingly the validity of their measurements. Are they really able to measure 'trust' specifically or just some diffuse attitude, opinion or mood? And is trust not too diffuse and elusive for precise measurement anyway? (It should perhaps be noted, though, that some trust researchers now work with neuroscientists to locate trust in the human brain; see Zak et al., 2004; Kosfeld et al., 2005; more generally, Camerer et al., 2005.)

Target-related surveys generally have an individualistic bias because the respondents are individuals influenced by subjective personal experiences in encounters with other individuals. This also draws attention to the affective element of trust captured in Larzelere and Huston's (1980) and McAllister's (1995) scales (see also Chapter 2). Somewhat ironically, the inclusion of affective items in a questionnaire may rationalize affect and turn the intended affective constructs into cognitive constructs. Raising the level of consciousness about affect by way of the questionnaire format – or indeed by any other research intervention – could misrepresent the respondent's affective perception of the target, as a result, say, of social desirability effects (Crowne and Marlowe, 1964).

In this section, I have focused on the problem of trust measurement. It goes without saying that in quantitative studies of trust a number of constructs apart from trust need to be measured, too. Their operationalization may be no less challenging than that of trust. For example, if we want to test whether trust enhances performance, there are countless ways of measuring the performance of an individual, group or organization (Venkatraman and Ramanujam, 1986; Dirks and Ferrin, 2001), and perhaps some of these are more likely to display correlations with trust than others.

Beyond measurement, more and more sophisticated methods of quantitative analysis are being developed, and they are not only a blessing, in that they provide new possibilities, but equally a burden, because it becomes harder to decide what kind of analysis is best suited to the task and whether older data can or even need to be reassessed by the new methods. Overall, advances in quantitative methods fascinate me, but where trust research is concerned I am sceptical about whether they are able to bring us closer to understanding core concepts like suspension. In the worst case, the concept of trust is reduced to fit into a given methodology (as in game theoretical work). In better cases, we end up with unwieldy scales and models that aim to include any possible aspect of trust (as in some of the survey-based trust research). In any case, the question is whether we can understand trust properly in quantitative terms at all, if the leap of faith is to be at the heart of the concept. Perhaps what we need are qualitative studies that can access the actors' experience of trust better.

6.3 QUALITATIVE STUDIES: UNDERSTANDING TRUST

The range of qualitative methods that can be used in empirical social science research is, of course, very broad (see, for example, Denzin and Lincoln, 1994). What they all have in common is that they gather and analyse non-quantitative data, which generally means that they deal with 'text' produced independently by the actors studied (for example, diaries, letters, e-mails, talks, pamphlets or press releases) or by the interaction of researchers and subjects (for example, transcriptions of formal interviews and discussions as well as casual conversations) or by the researcher act-ing independently (for example, field notes in the context of ethnographic methods, ranging from simple observations or more involved participant observation and action research). Although there are studies of trust that draw mainly on texts that were produced without the influence of re-searchers (such as my own analysis of a published diary, Möllering, 2005a) and some studies that constitute in-depth ethnographies based on rich ob-servational data (such as Uzzi, 1997; Tillmar, 2002), the most common qualitative approach by far is to conduct interviews, which are usually long enough (at least one hour) and open enough (semi-structured with open-ended questions) to generate rich insights into the interviewee's individu-al perspective on trust-related questions and problems.

In this section, I will first of all review in chronological order a num-ber of qualitative studies of trust that I believe are particularly instructive examples of what this methodological approach can achieve. Some of these studies have already been mentioned in previous chapters, but the focus here is on the empirical methods used. I will then point out some of the limitations and draw preliminary conclusions on the value of quali-tative work on trust. Since my aim is not to give a complete record of qualitative trust studies, I will only present studies published since 1996. Needless to say, we can still learn very much from older qualitative work, especially classics such as Garfinkel (1967), Henslin (1968) or Eisenstadt and Roniger (1984).

Rod Kramer (1996) adopts an autobiographical narrative methodology in his study of trust in dyadic relationships between doctoral students and faculty members, asking his respondents 'to recall and describe all of the significant incidents and behaviours that they felt affected the level of trust between them' (p. 230). While Kramer also uses quantitative meth-ods to analyse the data he generates, he points out that it is important to obtain thick and richly textured data, and he sees 'a need for more "naive theories" of trust' (p. 238), meaning by this the ways in which respon-dents themselves make sense of trust. Autobiographical narratives 'pro-vide data that are more representative of how individuals naturalistically operationalize variables such as trust and trustworthiness' and they 'po-tentially provide a rich and detailed picture of how a phenomenon is sub-jectively construed' (p. 239).

In a study already referred to briefly in Chapter 4, Sim Sitkin and Dar-ryl Stickel (1996) adopt a grounded theory approach and collect data by asking their respondents intentionally open-ended questions in interviews about their experiences with a quality management programme that was implemented in the research laboratory where the respondents work. The problems and dynamics of distrust caused by the quality programme come out in the interviews although the researchers did not set out initially to study trust. Since the researchers avoided a highly structured quantitative survey approach, they were flexible enough to react to the particular ways in which their respondents interpreted the issues they had with the programme. This is led to novel and well-grounded insights into the dynamics of distrust.

Brian Uzzi (1996, 1997) reports on an ethnographic study of 23 entrepreneurial firms in the New York apparel industry to demonstrate the network effects of embeddedness and, with regard to trust specifically, the way his respondents use trust as a heuristic in the development of a network of interfirm relations over time. Once again, the topic of trust was not central to Uzzi's project at the outset of the fieldwork, but because he collected rich data through interviews and observations over a longer period of time, trust could emerge as an important element in explaining the relationships between embeddedness, interfirm organization and economic performance in the specific setting Uzzi studied.

One of the practical problems faced by qualitative researchers after completing their studies is that the standard length of journal articles and chapters in edited volumes makes it almost impossible to convey the richness of the findings obtained. Fortunately, some detailed qualitative accounts of trust can be found in research monographs (for example, Huemer, 1998; Tillmar, 2002; Gambetta and Hamill, 2005; Six, 2005). Lars Huemer (1998) presents two extensive case studies of the business relationships between the truck manufacturer Terrain Tech and three of its suppliers as well as between the security service firm Securitas and two of its clients in Sweden. He finds rich and sometimes surprising aspects, for example that bases for trust can work in two ways: whilst some level of personal familiarity is required for trust, friendship is not and may even be undesirable or suspicious. The relationships he studied have survived severe tensions and the parties involved have been able to maintain or restore trust, which illustrates both the process nature of trust and the need for active trust constitution. Huemer's respondents feel strongly that – even when they cooperate and show concern for each other – there is always ultimately a commercial interest to be satisfied and a professional distance to be kept (see also Chapter 7). The 'rules of the game' (p. 323) are a strong relational variable besides trust.

In methodological terms, it is interesting to note that Huemer's field-work involved three interview phases. In the first phase, interviews were more open ended and Huemer deliberately did not probe for trust, although he paid particular attention to this issue. In the second interview phase, Huemer asked more structured questions, confronted the respondents with his own interpretations and addressed the issue of trust more directly. In the third phase, he sent transcripts to his respondents and followed up on their reactions, sometimes through a third interview. This kind of elaborate fieldwork not only has the advantage of generating extensive idiosyncratic data; it also deals openly with the problem that the researcher's interventions and interpretations need to be checked against the respondents' view of the world (about which see more below).

Those contemplating conducting their own qualitative studies might also like to look at the following studies for methodological inspiration. Julia Liebeskind and Amalya Oliver (1998) conduct interviews with scientists and others involved in academic research to describe the changes in trust relations resulting from an increasing influence of commercial interests on science and demonstrate that trust is 'the output of dynamic exchange relationships' (p. 140). In a longitudinal study, Sue Newell and Jacky Swan (2000) describe 'the evolution of trust within a particular interuniversity, multi-disciplinary research team' (p. 1287) providing rich insights from semi-structured interviews, non-participant observation and analysis of e-mails. As already mentioned in Chapter 5, Steven Maguire et al. (2001) 'explore the dynamics of trust and control' (p. 286) in the relationships between pharmaceutical companies and HIV/AIDS community organizations in Canada. Intensive fieldwork carried out over several years enables these authors to reveal the discursive construction of identification-based trust in particular.

Mark Saunders and Adrian Thornhill (2003) describe highly vivid findings from 28 in-depth interviews carried out in a UK public sector organization on the relationship of organizational justice and trust in the context of change, demonstrating how the 'real' experiences of respondents can inform the revision of theoretical frameworks. As also mentioned, in Chapter 4, Fréderique Six (2003) studies 'the dynamics of trust and trouble' in a Dutch professional services firm, drawing on qualitative material from almost 200 instances of trust and/or trouble in that organization and yielding a rich picture, although her analytical efforts are more directed at quantification than at capturing idiosyncratic experience (but see also Six, 2005).

Furthermore, Sally Atkinson (2004) interviews 30 senior managers in a range of sectors (including non-profit) and elicits from them extensive narratives about their most important work relationships. She distinguishes between 'personal relationships' and 'utility relationships' and analyses the role of trust in relationships that the managers have with colleagues above, below and at peer levels in their organization. Her approach is akin to grounded theory and, instead of defining trust narrowly in advance, she encourages her respondents to talk about their own understanding of trust and finds that the meaning of trust differs depending on the persons asked, the point in time at which they are asked and the relationship type they refer to. Interestingly, well-functioning relationships can also be based on mechanisms other than trust, and thus Atkinson sheds new light on the question of where trust has its place in a business environment.

At the end of Chapter 5, I presented three recent studies from the medical sector: Bernstein et al. (2004), McKneally et al. (2004) and Brownlie and Howson (2005). The first two are based on fairly open-ended interviews specifically designed and conducted to address the issue of trust. In contrast, Brownlie and Howson perform a secondary analysis of qualitative data collected for surveys that were carried out by other researchers and did not address the theme of trust as such. Acknowledging the uncertainties resulting from using such 'second hand' data, the researchers are still able to generate highly instructive findings, and it could well be argued that secondary analysis of existing but under-explored qualitative data is a fruitful alternative to the costly production of new original data. On the other hand, we clearly need new qualitative studies, too, and high-quality outlets where they can be reported (see, for example, Bijlsma-Frankema and Klein Woolthuis, 2005).

Before concluding this section I would like to give a special mention to recent fieldwork of trust that has gone to extraordinary lengths in obtaining ethnographic material. As both have already been referred to in previous chapters, I will only point to the underlying methodologies here. First, Malin Tillmar (2002) undertook extensive interviews and participant observations in Sweden and Tanzania, and it is clear, particularly in the African part of her study, how important it was that she immersed herself in the world of the people she studied. Second, although replicating James Henslin's (1968) much earlier work in many ways, Diego Gambetta and Heather Hamill's (2005) study of taxi drivers in Belfast and New York is fascinating due to the rich empirical data they are able to present from observing their respondents over a long period of time in the course of trust-related activities in their work. Through their high-involvement methods, both studies achieve something that is a primary but difficult aim of qualitative trust research: they manage to 'be there' at the very moments when people trust or make trusting choices.

It is indeed one of the disadvantages of most qualitative methods that they generally involve ex post or ex ante rationalizations and rarely capture the actors' 'pure' experience of trust. Needless to say, this is also a problem of quantitative approaches. Moreover, qualitative researchers face more general criticism with regard to the validity and generalizability of findings from a relatively small number of cases. In turn, the small number of cases that we usually find is a reflection of the fact that qualitative research is highly resource-intensive in all stages of the research process. Once we abandon simplistic conceptualizations of trust, however, it is clear that qualitative methods are required to understand trust as a complex idiosyncratic achievement by the embedded actor (see Chapter 5). It is important that qualitative work stays true to itself, aiming for richness, and that it also presents findings is such a way that they can make sense to others and be related to previous findings and future research questions. In other words, somewhat paradoxically, open-ended fieldwork on trust needs a clear frame of reference. At the same time, this frame must not be forced onto respondents but be used flexibly and self-critically at all stages of the research process. This is the main advantage over structured, quantitative studies, which inevitably have to be much more rigid.

6.4 COMPARATIVE STUDIES: CONTEXT AND HISTORY

I introduce comparative studies of trust as a separate category here in order to highlight the importance of studying the context and the history of relationships in which trust matters. Hence I agree with Reinhard Bachmann (1998) who argues that 'comparative research can ... show how strongly the *institutional* framework shapes the forms and quality of economic relationships' (p. 299; emphasis in original). In this section, I will review examples of studies that demonstrate this importance empirically because they compare the constitution of trust in different contexts and/or at different times.

The comparative approach dates back to the sociological classics such as Alexis de Tocqueville and Max Weber who, as part of their larger scholarship, sought to understand modern societies by comparing them. More specifically on trust, Alan Fox (1974) applies a distinction between high-trust and low-trust systems of management, not only at the level of individual organizations but also, more famously, at the institutional level of national bargaining structures, concluding that British and American systems are 'low-trust' while the German and Japanese equivalents are 'high-trust'. The point to note here is that trust relations within organizations mirror the trust template inherent in the institutional provisions and vice versa. This general finding is also confirmed in a comparative study by Wolfgang Streeck (1992), who observes that legal regulation, especially that governing industrial relations, has an effect on the development of trust in the workplace. Shmuel Eisenstadt and Luis Roniger (1984) present another classic comparative and partly historical analysis of interactions between interpersonal trust relationships and larger social structures, covering an impressive selection of societies ranging from European and African countries in the Mediterranean to Latin America, several Asian countries, and both the United States and the Soviet Union.

Perhaps the best-known work in this regard is Francis Fukuyama's (1995) wide-ranging analysis of trust in different societies. Fukuyama adopts a historical perspective in order to reveal the origins of contemporary differences in the constitution of trust in different parts of the world, claiming that the prosperity of nations depends on trust (or, more precisely, on the social capital and spontaneous sociability that trust engenders). While impressive and thoroughly researched, Fukuyama's book does not offer a comparative empirical study in the narrower sense of a research project on trust that gathers and analyses data systematically at different points in time and/or space. Such studies do exist (for example Sako, 1992, 1998; Stolle, 2001; Dyer and Chu, 2003; Cook et al., 2005b; Rus, 2005), and in the following section I present the Cambridge Contracting Study as a prime example.

From 1992 to 1997, a team of researchers at the University of Cambridge studied the connections between the contractual environment, actual contracting practices and trust in a project referred to here as the Cambridge Contracting Study (Deakin et al., 1997). It is a comparative survey of contracting practices in Britain, Germany and Italy, covering the two sectors of mining machinery and kitchen furniture (fitted kitchens) in each country and drawing on interviews with both buyers and suppliers in each sector. The researchers conducted semi-structured interviews between November 1993 and December 1994 with 62 respondents in total, 14 of which represent buyer firms (6 German, 4 British, 4 Italian) and 48 suppliers (17 German, 16 British, 15 Italian) 'spread more or less evenly over the two sectors concerned' (Arrighetti et al., 1997, p. 176). In addition to the interviews, the Cambridge researchers studied various secondary sources and consulted industry experts (Lane and Bachmann, 1996; Lane, 1997).

Brendan Burchell and Frank Wilkinson (1997) report in detail on the respondents' perceptions of trust in business relations. They find that, overall, country differences in the understanding of the substance, functions and sources of trust are a matter of degree rather than kind. The basic notion of trust is highly similar among British, German and Italian buyers and among suppliers in both mining machinery and kitchen furniture. There is also a consensus among the respondents that trust has become more important in vertical relationships compared to the five years prior to the interview. Above all, trust to the respondents means adhering to agreed terms and behavioural norms and to have favourable past experience of each other. The last aspect is particularly relevant to Italian respondents who, however, do not associate trust with behavioural norms.

On the question of which strategies firms use to establish themselves as trustworthy there is more variation between countries, but the primary strategy in all countries is the creation of a 'reputation for competence, reliability and straight dealing' (Burchell and Wilkinson, 1997, p. 224). Cooperating and responding quickly is another common strategy. In Britain, the establishment of personal contacts is used much more than in the other two countries as a means of displaying trustworthiness. When asked how, in return, firms generally decide whether they can trust another firm, long-term experience, satisfaction with performance, the results of inquiries and having personal contacts are given as the main bases for trust. Italians do not instigate inquiries as much as the Germans and do not rely on personal contacts as much as the British (Figure 6.2). Across the three countries, the dominant response to untrustworthy behaviour on the part of another firm is to terminate the relationship (53%), but while this seems to be the almost inevitable and exclusive response in Italy (88%), many German firms (41%) also make contractual provisions to cover risk and 25% of the British firms will try to sort out the differences.

Burchell and Wilkinson report further that two show cards with twelve items each were presented to the respondents, who were then asked to rate the items in terms of importance for the development of trust in business relationships. Once again, the country differences are not dramatic,

Percentage of firms*	British	German	Italian	All
Meaning of trust in business relationships:				
– Adhering to agreed terms	25	26	33	28
– Adhering to behavioural norms	35	30	0	23
– Favourable experience	10	22	67	31
Strategies firms use to establish their trustworthiness:				
– Create reputation for competence, reliability and straight dealing	50	83	39	59
– Cooperate and respond quickly	26	13	22	18
– Establish personal contacts	35	9	6	16
How firms decide to trust other firms:				
– Long-term experience	40	43	33	39
– Satisfaction with performance	25	22	44	30
– Instigate inquiries	30	39	11	28
– Personal contacts	30	17	6	18
Number of respondent firms	20	23	18	61

* Respondents could give more than one answer per category.
Source: Burchell and Wilkinson (1997, pp. 224–25).

Figure 6.2 Perceptions of Trust in the Cambridge Contracting Study

but an interesting pattern emerges according to which British firms associate trust most importantly with flexibility outside of the contract, while flexibility beyond the contract is most important for trust in the German sample. Strict contract adherence, although seen as important in all three countries, characterizes the Italian attitude in particular. In other words, relatively speaking, in Britain trust is regarded as somewhat separate from contractual obligations; in Germany it is something that builds on to contractual relations; and in Italy it is primarily about honouring the contract as such.

On the question of how trust can be developed in business relations, the overall finding is that 'Italian firms identified reputation for fair trading as more important for developing trust than long-term relationships, whereas for the German and British respondents this ordering was reversed' (Burchell and Wilkinson, 1997, p. 229). Overall, it is striking that different trust perceptions and contracting practices cannot be traced back to differences between the mining machinery and kitchen furniture industries as much as to differences in the conditions under which vertical relationships are established in Britain, Germany and Italy (Arrighetti et al., 1997). The researchers investigated these conditions or 'contractual environments' in more detail, looking at contract law, trade associations and technical standards in particular (Lane, 1997; Deakin et al., 1997).

The publications from the Cambridge Contracting Study conclude unanimously that the contrast between the British and German contractual environments demonstrates how a comprehensive, consistent, transparent, integrated and legitimated institutional system, like the one in Germany, provides stability, predictability and therefore reduced uncertainty and risk in vertical relations (Lane and Bachmann, 1996; Deakin et al., 1997). Moreover, as both general principles, such as 'good faith' and the protection of weaker parties, and informal norms are supported by the German institutional system, too, it is no longer surprising that German firms are able to develop a long-term cooperative orientation in their vertical relationships, while in the British environment contracting will be more competitive and short-term (Arrighetti et al., 1997). With regard to trust, the researchers infer that reliable institutions also foster the trust that is required for long-term cooperation, drawing on the Luhmannian complexity-reduction argument, whereby institutions reduce complexity to a level where the further reduction of complexity by trust becomes possible, which, in turn, enables the endurance of increased complexity from enacting trust (Lane and Bachmann, 1996). More by inference than on the basis of their interview material, the Cambridge researchers conclude that German firms have more system trust than British or Italian firms and that this promotes the interfirm trust required for a long-term commitment to cooperation (Deakin et al., 1997).

The Cambridge Contracting Study reveals on the basis of rich empirical material compelling connections between contractual environments, contracting practices and perceptions of trust which explain the distinct, self-enforcing patterns of interfirm vertical relations in Britain, Germany and Italy. The study does have unfortunate limitations, though, primarily in two respects. First, on the basis of the material generated, only very tentative performance effects of different contractual environments and corresponding practices can be shown. Christel Lane (1997) argues that the long-term cooperative orientation of German firms and the effectiveness of German technical standards may explain why German firms appear to achieve very high levels of quality, which gives them an advantage in those markets where quality rather than price is the major selling point (see also Lane and Bachmann, 1996). Whether the German system is 'better' than the British or Italian thus depends on the markets served and on whether there is actually a trend towards higher quality standards or not. Moreover, as Simon Deakin and Frank Wilkinson (1998) report, no correlations can be detected at the level of the individual firm between the adoption of cooperative contracting practices and firm performance measured in terms of changes in turnover and number of employees. They do find evidence, however, that the general level of firm performance is higher in German and Italian industries than in Britain, which could indicate that firm performance is affected by the institutional system.

Second, the Cambridge Contracting Study cannot answer directly the question of whether there is more trust or greater trust in one of the countries, sectors or individual firms than in the others, because the researchers only asked respondents to talk about their general orientation towards trust in business relations. They did not ask to what degree the respondents trust their own suppliers or buyers, or how much confidence they have generally in the firms and institutions relevant to their sector. The researchers therefore have to make strong assumptions and infer, for example, that the long-term orientation in Germany coincides with higher levels of trust while the preparedness of British firms to readily take legal action over breach of contract speaks for a lower level of interfirm trust in Britain. While the evidence might be stretched to support such inferences, at least tentatively, the solid conclusion from the study can only be that in different institutional contexts trust is understood and produced in different ways with the result that, for example, in Germany trust in vertical relationships seems to be more institution-based than in Britain. It is possible, though, that British firms are able to develop strong trust in a less institutional way. Overall, however, this limited insight supports the argument that 'firms' strategies for achieving co-operation are heavily influenced by institutional forces' (Deakin et al., 1997, p. 118) and it also underscores the view that institutions are possible bases for trust.

If we recognize the importance of the institutional context for trust and trust-building processes in the way that comparative studies reveal, then a further problem of particular interest in trust research can be derived quite easily: what happens when the British, German and Italian buyers and suppliers interviewed in the Cambridge Contracting Study start doing business outside their own countries? How can trust be built if trustee and trustor are situated in different institutional contexts and trust has to cross boundaries associated with national or regional cultures, legal systems, professions, social networks and the like?

This problem has been addressed by many empirical studies, especially in the literature on international business and management (with regular publications in the *Journal of International Business Studies*). For example, Jean Johnson and her colleagues (1996) study Japanese–U.S. cooperative alliances; Marjorie Lyles and Jane Salk include trust in their work on international joint ventures in Hungary (Lyles and Salk, 1996; Lane et al., 2001); John Child (1998) investigates trust in Sino–foreign joint ventures; Angela Ayios (2004) discusses trust in Western–Russian business relationships; and Torsten Kühlmann (2005) looks at the formation of trust in German–Mexican interfirm relations (see also Faulkner, 1995; Salk, 1996; Inkpen and Currall, 1997; Child and Faulkner, 1998; Mohr, 2002). In such empirical settings, the development of trust is not only influenced by the heterogeneity of contexts as such, but also by the way in which actors are sensitive to this issue and deal with it proactively (Child and Möllering, 2003). How difficult and precarious this can be in practice comes out particularly well in qualitative studies, whereas quantitative studies offer more generalized findings and explanations.

I expect that the topic of trust across contexts, meaning generally across boundaries and more specifically across cultures, will attract continuous interest and increasing research efforts. For years to come, globalization will not lead to the dissolution of differences and boundaries as much as it will require people to build relationships with 'strangers' who come from and interact within heterogeneous and dynamic contexts. (On trust within and across groups, see Williams, 2001.) I also believe that the challenge is much bigger than suggested by simple intercultural training courses. It comes close to what Anthony Giddens (1994b) calls 'active trust' and it will involve more pronounced leaps of faith (see Chapter 5). As long as comparative studies are not too static, simplistic or detached from individual experience, they can be a very good starting point for studies of boundary-crossing trust relationships.

6.5 CALLING FOR INTERPRETATIVE STUDIES

The purpose of this chapter has been to give an idea of the broad range of empirical approaches to studying trust that are possible and have been tried in prior research. While my personal preferences have already come through, it has to be stressed again that all methods can contribute to our understanding of trust, depending on the particular aim and focus of study. However, empirical work that takes the concept of trust that I have developed in the previous chapters of this book seriously needs to be highly ambitious in its methodological strategy. It requires a *process per-spective*, obtaining a rich (typically qualitative) picture of actual *trust ex-periences*, understanding the *embeddedness* of the relationships under investigation and taking into account the *reflexivity* not only in trust de-velopment as such but also in the research interaction itself. The general orientation should be to get away from measuring predefined variables and get closer to the respondents' idiosyncratic experiences and interpre-tations (Möllering, 2001).

More specifically, to begin with, manifestations of trust (or distrust) at any single point in time can only be understood against the background and history of the relationship and in the light of the present and future issues that the actors involved are aware of (Sabel, 1993). Researchers should adopt a process perspective (Poole et al., 2000; Van de Ven and Poole, 2005) that aims to reflect both the trust-building process and any concrete manifestations of trust (see Chapter 4). This could result in two complementary research strategies. On the one hand, it would be desir-able to carry out longitudinal studies of trust relationships. In some cases, researchers may be in a position to conduct an ongoing observation of a trust-building process, as for example in the ethnographic studies referred to above. More commonly, researchers could have several points of meas-urement which enable them to reconstruct a trust-building process over time (Robinson, 1996; Newell and Swan, 2000). On the other hand, it could be argued that the idea that a trust-building process can be objec-tively reconstructed through longitudinal analysis is partly misguided due to a positivistic epistemology (Denzin and Lincoln, 1994; Alvesson, 1999). For instance, this logic would assume that actors have a stable in-terpretation of past events over time. In reality, though, something that an actor used to see as evidence of somebody else's trust, for example an absence of monitoring, may later be reinterpreted very differently in the light of new information, for example as disinterest rather than trust (Luh-mann, 1979; Sabel, 1993).

More important than having several points of measurement in a longi-tudinal study is being able to determine at any point in time the current interpretation of past, present and future by the respondent and how it relates to their trust then (Alvesson and Sköldberg, 2000). In other words, a process perspective can be adopted by addressing, but not necessarily observing, the process of trust development. Questions along the lines of 'How much do you trust?' need to be followed up by asking 'How did you come to trust this much?' and/or 'Have you always trusted this much?' This extension is subtle but crucial.

Secondly, trust as a highly idiosyncratic phenomenon encompasses the specific knowledge, attributions and, ultimately, irreducible faith of the actors involved (Giddens, 1991; Seligman, 1997). It therefore has to be assumed that the actors' experience of trust needs to be understood in rich detail and with sensitive methods (Denzin and Lincoln, 1994; Guba and Lincoln, 1994; Smith, 1995). Clearly this is difficult to achieve by means of highly standardized instruments, such as the quantitative surveys used in much trust research. Instead, qualitative methods are suggested and the richer the picture that they generate the better. It is important that the method accesses the actor's own experience and does not merely confirm the researcher's expectations and observations (Schwandt, 1994; Alvesson and Sköldberg, 2000). The respondents need to be stimulated to talk about their experiences, which will commonly happen in an interview (Fontana and Frey, 1994; Smith, 1995).

The difficulty for the researcher is to empathize with the respondents and at the same time to assess whether their accounts are honest in the sense of truthful, to the best of their knowledge, and not deliberately distorted or misleading. In dyadic trust relationships, both sides of the dyad should be interviewed (Huemer, 1998) – not so much as a means of confirmation or triangulation (Altheide and Johnson, 1994) but rather as a means of taking in multiple perspectives that allow reflection on the idiosyncrasy of trust experiences.

Thirdly, trust development processes and trust relationships do not exist in isolation but always have to been seen in their wider context, which, after all, is always relevant as a potential basis for trust (see Chapter 3). Empirical research therefore needs to capture the embeddedness of the relationship under investigation (Granovetter, 1985; Uzzi, 1997; Sydow, 1998). In practical terms this might well mean that researchers have to spend most of their time trying to understand their respondents and the relationships that they are engaged in generally before the investigation can address trust specifically (Huemer, 1998). Understanding embeddedness also means seeking insights into how a particular trust relationship under investigation is related to the individual respondent's other relationships (Burt, 1993).

Fourth, as the previous points have already made clear, trust research should be highly reliant on the respondents' interpretations. This raises a number of methodological issues (Alvesson and Sköldberg, 2000; Möllering, 2001), the first of which is naturally the fact that in most forms of investigation respondents' interpretations are triggered by the researcher (Guba and Lincoln, 1994; Smith, 1995). Because the respondent is asked to give an interpretation, the description of the original trust-relevant experience will already be biased in a certain uncontrollable way (Fontana and Frey, 1994; Sitkin and Stickel, 1996; Huemer, 1998). Moreover, the researcher's own interpretation of the interpretation introduces further distortions (Schwandt, 1994; Smith, 1995).

There is no easy solution to these typical problems of in-depth qualitative research, but at least researchers should acknowledge and reflect on the reflexivity of their work (Steier, 1991; Denzin and Lincoln, 1994; Smith, 1995; Alvesson and Sköldberg, 2000). The respondents' interpretations should be seen in the light of the interaction with the researcher, and researchers themselves need to be able to step back and appreciate critically their subjective involvement in generating and analysing interpretations (see Mauthner and Doucet, 2003). This point is of particularly delicate relevance in trust research, where a respondent's willingness to interpret his trust relationship with another actor – to whom the researcher may also talk – depends not only on the trust in that relationship but also on the respondents' trust in the researcher who, for example, may or may not maintain confidentiality (Fontana and Frey, 1994).

In conclusion, when studying trust our empirical methods have to evolve with the level of complexity and sophistication achieved in our theories and conceptualizations of trust. I draw this conclusion partly from personal experience because I have also worked with relatively simple empirical frameworks (Möllering, 2002; Child and Möllering, 2003) which had certain advantages but made me realize that we were not getting as close to the essence of trust as I would have liked to (Möllering, 2001). In the following chapter, I present three exploratory cases of trust in buyer–supplier relationships in the British printing industry. I will show that it is possible to get closer to the 'ideal' outlined above, which means, first and foremost, to try and understand the experience of trust through rich interpretation.

7

EXPERIENCING TRUST

7.1 AN EXPLORATORY STUDY OF BUYER–SUPPLIER RELATIONS

With suspension at the heart of the concept, trust ultimately represents an idiosyncratic accomplishment by actors in their stream of experience and interpretation. As I concluded in the previous chapter, it follows that empirical research on trust requires a process perspective, obtaining a rich (qualitative) picture of actual trust experiences, understanding the embeddedness of the relationships under investigation and taking into account the reflexivity of the research interaction itself. To date, such a methodological strategy is still rare in trust research, but I adopt it explicitly in the empirical work presented in this chapter.

In what follows, I explore the contribution that qualitative case material can make, drawing on interviews with purchasing managers of UK printing companies and representatives of their paper suppliers. Three different cases of buyer–supplier relations are presented with regard to relationship background, level of trust, meaning of trust, bases of trust, trust building and some other observations. I seek to let 'real' actors speak about their trust experiences and interpretations in a rather common micro-social setting. The cases are instructive in the way they reveal the concurrent simplicity, complexity and ambivalence of experienced trust. And they allow critical reflection on the limits of accessing trust in empirical research. I also have the feeling that theorizing and measuring trust might have led us further and further away from the reality of trust as an experience of individuals in various micro-social settings and as a reflexive process that requires rich interpretation by actors and observers in order to arrive at understanding (see Möllering, 2001 and the previous chapter). Hence, another issue addressed in this chapter is whether the actual experience of trust squares with our models. Is the Trust Wheel (Chapter 5) a useful analytical frame when it comes to concrete empirical cases? In this first section, I present the background to the three cases which make up the three main sections of this chapter and follow them with some discussion and conclusions.

Buyer–supplier relations represent one of the most common types of interorganizational relationship and, although the basic set-up might suggest arm's-length, market-based repeat transactions, it has long been recognized that, far from being anonymous and transient, these are indeed 'relationships', that they require more or less close cooperation from the parties involved and that trust plays an important part because the threat of opportunism and vulnerability is acute even when there is a mutual interest in continuing the relationship (see Ford, 1980; Dwyer et al., 1987; Heide and John, 1990; Sako, 1992; Lamming, 1993; Lane and Bachmann, 1996; Smeltzer, 1997; Huemer, 1998; Zaheer et al., 1998; Blois, 1999).

Following up on a quantitative survey of buyer–supplier relations in the UK printing industry (Möllering, 2003), I decided to obtain a richer picture of these relationships by conducting semi-structured interviews with representatives from both sides of the buyer–supplier dyads studied. From the outset, this qualitative empirical work was conceived as a small-scale, exploratory study complementing conceptual development and not as a comprehensive and extensive field study. Nevertheless, the cases are highly instructive.

Typical printing companies are of small or medium size, have very limited storage space, require high flexibility and are immanently concerned with quality whilst at the same time experiencing high cost pressures (Porter, 1994; Green, 1994; Birch, 1994). They are typically not vertically integrated with their material suppliers, despite having long-term and regular business relationships with them. The overall picture of the industry given in industry reports (Beatt, 1993) and by the British Printing Industries Federation (BPIF) confirms this: 'The printing industry is one of the largest of the UK's manufacturing industries but is among the least well documented. … Its structure reflects the diversity of its products and fragmented nature of its market with a few integrated groups, a number of medium-sized companies which tend to specialize in a narrow range of products and a vast army of small firms which usually cater for the local market' (BPIF, 1996, p. 1).

At the time of my quantitative and qualitative fieldwork from 1997 to 1999, the printing industry was the sixth largest manufacturing industry in the UK with an estimated turnover of approximately £9 billion and 150,000 employees in 10,000 companies (excluding newspapers), 3,000 of which are reported to be members of the BPIF (1995). In 1995, 39% of the BPIF members had less than 10 employees, 87% less than 50 employees, and only 7% employed more than 100 people.

In the mid-1990s, new sourcing strategies had been suggested in the UK printing industry, as one commentator reported at the time: 'Many print companies are now moving away from the traditional ideas of dual sourcing "to keep suppliers on their toes" and are instead using a single supplier, building on a situation of mutual trust' (Green, 1994, p. 200). Industry leaders like John Holloran (1994, p. 23) pointed out that they regarded supplier relations 'in rather more personal terms as a partnership', but nobody could say how strong this perceived trend actually was and whether the basis of trust between printers and their suppliers was strong enough to move to single sourcing or other more collaborative forms of supply management (Lamming, 1993).

The picture that emerged from my quantitative survey of 196 buyer–supplier relationships in 1997 (Möllering, 2003) revealed, on the one hand, a very positive atmosphere between paper buyers and suppliers – surprisingly for the experts – as respondents expressed very high levels of satisfaction, reciprocity and trust overall. On the other hand, there was enough variance within the sample and a cluster analysis showed that 55.6% of firms could be classified as 'traditional wary traders', 14.3% as 'controlled routine partners' and 30.1% as 'committed flexible partners' (Figure 7.1). Only the latter cluster seems to have relationships that actually benefit from strong trust, while the other two clusters primarily seek to limit their vulnerability, although they do not actually distrust their business partners either.

In February 1999, I contacted twelve of the respondents that had participated in the quantitative survey, explaining that I would like to follow up my research by conducting an interview with them. Given the exploratory nature of this exercise, the sample aimed for diversity rather than representativeness in terms of the size and business areas of the printing companies approached (see Morse, 1994). In particular, I managed to gain access to one case from each of the three clusters identified above. The

Traditional wary traders (55.6%)	– much lower levels of trust and performance – believe that the relationship with the supplier works well – do not distrust the supplier – relationships lack openness, flexibility and strong trust – traditional ways of trading used – focus on the immanent, isolated deal
Controlled routine partners (14.3%)	– high trust, performance and reciprocity – rely heavily on formality and strict following of agreed terms – exchanges like a highly reliable but unstoppable routine – inflexibility, attitude against exceptions and lack of openness – may break apart when unexpected changes occur
Committed flexible partners (30.1%)	– very high levels of trust and performance, strong reciprocity – very likely to see their suppliers as partners with mutual interests – relationship is relatively informal – both sides are prepared to make exceptions – suppliers are valued beyond prices and competence – buyers feel reassured and well understood

Figure 7.1   Typology of Supplier Relations

three printing companies described in the following sections were available at relatively short notice and interviews were arranged in March 1999. Crucially, all three companies also helped to establish contact with one of their paper merchants, who agreed to be interviewed as well. In one case it was possible to conduct an additional interview with the representative of a paper mill, resulting in a fourth dyad and giving eight interviews in total.

The interviews typically lasted for two to three hours (only one hour in one case and three and a half hours in another case). They were tape-recorded and transcribed in order to facilitate analysis. Additional information about the companies was obtained from the questionnaires they had filled in for the original survey, from company brochures and, where applicable, from the companies' websites. The interviews were semi-structured and based on a comprehensive but also flexible interview schedule which was divided into three parts plus a brief structured part on personal background information. The first and largest part of the interviews was devoted to understanding the buyer–supplier relationship and the individuals involved in it in as much detail as possible without yet raising the question of trust (see also Huemer, 1998, who used a similar strategy). The respondents were then asked about perceptions of trustworthiness, thus providing a transition to the topic of trust.

The main tool for accessing the meaning of trust in the relationship was to invite the respondents to recall typical incidents where they trusted or distrusted their business partner either personally or as a company. This was inspired by the autobiographical narrative method used by Rod Kramer (1996). Finally, towards the end of the interviews the respondents were asked about their general views on trust in business relationships beyond the specific dyad that the interview focused on. Only if the respondents themselves brought the topic of trust up at an earlier stage of the interview did I ask trust-related questions earlier than planned (as suggested by Smith, 1995).

Although the interviews are single points of measurement, I adopted a process perspective by asking the respondents to describe the past, present and future of the relationship and to recall key events related to the development of the relationship. I attempted to access the experience of the respondents by emphasizing that I would like to know their personal views of what goes on in the relationship and by prompting them to recall incidents that they personally considered important. The embeddedness of the relationships in question was captured by asking extensively about context (probably for two thirds of the interview on average) rather than addressing immediately the issue of dyadic trust. During the interviews, acknowledging reflexivity meant by and large being careful not to ask closed or suggestive questions, not to be judgemental or, at least, to indicate clearly which questions or comments from my side reflected my own opinion or interest, and to be sensitive generally to the dynamics of the interview situation. This is a typical challenge in interviews as pointed out, for example, by Fontana and Frey (1994) and Smith (1995).

Each interview was read and annotated numerous times (and the tapes listened to repeatedly) in order to extract a picture of the respondent's personal view of the relationship (see Smith, 1995). Next, the interviews with both sides of a respective dyad were compared and integrated to give a picture of the relationship that reflects the commonalities and differences in the views expressed by the respondents. This was followed by a comparison of the three cases, looking once again for both overlap and divergence between cases (as suggested for example by Stake, 1994; Huberman and Miles, 1994).

The advantage of working with only eight interviews was that it was possible to always refer directly to the annotated transcripts instead of abstract coding tables and thus to maintain the richness of the material analysed while remaining highly sensitive to themes brought up by the

give them an order, we're trusting them to deliver it on time and to our specification. And basically, if they don't, we can't print that paper. And we are going to upset our customer.' A common problem is whether the presentation of the sheets on the pallet is such that the paper can be fed into the machine efficiently. Problems in this area as well as with timely delivery and quality are most likely to be caused by the paper mill, but Jill trusts her merchant John of BPP, who then trusts the mill to perform. Another instance mentioned by Jill where trust is involved is when she needs supplies at short notice and can expect that John and the mill will go out of their way to make it happen. Overall, her idea of trust is captured in the following statement about BPP: 'I feel that if they say they can do it by a certain day, I know they do everything in their power to achieve that.' Moreover, Jill says that in a trusting relationship such as that with John it is possible to talk about more confidential issues with an unspoken understanding that nobody else needs to know. And it is also possible to discuss issues beyond the specific business between Uni Press and BPP: 'I will sometimes ask their advice, even if it's got nothing to do with them. I will ask them what they know about this, because I suppose I trust them to give me correct information' (Jill).

In return, when asked what trust in Jill means for John he says: 'My trust in the Printing Division is that I trust them to combat the pressures from the Publishing Division.' In particular, he trusts Jill and her colleagues to point out to their internal customers that cheaper paper means compromising on quality, service, availability and on the efficiency of the printing process. While cost cutting and other pressures are common in the industry, especially at times when the business cycle turns to the disadvantage of paper suppliers, the difference that trust can make in a supplier relationship, according to John, is that Jill will not change supplier quickly but first give him an opportunity to defend his business, for example by offering a different type of paper. His trust in Jill does not guarantee long-term successful trading relations with Uni Press but it certainly strengthens his position. John says that 'trust is everything in business' but always in relation to what the deal is about.

As an instance where his trust in James of Scott Mills might come to the fore, John talks about situations where he and James will settle a customer's complaint in favour of the customer for the sake of not disgruntling the customer over a relatively minor issue, although they are both convinced that the complaint is really unjustified. Trust is thus required 'where you're making your own decisions in what you feel to be the long-term interest of the company, but wouldn't necessarily be supported by the man in back base' (John). Generally, John says that 'you trust each other in helping each other' and means this especially with regard to the kind of short cuts that are sometimes necessary but nobody else needs to know about.

Interestingly, the incident recalled by James is similar to that told by John, but this time not in favour of the customer. James says that one time when he felt very much that he could trust John was when John immediately sided with him against a customer whose complaint was difficult to deal with. It is important to understand that John as the merchant and middleman could have also sided with the customer and blamed the fault on James as the representative of Scott Mills who delivered the paper concerned. This would probably have been the easier way out for John, but instead he supported James in negotiating a favourable settlement of a very substantial complaint. James recalls more of such incidents even involving Jill, too. However, remembering that Jill trusts John as well, John's trustworthiness seems to lie in his pragmatic, competent and honest approach to problem solving, conveying the message that everybody should be reasonable and helpful instead of making each other's lives unnecessarily difficult. At the most general level, trust for James and for the other two respondents is to be able to expect that the other takes one's interests into account and tries to be helpful and cooperative.

Bases of Trust

The respondents also talked about the bases for their trust, prompted mostly by questions eliciting how they know they can trust the other or what enables them to trust the other. Jill has a very clear view on this: 'I think you can only trust someone when you know them. I don't believe in blindly putting your faith in someone to come up with something. Unless you really have no alternative. Respect has to be earned over a period of time. And that can really only come with experience.' She also says that she trusts most of her current suppliers including BPP 'because of past history and experience of them' and that she 'would be wary of a lot of new suppliers, purely because they don't know us and I don't know them.' However, apart from 'experience', Jill also points out that Uni Press have an inspection procedure and reporting process, whereby any problems occurring are brought to her attention so that she knows about them immediately. Jill therefore sees the first basis for trust in BPP in 'their ability to achieve what they say they can achieve and their consistent ability to achieve their promises.' This is not to deny the benefits of a closer supplier relationship such as that with John of BPP: 'We feel that BPP know what we require. And that's through experience.'

This is underlined by John who claims that he knows if he can trust 'through nothing other than experience'. Like Jill he not only means by this his own personal stock of experience but the mutual experience from interaction with others over time. In the first interview, John talks a lot about his own approach to doing business and from that can be inferred what he might consider to be a particularly trustworthy buyer or supplier. The ideal combination, epitomized by the late Sales Director of Scott Mills, would be personal liking coupled with recognized competence and business acumen. Just as much as he believes that it is terribly important to get on well with the people you deal with, John insists that business interests as such should always come first and need to be respected. A good basis for trust should therefore balance friendship and professionalism. In the second interview, John distinguishes between 'old school' and 'new school' as general approaches to business, associating himself with the former. In short, 'old school' stands for the traditional, hard-learned, down-to-earth traders of John's own generation, while the 'new school' represents modern, superficial, faddish practices that younger managers in particular adopt who 'come out of the university and think they know it all' and 'who change things for the sake of changing things and then move on' (John).

Another very telling example of the difference between the schools is that, as John says, the new school have all the figures but no answers, whereas the old school have the answers but no figures. Irrespective of whether this distinction is sensible and realistic or maybe a bit too 'cynical', as John himself suspects, it is interesting to note that John apparently uses it as a heuristic to determine whom to trust. John describes James as belonging to the old school but having taken up many new school practices, not least because his superiors would demand them. Furthermore, John thinks that 'trust can be built in many ways: respect, admiration, the fact that you like each other, the fact that you need each other.'

Like Jill and John, the role of experience is also emphasized by James, who says that 'any trust comes from experience and judgement of people. You make a judgement of a person and then you think, "I can trust him." And then you do trust him. If you find that that trust is well founded, then all the way you go. It can work the other way round. You can think, "Oh,

I believe him and I'll trust him" and then you are sadly let down, but you've learned your lesson. And you learn whom you can trust and whom you can't.' Asked about the basis for his trust in John, James points out that 'whenever I've given my trust to him, he's not betrayed it. He's never let me down.' James also thinks that that it helps that 'we both come from honest working class origins', that is a common background despite their very different educational careers. But overall: 'It's purely experience. I know from experience that I can trust him.'

On the other hand, although experience gives the basis for trust, James describes very graphically – and notably without any cues from the questions I asked – how trust always entails uncertainty about the other, when he calls trust 'a substitute for telepathy' and notes: 'You can never know what a person is thinking. And trust is the sort of bridge between having a good idea and having total knowledge of what a person is thinking. It is like faith. It's the jump that you make. The jump into the unknown. And if you land on something on the other side, then you know the trust is there. And if you don't, if you fall then through space, then you know to play it a bit more cautiously next time. It's faith.' James connects this view with the idea that trust is experience-based, because the 'leap of faith' in trust means 'to put it to the test' and thus have a trust-relevant experience with the other.

Trust Building Process

As was already mentioned above, Jill says that she would be wary of a lot of new suppliers that she does not know. Generally, she points out that 'trust with experience is deeper than initial trust for a new supplier.' She gives the example of a short-notice order with a new supplier, where she would trust the supplier to deliver but write explicitly on the order sheet that the paper must not be late, whereas with a more deeply trusted supplier such as BPP she would agree the date and then not worry about it any more. The main thing to do in creating trust in new relationships, according to Jill, is 'both parties letting the other know what is expected of them and what they expect of the other one.' While this openness in building trust is required, it must not interfere negatively with existing relationships. Part of building trust with new suppliers is to maintain the confidentiality of established suppliers.

John emphasizes early on in his first interview with me that it is very important to him that he only deals with companies that are well known to him. Thus the process of building trust begins with and depends on what he already knows about the other. John points out that a relationship like the one with Jill at Uni Press 'is built up by constantly speaking to people', by helping each other out and by doing each other favours. At the same time, John explains that small companies in particular need to build relationships gradually not least in terms of financial commitment and cash flow considerations, which means that it is sensible to grow the business with a new customer 'in a controlled way year by year'. Trust develops over time through successful interaction and especially through proving oneself on 'vital orders', where the buyer is particularly vulnerable and 'it's all about trust' (John). The 'principle of gradualness' applies to the building up of trust more generally, as John states in the second interview: 'You obviously tread very carefully to begin with and then you build up the trust. You start with a little one and then move up to a bigger one.' All in all, building trust means 'doing things together and taking chances' (John). Socializing, having a private rapport outside of business and simply 'spending time' with each other are things that John considers to be extremely helpful and also enjoyable in trust building, but not absolutely necessary.

The statements from James quoted in the previous section already indicate that he also sees trust building as a gradual process of learning, experimenting and testing whether trust is 'justified', even if it ultimately remains a matter of faith. The building up of trust does not rule out the negotiation of relatively detailed contracts, according to James, although his company Scott Mills do not have a formal long-term contract with BPP. At any rate, contracting appears to be more a means of clarification and expressing commitment to the relationship than a legalistic threat: 'It's not worth being found out. That's what a contract is for' (James). Asked whether one can consciously build trust in a new relationship, James replies that all you can deliberately try to achieve is to get on with the other and to find some common ground, but he does not think that one can set out to create trust; it is 'something that comes from a relationship when that relationship is put to the test.' Accordingly, James finds it difficult to trust people whom he does not get along with, but thinks that it is possible to get on with people without having to trust them, because the question of trust may not come into it. However, I think the view that 'you can only establish trust, if you put it to the test' (James) does not imply the suggestion that occasions for testing trust should be consciously created.

Other Observations

It is much reflected by Jill, John and James that their dyadic personal and professional relationships are embedded in a wider business context involving a number of other key individuals and organizations. Jill is highly dependent on her superiors and her internal customer at Uni Press. The supplier relationship with BPP has to be seen in context with other existing and potential suppliers. James is in a similar situation at the other end of the supply chain, because his work is shaped by the decisions of his superiors and others at Scott Mills. BPP is his biggest customer but by no means the only one. John as a typical paper merchant has a web of paper mills as suppliers and printing companies as buyers around him, who compete more or less with each other and with BPP. Pressures on the dyadic relationships between Jill, John and James may therefore be due to the other relationships that they maintain. Trust for them means handling this complexity while respecting as far as possible each other's interests. While there can be a strong personal element to this trust, John in particular points out that he likes to avoid dependence on one person and always seeks to establish rapport with the staff either 'coming behind' and currently working for his current contact person or standing as decision makers above that person. Although the day-to-day business relies on individuals, the three respondents recognize – not least due to the experience of unexpected deaths or resignations – that supplier relationships usually have a longer-term orientation at the company level than at the level of the individuals involved.

Finally, another interesting observation in the case of Uni Press, BPP and Scott Mills is that the respondents are quite aware that the paper trade has pronounced business cycles, whereby the buyers and suppliers alternate at regular intervals between having the upper and lower hand. The exact economic reasons for this phenomenon are immaterial here, but it is interesting to note that buyer–supplier relationships apparently survive these cycles and the role reversals from being advantaged to disadvantaged and back again. My respondents did not put it this way, but it is plausible that these role reversals are a 'shadow of the future' that prevents excessive exploitation of strong market positions, and that trust can be both a means and a result of softening the cycle, establishing an open-ended reciprocity and looking out for each other in difficult times. In this respect, the position of merchants such as John is quite interesting, because he acts as a buffer in the paper trade, absorbing uncertainty and at times serving as a trust intermediary who uses his trustful relationships to give and request favours from either side of the supply chain.

7.3 CASE II: BLUECHIP PRINT AND MERCH PAPERS

Background to the Relationship

Bluechip Print is an independent printing company that employs about a hundred people. According to the typology in Figure 7.1 above, it would be classified as a 'traditional wary trader'. Bluechip Print was founded in 1992 and assumed its current form in 1994, when it acquired and restructured an established financial printing company. Bluechip Print's customers are primarily in the financial and service sectors and principally located in the City of London. In terms of technology, Bluechip has set out from the start to take full advantage of digital printing and publishing facilities, aiming to serve the short-notice and often urgent overnight requirements of its City customers. Bluechip has eight regular paper suppliers in total, four of which are considered 'core suppliers'. One of these is Merch Papers, which has supplied Bluechip for five years, currently accounts for about 30% of the latter's annual paper purchases and is therefore one of its biggest suppliers, but far from being in a dominant or exclusive position.

Merch Papers is a fairly sizeable paper merchant with a turnover of over 100 million pounds, trading offices around the United Kingdom and its own warehouse facilities. The company is owned by a Scandinavian group that represents a big player in the global paper industry. Merch Papers sources about 60% of the paper it sells from mills within the group. The sales to Bluechip Print account for less than 0.2% of Merch's total turnover. However, although the sales to Bluechip are not vital to Merch Papers as a whole, the company 'would be considered a good customer' and 'it would be bad to lose them, but it wouldn't be the end of the world' (Tim of Merch Papers). Respondents from both companies think that Bluechip is more important for Merch than vice versa, because Bluechip could easily find a new supplier for the materials it needs.

At Bluechip Print, I conduct an interview with Tony, the Purchase Manager responsible for all paper buying, who has been in his current position for four years and with the company for 13 years, which means that he already worked for the printing firm that was bought by Bluechip in 1994. Tony is 54 years old and joined the company originally as a van driver with no formal educational or professional qualifications (having left school at 15) but he learned the printing trade and is now among the most important staff in the operations of Bluechip. In his job, he is fairly independent and 'just gets on with it', but he is also influenced by one of the directors of the company, by the team of production, pre-press and sales staff that he works with and by the requirements of important clients.

My respondent at Merch Papers is a man called Tim. He is joint Branch Manager of the Merch trading office supplying papers to Bluechip Print. He is in his late thirties and has been a Branch Manager of Merch Papers for the past seven years. He worked for other paper merchants in sales jobs before that and has been employed in the paper industry since 1978, after finishing his school education with four O-levels. The branch that Tim manages has about twenty employees and operates as a profit centre of Merch Papers. He reports to a Regional Sales Manager, who again reports to the Managing Director of the company. Tim says 'we're very much left to run the business as we see fit.' They are in close contact with Merch's main warehouse and credit control department as well as with the paper mills. Important people for Tim personally in his day-to-day job are the other Branch Manager in his office and the inside sales team of the office, in particular one very capable person on that team. Tim does not give a specific figure, but he seems to have around forty to fifty different customers that he looks after, of which Bluechip Print is an important one but not one of the biggest.

Tony actually places the orders of materials himself by phoning the inside sales team of Tim's office. Given that the print jobs of Bluechip are usually urgent from their own customers' point of view and given that Bluechip have almost no storage facilities, the paper orders are also usually placed at short notice, practically requiring just-in-time delivery on the same day or overnight. Therefore, Tony is in touch with Tim's office every day, but he only speaks to Tim himself whenever there is a problem or when, for whatever reason, the price of a certain type of paper needs to be (re)negotiated, which means that Tim is still the main contact for Tony although he does not normally get involved in the day-to-day ordering of papers. Tony and Tim meet about once a month in person. On these occasions, Tim visits Bluechip's premises either to sort out a specific problem or just as a courtesy call 'making sure that we look after him okay and that our prices are okay, seeing if there are any issues that have cropped up, perhaps introducing a new product' (Tim).

General Level of Trust

Tony says that 'without a doubt' Tim and also Merch Papers as a company are trustworthy. And he describes Tim as 'quite open and honest' and as 'a man that tells the truth'. At the same time – and this is an interesting use of the concept – Tony thinks that he does not need to trust Merch Papers, because 'they do what they say they'll do; they're just very efficient.' He thinks that 'trust is a very strong word' and so he probably would not describe as 'trust' his seldom disappointed reliance on Merch Papers to deliver as agreed: 'They don't promise really, they just deliver – full stop. It's like buying something at Woolworth's.' In the same vein Tony says that while he would like to think that Merch find him trustworthy, they actually 'don't need to trust – they know', for example, that when he has a complaint it is a genuine complaint. Tony's view that the relationship with Merch is not a matter of trust could also mean that in his trust 'without a doubt' he has suspended effectively the irreducible vulnerability and uncertainty that remains on Tim's side as well as his own.

Tim 'definitely' finds Tony trustworthy and describes him as honest, straightforward and nice. However, he is a bit more cautious with regard to Bluechip Print as whole. While the company is generally trustworthy, Tim thinks that 'they play the game a bit' when it comes to paying invoices on time, which for Tim is a common problem that merchants need to learn to deal with. It means that smaller printers in particular tend to manage their own occasional cash flow problems by delaying the payment of invoices, which they can do as long as they have several suppliers to 'play cat and mouse with' (Tim). He does not doubt, though, that Bluechip are creditworthy, that they always intend to actually pay and that they 'are a lot better than some others'. However, the fact that 'you have to chase the money quite hard' certainly makes Bluechip less trustworthy than they could be in Tim's view. This has nothing to do with Tony personally, however, nor with the process of ordering paper. All in all, Tim would say that there is trust between the two companies, but then again he points out that 'there is always a little bit of mistrust on both sides', too, because they all know that they are bargaining for the best price from their own point of view: 'He knows it. I know it. It's business.'

Meaning of Trust

Instead of talking about 'trust', Tony prefers to point out that Merch Papers 'are as good as you're goin' to get anywhere.' A proxy for his trust in Merch Papers may therefore be the various statements that express his reliance on and satisfaction with the supplier. For example, Tony says that 'if you've got a complaint, they act quite quickly on it' and that 'they're very helpful', 'they do as much as they can to help me', 'if you need help, they help you'. He also says that if there is a problem, they 'just stitch it', 'they always try and find a way around the problem', 'they ring and let you know' about an alternative. Probably the assurance that Merch Papers responds quickly and constructively to Tony's problems is the best expression of his trust. And Merch's ability to trust in Tony is best expressed by the fact that, according to him, he would never make an illegitimate complaint. Helpfulness and truthfulness thus appear to capture the meaning of trust for Tony.

Tim is able to give a number of examples where the term 'trust' might apply in supplier relationships and in particular in his relationship with Tony. First, whenever printers have a problem with a paper in the printing process, they may fraudulently exaggerate the problem and request compensation from the supplier for lost machine hours etc. far in excess of what they have actually lost. Tim is sure that 'Tony wouldn't do that' and that it is an issue of trust because it is difficult to prove how big the damage really is and the printer could exploit the situation. Thus to trust means to expect that the other will be honest and not exploit situations of vulnerability which may arise.

Second, Tim refers a few times to situations where he would hope that customers give him the 'last phone call' before actually placing an order and thus the opportunity to defend his position. In the end, the best price wins the order but the supplier who gets the 'last phone call' is in the privileged position to make the last bid. To receive this call is both a sign of trust and trustworthiness. Trust in this sense means to be able to expect that somebody takes into account one's interests alongside their own. Thus Tony would give Tim 'the opportunity to move down price' whenever he receives a competitive offer from another supplier.

Third, and closely connected to this notion of the 'last call', Tim realizes that trust is involved when you receive the call and you cannot know whether the buyer is bluffing a low price level or telling the true best-price-so-far: 'I would say that Tony was telling the truth, but he might just be trying it on.' He associates trust in this kind of telephone bargaining with an expectation that the interlocutor is honest and tells the truth, although he could easily bluff.

Finally, Tim sees trust in many 'little ways' such as: 'They trust us to deliver what we say we're goin' to deliver. They trust us to invoice the price that we verbally quoted. We trust them that sometimes if we give them a price, they don't tell anybody else.' However, he also adamantly points out that he does not think that this kind of trust is generally decisive, but rather that 'when it comes to price, trust seems to go out of the window.' Only if the price were exactly the same for a given purchase might trust or personal liking come into play, according to Tim. This might actually be debatable to a certain degree in the light of Tim's own example of the 'last phone call': how many calls a buyer makes and whom he calls last might well depend on more than just the expectation of getting an even better price.

Bases of Trust

From the interviews with both Tony and Tim, it appears that any trust that they have in each other – irrespective of how important or prominent it may be in their ongoing interactions – is based on the positive history of the relationship hitherto. Both sides have a high level of satisfaction plus a high level of mutual respect and admiration which neither Tony nor Tim take for granted in supplier relations in the paper trade. Thus, Tony says about Merch Papers very early on in the interview that 'they're a nice company', 'they are just nice people', and that the relationship with them has become 'more personal; you tend to like that person'. He adds that whenever the price is the same he gives the order to the supplier that he likes more (see above). He values that Tim and his staff are straightforward, honest and friendly. Interestingly, these are exactly the things that Tim likes about Tony. In other words, one could say that their satisfaction with the relationship and probably also their trust comes from the mutual understanding that there is no need in supplier relationships to make each other's lives unnecessarily difficult. Tony's maxim is: 'If you can't do anyone any good, don't do them no harm.'

This is confirmed by Tim: 'Tony's attitude is: Why have a difficult relationship when you can have an easy relationship with someone?' Tony as an individual makes the relationship between Merch and Bluechip better than average and turns it into a kind of partnership according to

Tim, who says about Tony that 'he tries to get through the day with a smile and is not confrontational', 'knows exactly what he wants' and 'is a nice man to deal with'. Tony and Tim actually know a fair bit about each other's private life, but Tony does not (yet) socialize with Merch staff except for attending their annual Golf Day. They both value the personal rapport and find it useful in the context of their business relationship, which, they both agree, has to come first but need not be unnecessarily confrontational. Personal rapport and mutual understanding emerged in the very first contact between Tony and Merch's sales team, developing further as the business relationship itself developed. Thus the basis for trust today lies also in the positive experiences that both sides have had with each other over the past five years of trading. When asked specifically how he could know that Merch are reliable and will keep their promises, Tony replies: 'Well, they've always done it. Oh yes, it's gone wrong a couple of times, but they'd put it right.' Tim in return says the following about his basis for trusting Tony not to exaggerate complaints: 'I trust him on the basis of the fact that I have known him for five years and it would be uncharacteristic of him to do that. And he wouldn't do it.' Tim realizes that although he is sure that Tony would not be opportunistic and would therefore not dispute his claims, he cannot actually be absolutely sure about this. Tim's experience with Tony serves him as a good, but ultimately imperfect, basis for believing that Tony tells the truth. It enables him to suspend the possibility that Tony tells lies, because this would be untypical.

Trust Building Process

The interviews with Tony and Tim are not very informative regarding the process of building up trust. Tony merely says that the business with Merch has 'gradually grown really' and the relationships between the people involved in it have evolved along with the business relationship, probably also in terms of trust, from the first small order five years ago to the current stable level of sales to Bluechip. Successful joint problem solving and price negotiations would seem to be occasions where both sides can test the strength of the relationship, but such occasions would not be brought about deliberately for this purpose.

Tim agrees that the business relationship has developed 'fairly gradually' like a 'snowball effect'. He relates the interesting detail that the reason for the first order five years ago was the request by one of Bluechip's customers that a particular paper of Merch be used. It was thus a kind of coincidence that first brought together Merch and Bluechip and then it just carried on from there. According to Tim, the relationship has 'not really' changed over the years in terms of trust: 'Obviously, we have got to know them better and they know us better, but it's worked pretty smoothly really.' Tim also tells me that to get to know each other is very important in building new relationships. With a new customer, Merch would thus 'try and go and see them straight away' with the aim that 'they can find out about us and we about them and where the common ground is' (Tim). By implication, part of what my respondents mean by 'relationship building' is to build trust by understanding each other.

Other Observations

A semantic observation that applies to all my interviews is that to all my respondents 'having a relationship' already expresses that there is more between two organizations and their representatives than just straight business transactions. It implies a long-term orientation, mutual under-standing and goodwill. To have a 'relationship' is something special and probably implies a certain degree of trust. However, all my respondents also make it very clear that 'relationships' are still primarily about busi-ness. The business orientation is particularly strong in this case of Blue-chip Print and Merch Papers but, as has been shown, the respondents in this case equally value their 'relationship' instead of just arm's-length or even confrontational interactions.

7.4   CASE III: RETAIL GROUP PRINT UNIT
AND REPUTE PAPERS

Background to the Relationship

Retail Group is one of the largest retail businesses in the United Kingdom and runs an in-house print unit that provides for any printing require-ments of the two dozen department stores and 120 supermarkets owned by the Group as well as various other operations and administrative divi-sions. According to the typology in Figure 7.1 above, the Retail Group Print Unit would be classified as a 'controlled routine partner'. It has 16 employees and produces 92% of the printed items required by its internal customers such as forms, pamphlets, leaflets and point-of-sale material. It is also responsible for outsourcing most of the remaining more specialist printing jobs. Retail Group constitutes a very sizeable, though not huge, buyer of paper products, which it purchases almost exclusively (95%) from Repute Papers, one of the largest traditional paper merchants in the United Kingdom, with numerous trading offices and warehouses around the country. The special position of Repute Papers as the predominant paper supplier of Retail Group is the result of the latter's deliberate move to reduce its supplier base many years ago. Both sides know, though, that Retail Group could switch to another supplier relatively easily if it wanted to. However, the business relationship goes back 15 years and Repute Papers is only in this special position because Retail Group has been particularly satisfied with its service over the years, the upshot being that there is no intention on either side to end the relationship. The print unit of Retail Group requires about 150 different papers and has very limited storage facilities so that most of the deliveries by Repute Papers have to be made on a just-in-time basis, with orders being placed in the afternoon to be delivered by 8 or 9 o'clock the next morning. Repute's ability to achieve this is highly valued by the Retail Group print unit.

My respondent at Retail Group is Albert, who has been the Print Unit Manager since 1988. Now at the time of the interview in his early fifties, he has worked at Retail Group for over 35 years, starting off straight from school (without formal qualifications) as a trainee compositor, attending courses at the London College of Printing and then gradually working his way up within the print unit into more and more managerial positions. He describes his current position as 'unique' in the sense that, although his department is relatively small, it is very independent, because nobody else in Retail Group has the expertise on printing that the print unit and especially Albert himself possess. Nevertheless, his job is influenced very much by his internal customers and by the general management of the branch in which the print unit is located.

The second respondent for this case is a Key Account Manager at Repute Papers called Alan, who looks after the trade with Retail Group and represents Albert's opposite number and main contact. Alan is a 27-year-old university graduate in Industrial Economics who joined Repute Papers in a Head Office administrative function at graduate entry level four and a half years prior to the interview, moving just over two years ago to his current position in one of the regional divisions of Repute Papers, where he reports to a sales manager. He is responsible for about 40 customers. Retail Group is one of the most important of his customers as well as a 'key account' among the thousands of accounts of Repute Papers as a whole.

Seeing that the Retail Group Print Unit already purchases almost all of its paper from Repute, it is not an account that offers great scope for development but rather needs to be maintained at this high level by continuous good service. Alan took over the account half a year ago. His predecessor only managed it for a short period, but the representative before that had dealt with Retail Group and Albert successfully for about ten to twelve years. It should therefore be noted that, although the relationship between the two companies is fairly mature and was built up over many years mainly by Albert and his then opposite number at Repute, Alan's involvement in this relationship is much more recent.

As with the previous two cases presented earlier, my respondents are not normally involved with each other in the day-to-day operational placing and taking of orders, which is conducted over the phone (followed by written confirmation) by the people who work for them. Albert and Alan do have overall responsibility for the transactions, though, and they regularly deal with each other on any issues arising. They meet in person at least once every two weeks and this would normally entail a visit to the print unit by Alan, who thinks that it is important to have frequent meetings because 'it gives you the opportunity to potentially exploit other opportunities, allows you to pre-empt any potential problems, reassures customers and gives them a certain comfort factor that you are responsible for all aspects of the account and that you are on call to assist them with any projects; that you are taking an active interest in the account and that you have a genuine personal and business interest in their business and their activities rather than simply being a sort of faceless organization at the end of the telephone.' Given the constant and not just latent threat of competitors offering to supply to customers like Retail Group, the cultivation of the relationships is necessary although it has been successful for 15 years and at a fairly high and stable level of business in recent years. Albert knows this, of course, when he says that 'the bottom line is that they know that I can go elsewhere, if we want to, but we don't have to say it.'

General Level of Trust

Albert volunteers right at the beginning of the interview that one reason for buying 95% of their paper requirements from Repute Papers is that 'we have built up a sufficiently good relationship and trust in Repute.' He clearly finds Alan trustworthy and also states regarding Repute Paper generally that 'my personal experience is that Repute as a whole are very trustworthy. They've never let me down.' His trust is closely associated with his general satisfaction with the relationship with Repute, which is 'pretty near perfect'. Reliability and responsiveness are the basis for this strong satisfaction and also the basis for Albert's trust (see below). He thinks that the trust is mutual because 'Repute know with us that if we say we've got a problem, it is a genuine problem. We don't complain for the sake of complaining.'

Interestingly, though, Albert recalls upon my probing one exceptional incident where Alan's predecessor, who was at the same time the successor to the Repute representative who had built up the relationship, did not tell Albert about a problem. It turned out to be an administrative misunderstanding and was quickly rectified, with an apology tendered; however, it meant that Albert doubted for a moment the reliability of Repute. More precisely, though, it was the specific representative's behaviour that caused the doubts, and one consequence was that Alan became the new representative responsible for Retail Group. Albert considers the previous representative as untypical because 'Repute are not like that', whereas he now trusts Alan as much as the first representative and the supplier in general.

In return, Alan volunteers that 'that whole business for the last 15 years has been run on the basis of trust between the two companies.' Alan says about Albert: 'I know I can trust him' and has 'no reason to doubt' that Retail Group as a whole are also a trustworthy company, which he frequently attributes to the company being 'fair, ethical' and thus just like his own company, which he thinks Albert 'certainly finds trustworthy', too. Interestingly, Alan also explains that 'I'd certainly hope he finds me trustworthy, but from a business point of view the most important thing is that he [Albert] finds Repute Papers trustworthy.' The reason for this is that Alan assumes that he will move on to another job in his company within the next couple of years so that it is essential that the relationship between the two companies lasts far longer than that between Alan and Albert.

Meaning of Trust

Trust for Albert essentially means the experience and assurance of not being let down by a supplier. Whenever a problem does occur, he very much values the swift responsiveness of the supplier, seeing it as evidence of their trustworthiness. He frequently mentions in connection with his trust in Repute Papers and Alan personally that they 'respond very well'. More specifically, when asked to recall incidents where his ability to trust Repute was particularly important and acute, Albert relates that sometimes Repute help him out by giving him an exceptional price to prevent him from losing an order from one of his internal customers (who are in principle free to buy from outside printers as well as from the in-house print unit): 'They've put the price down simply so that I can get the work from our customer internally.' Albert associates with trust exceptions of this kind, which Repute are by no means obliged to make, where they put Albert's interest before their own. More generally, though, he understands trust in the sense of knowing 'that if my supplier says he's goin' to do something that he's goin' to do it' and thus, notably, 'I haven't got to keep following up. I've got no more worries. I can forget that side of it and get on with the other worries that I've got.' In other words, to be able to trust for Albert means to be able to suspend any doubts that one could have otherwise had regarding a supplier's performance.

Alan very much realizes that Albert's trust and his satisfaction more generally hinge on Repute Papers' reliability and responsiveness. While reliability is key, it appears to be accepted in the industry that problems occur occasionally – if only because 'paper is a natural product', as several of my respondents point out – and, when they do, a good and trustworthy business partner will handle them competently, constructively and cooperatively. Thus Alan says: 'The way in which a supplying organization deals with a problem is the biggest test.' And accordingly he thinks that trust 'means acting in a way that simply is long term. An honest approach to problems and working collectively as a team to sort out problems. It means from my point of view Albert not switching his orders to a competitor because of a potential price advantage and really to retain some loyalty with Repute Papers.'

Trust as an expectation of loyalty does not override the acceptance that Albert must get the best price for his company. Rather, similar to the understanding of trust from the supplier's point of view in the previous two cases, trust in a buyer means being able to expect that one will be given the opportunity to defend one's position before the buyer switches to another supplier: 'If you have a good relationship, there is an opportunity for you to do something about a competitor' (Alan). As Albert says: 'We would always give our supplier a fair warning of our intention [to change supplier] and give him or her the opportunity to look at their own price structure or whatever other area we're critical of and see if they can improve.' This had happened not long before the interviews and is seen by Alan as 'a good indicator of the trust'.

Other incidents that reveal the meaning of trust for Alan and, for that matter, also for Albert refer to the making of exceptions in the interest of the other. For example, in return for an extremely low price for one type of paper, Albert may accept a slightly higher than necessary price on another type of paper, thereby taking into account not only his own interest in getting the lowest possible price but also Alan's need 'to make a living'. As described above, Repute generally reciprocates by making exceptions, too, and this is what trust entails for both the buyer and the supplier. Note, though, that these exceptions do not defeat the basic price and service-based nature of the relationship; nor are they done in a straightforward tit-for-tat manner and definitely not as a corrupt practice. Instead, these practices show that trust simply means to be able to expect that the other recognizes and respects one's interests alongside their own.

Bases of Trust

Both Albert and Alan know very well – and keep pointing out – that the overall basis of the good relationship between them personally and between their companies is that Repute Papers keep giving Retail Group 'good service' in terms of price, reliability and responsiveness. These factors are also bases for the trust that Albert has in Repute Papers. In addition, it appears to be a particularly trustful rather than simply well-functioning relationship, because both sides perceive that there is a 'mutual understanding' in at least two respects. First, Albert values in a mainly technical sense that 'they know our needs and what type of work we have.' This knowledge resides very much with the individuals involved in the relationship, the result being that Albert was concerned when Alan became the new representative that 'it was a case of having to start all over again' and that the knowledge that the previous contacts had built up 'of my business as much of their own' would be lost. In practice, Alan managed to dispel these concerns very quickly, but it goes to show that understanding the other's technical set-up and requirements is a basis for trust that may be eroded when individuals involved in a business relationship change. Second, 'mutual understanding' also means the other's respect for one's own interests as a basis for trust. Thus Albert remarks early on that 'there's a mutual agreement that we've both got to make a living.' Technical knowledge and appreciation of interests are therefore both referred to in the following statement by Albert: 'It's a very good working relationship that we've got with a lot of mutual understanding for each other's needs. And we just progress on that.' This understanding comes from a history of interaction that spans 15 years and has produced countless positive and a few problematic experiences.

Alan, on the one hand, refers quite specifically and several times to the fact that 'we both know our mutual benefits' as a basis for trust and that with Retail Group 'there is a feeling that they are in the same boat'. This encapsulated interest makes the relationship 'perhaps more of a part-nership'. On the other hand, this fundamentally commercial basis for trust is matched according to Alan by the fact that the two organizations are culturally very similar in the sense of valuing fair, ethical, loyal trading relationships: 'Retail Group are the same, they have the same sort of cul-ture. We deal with our suppliers in exactly the same way that we would like our customers to deal with us. And Retail Group are a similar type of organization culturally and that's one of the keys to the success.' This description is confirmed by Albert's description of his own company's values and those of Repute Papers. In other words, the trust between Re-pute Paper and Retail Group is based at least partly on their generally trustful and trustworthy dispositions at the organizational level, which they recognize in each other and thus expect of each other.

Interestingly, when asked to relate more specifically how he knows whether another company or one of its employees can be trusted, Alan admits that he works on 'gut feeling' and that 'you don't actually know' whether the other is truly trustworthy and will honour the trust placed in him: 'You have a feeling for someone, and their actions and deeds will lead you to the conclusion that actually you [can or] can't trust them. It's a very difficult thing to put your finger on. I tend to work on gut feeling.' Alan applies this to Albert, for whom he has the feeling that he is trust-worthy and 'the way he acts and the way that he's treated us as an organi-zation and me personally only go to bear it up.' Trust is thus based on a very diffuse and imperfect feeling that is reinforced or revised over time in the process of interaction. Alan realizes that he cannot be absolutely sure that Albert only purchases from Repute and not from anyone else. When he feels nevertheless that Albert will stay loyal and therefore trust-worthy, he suspends the possibility that he is not.

Alan also comments on the practice of obtaining credit ratings for new customers and makes clear that he does not see this as a sign of distrust by the supplier in the buyer. The same applies to the practice of written confirmation of orders, which is also simply a sound standard business practice that would be common with both a very trusted and a less trusted customer. That they may still function as a basis for trust could be implied, however, by the fact that Alan would be suspicious of any customer that refuses to participate in such common practices as credit checks and administrative paperwork: 'Frankly, if somebody found that unreasonable, I would find it very difficult to sustain a long-term business relationship with them.' In other words, trust and control are positively related here.

Trust Building Process

Albert's unprompted remark that 'trust builds up' in supplier relationships is not corroborated by a more detailed concept of how this happens, other than that the development of trust goes hand in hand with the general positive development of the business relationship evidenced by continuous and consistent 'good service' and the experience of 'not being let down'. Alan has managed to win Albert's trust mainly by continuing the competence and responsiveness of his predecessors: 'He knows his business, he knows his papers, he responds very well to anything that I put in front of him' (Albert).

Alan for his part relates how the business relationship has 'evolved' and grown 'organically but not dramatically' over many years and says that the most important thing that Repute Papers has been able to do to win both the orders and the trust of Albert and Retail Group has been to provide excellent service. Apart from the 'smooth running of the account', however, any problems and issues arising, and especially the way they are handled, provide the opportunity to build and reinforce trust: 'The basis of how you handle that is how you judge anything really as an organization' (Alan). Equally, the trust he has in Albert and his company 'has been borne out of events in the past, his length of relationship and loyalty as a customer to Repute Papers and the events that have happened certainly under my account management' (Alan). In other words, trust builds up over time through successful interactions where trust is at stake, such as joint problem solving. The actors build up trust by experiencing each other as trustful and trustworthy. Alan gives the advice: 'Don't make too many promises, because the surest way not to have any trust is when you let somebody down.'

Other Observations

The case of Retail Group and Repute Papers provides further insight into the organizational embeddedness of the relationship between the representatives of the two companies. In their interactions, Albert and Alan recognize the fact that the relationship between their two companies began (long) before they themselves came to be involved in it and in contact with each other. Alan in particular assumes that his own involvement will only be temporary, a matter of a few years, before he moves on to other responsibilities. He also comments that it was very easy for him to take over the account of Retail Group because 'I was inheriting a business which had been looked after reasonably well. So it was reasonably open and friendly from the start.' Alan was able to benefit from the goodwill earned by his predecessors. In the same vein, he perceives a responsibility to cultivate the relationship and pass it on one day in good shape. Interestingly, this means that he has almost no choice but to try and develop a good personal relationship with Albert as a means of cultivating the business relationship. In a buyer–supplier relationship the personal and the business level are entwined, even though the business level, at least in this case, is more durable and the personal relationship probably only temporary. Thus Alan describes himself as 'an ambassador for the company', who has to act in a way that is regarded as typical for Repute Papers' employees.

In return, he says that 'Albert is Retail Group personified really', meaning that his attitude and behaviour are typical of his company. Albert confirms this independently when he remarks that after over 35 years in the company he has definitely internalized its fair and ethical philosophy. However, it is clear from Albert's comments that, while you would expect the representatives of a company to act in a certain, distinct way, they are nevertheless not easily replaceable or interchangeable due to the specific knowledge that they gain about the other company (as already referred to above). Once again it is clear that individual actors are the carriers of business relationships generally, and in particular with regard to trust, even though they only act 'on behalf' and 'in the interest' of their employers.

Finally, an observation needs to be noted that applies to all three cases described in this chapter. When trying to describe what kind of a trust relationship they have with the respective representative of the supplying or buying organization, several of my respondents pointed out that their willingness to talk openly about the relationship in an interview with me

– and to accept that their opposite number was doing the same – was a strong sign of their mutual trust. If they did not trust each other, they would not agree to participate in my interviews, because they could clearly convey in the interview much confidential and personal information about themselves and about the other. Some respondents then remarked as well that it was because of the confidential nature of the interview that they had to trust me, too, even though they hardly knew me. Altogether, my respondents were well aware of the vulnerability that the interviews signified and they could even use their willingness to make themselves vulnerable as an example of their trust in the respective business partner and also in myself.

7.5 INTERPRETING TRUST RELATIONSHIPS: LESSONS FROM THE CASES

The three cases show that respondents in buyer–supplier relations can relate to the category of trust as an element of the good 'relationship' that they enjoy with a business partner. What the case descriptions conceal, however, is that the respondents actually found it difficult to express the meaning and role of trust verbally. They typically needed to think for a moment before they could put their thoughts about trust into words. Their statements are very instructive but, unsurprisingly, they hardly reflect fully and directly the complexity of trust as revealed in the previous chapters of this book. Moreover, in line with Huemer's (1998) findings, the respondents oscillate between rating very highly the importance of trust for doing business successfully ('Trust is everything in business') and pointing out that 'business' always comes first with trust as a secondary issue ('When it comes down to price, trust goes out of the window'). Despite such difficulties and inconsistencies, the three cases described above provide valuable illustrations of the elements of the Trust Wheel and the concept of trust that I have proposed.

First of all, it is clear that trust in buyer–supplier relationships forms and develops in a reflexive process along with the development of the relationship in general. It is not possible to understand why a buyer trusts a supplier, or vice versa, at a particular moment in time without looking at what lies behind and what lies ahead of them. All respondents regularly refer to the history of the relationship and also to the fact that they would like to continue the relationship.

Second, it is striking that the respondents definitely consider the trustworthiness of their business partners in fairly utilitarian terms, besides their more personal and intuitive perception of trustworthiness. In the interview situation, at least, the respondents are able to rationalize the utility of the relationship and, as they would put it, the need for buyer–supplier relations to be good for business. This is why categories such as price, order levels, service, quality and so on are referred to all the time. Moreover, the respondents are very aware of the exit option that is available to both sides in principle and the fact that they would have to discontinue the relationship if they found it to be against their own interest. At the same time, the respondents do recognize mutual interest and benefit, and they also indicate that they would not easily end established relationships without trying to rescue them first. Overall, there is clear evidence that in these relationships trust is a matter of reason, even in the fairly calculative sense as advocated by rational choice, institutional economics and game theory. On the other hand, this cannot be the whole story either.

Third, although parts of the interview guide were specifically targeted at this aspect of trust, the respondents could not say very much about how the trust in their business partners depended on routines and institutional arrangements, although certain 'rules of the game' were evident in the accounts they gave. The case descriptions above show that the respondents recognize the embeddedness of their relationships in the larger organizational contexts, but they do not really connect this with the issue of trust. One exception is that several respondents referred to interaction effects between personal trust in the people they deal with directly and trust in the organizations they represented (see also Currall and Judge, 1995; Zaheer et al., 1998; Currall and Inkpen, 2002; Inkpen and Currall, 2004). In my observation, the respondents also placed their trust very much in role expectations (like being the buyer), in organizational rules (such as reporting structures, the amount of business they could sign) and also in the customs of the paper trade (in particular, technical tolerances, confidentiality), but such things are probably too taken-for-granted to become salient in an interview without direct and insistent probing. Interestingly, their trust also seemed to refer to role negotiability, the fact that exceptions to rules are usually possible and that customs need to be interpreted creatively. Thus, it is possible to say that institutionalized routines – and how they are performed – do play an important part but do not fully determine the level of trust in buyer–supplier relationships.

Fourth, the interviews were most instructive on the question of how trust-related experiences provide a basis for trust and how trust can emerge reflexively. The relationships described had been established for at least five years and generally much longer. Nevertheless, in the case of Bluechip Print and Merch Papers the respondents recalled how the relationship started by chance with a first relatively unimportant order. The two companies trusted each other more or less 'blindly' in this first interaction, but this then served as the basis for developing a more solid relationship. Moreover, several other comments showed that many relationships can be ongoing without trust becoming an issue until 'it is put to the test', usually because a problem emerges that needs to be dealt with. This can be interpreted as an implicit and unreflected granting of trust on the first occasion and thereafter 'until further notice' and 'as long as things are going fine'. The partial 'blindness' of trust throughout the duration of a relationship also comes through in that exceptional incidents such as 'being let down' or 'being helped' appear to raise the issue of trust while it is normally not constantly reflected upon.

Almost all respondents express the view that their trust in their respective opposite number and/or that person's company is based on past experience. Process-based trust (Blau, 1964; Zand, 1972; Zucker, 1986) thus seems to be a category that respondents can relate to very well. They frequently state how important it is to get to know the other and to have common experiences that serve as evidence of trustworthiness and reliability. Clearly new relationships are handled very differently from established relationships and, as a rule, the respondents express a preference for continuing relationships rather than frequently starting and ending relationships, because they recognize the importance of mutual knowledge not only in a technical and commercial sense but also in the sense of personal rapport. The 'principle of gradualness' (Luhmann, 1979) is a notion that the respondents introduce themselves when they say that trust tends to build up gradually alongside the more general development of a business relationship. It is clear that, while the respondents are generally familiar with what a printing company or paper supplier does, they also experience unfamiliarity in the sense that every company and individual is unique and that it is therefore necessary to familiarize oneself with the other by getting to know them and identifying the common ground which may make it a trustful relationship.

Giddens' (1994b) idea of 'active trust' as expressing the reflexive constitution and continuous communication involved in trust can also be illustrated and perhaps clarified further by the cases described. The active element in building up trust is evident in the respondents' consistent view that trust in business relations matters most and actually develops whenever it is 'put to the test', for example whenever a problem or complaint arises. Whether trust is reflexively reinforced or destroyed depends very much on the way in which the actors deal with such emergent issues. Interactions where the actors actually experience each other as trusting and trustworthy (or not, as the case may be) are apparently more important for trust development than any abstract deliberations about the other's motives and expectations.

It is also clear, especially from the comments made by the paper suppliers, that successful and trustful relationships still need to be 'worked on' continuously to ensure that the basis of the relationship is reproduced and/or adapted when necessary. In all three cases this is facilitated by the fact that the companies are mostly in contact with each other on a daily basis. Face-to-face meetings are less frequent but considered essential by the respondents for cultivating the relationship. Thus the constitution of trust appears to happen through successfully resolved trust crises while the relationship in general is maintained through continuous communication. Lest active trust be understood too much as a kind of daring or even foolish form of trust, it has to be said that no respondent suggested that trust should be put to the test deliberately. On the contrary, bringing about a problem just to see how the other reacts would definitely be seen as destructive to trust. Nevertheless, the constitution of trust appears to be more than a 'by-product' (Elster, 1983) of successful cooperation and problem solving, because the respondents realize that when they work on a problem they also 'work on' trust (Sydow, 1998).

Furthermore, the cases offer some insight into suspension and the Simmelian notion that there is an element of faith in trust. In this regard, the statement by James of Scott Mills is remarkable, although he is the only respondent who explicitly connects trust with faith in others. James even uses the metaphor of the leap required for trust when he describes trust as a 'jump into the unknown'. Several other respondents recognize that their trust has to rest on imperfect knowledge and that they could not possibly be absolutely sure about whether or not their business partners actually honour or exploit their trust and to what degree. With a trusted partner, they simply cannot imagine that the partner exploits trust, although the possibility cannot strictly be ruled out and they trust nevertheless. Implicitly, the respondents thus acknowledge that suspension is at work here.

Explicitly, the buyers in the three cases (Jill, Albert, Tony) refer to the benefit of this suspension in trust when they say that with a trusted supplier they can place an order and then not worry about it anymore, which frees them to deal with their 'other worries' (Albert). On the suppliers' side there were corresponding remarks to the effect that with a trusted customer you could suspend, for example, the idea that they might make an unjustified complaint.

Finally, the reflexivity of the research interaction is evident, too. The case descriptions and this discussion involve strong interpretations on my part. Moreover, the interviews and, consequently, the raw material for the cases were already skewed by my intervention, my interview schedule and my rapport with the respondents. To what extent the accounts that the interviewees have given me as a researcher actually reflect their day-to-day reality in buyer–supplier relations is difficult to say. At least, the respondents appeared to be open and sincere, and they definitely welcomed the opportunity to talk about their experiences and practices. These qualifications are typical of qualitative research and they should not distract us from the main aim of this chapter which has been to get closer to the experience of trust. The interpretations offered in this chapter not only 'make sense' in terms of the Trust Wheel but give empirical meaning to this analytical framework and therefore further our understanding of the concept of trust.

Methods capturing process, experience, embeddedness and reflexivity are particularly suited to empirical trust research. They help to bring out the richness of trust as a phenomenon even in a rather common micro-social setting, by letting 'real' actors speak about their experiences. The concurrent simplicity, complexity and ambiguity of trust become apparent. The study would have benefited from more interviews, either with more respondents or more often with the same respondents. As an exploratory project, however, the study does make a valuable contribution by sensitizing us to the difference between studying trust as an idiosyncratic accomplishment and studying trust as a numerical value on an elaborate scale, and by illustrating the insights into trust that respondents can express in open interviews. Perhaps case descriptions such as the ones presented here are needed if only as a constant reminder that behind our constructs and models of trust there are real people and unique relationships.

8

POSITIVE EXPECTATIONS

8.1 CORE INSIGHTS AND CONTRIBUTIONS

As stated in the introductory chapter, it has been one of the aims of this book to demonstrate how multifaceted a phenomenon trust is and how instructive it is to look at it from many different perspectives. Chapter 5 already contains a summary of the concepts that I have discussed and the two empirically oriented chapters preceding this concluding chapter have brought out the more practical meaning of key abstract ideas. Hence, in the following sections of this short final chapter, I will not offer another summary, but rather focus on the core insights of the book again and put them into greater perspective.

Quite simply, I argue that at the heart of the concept of trust is the suspension of vulnerability and uncertainty (the leap of faith), which enables actors to have positive expectations of others. I propose that 'trust research', in the narrower sense, needs to address, understand and explain this essential feature of trust, whereas 'trust-related research', in the broader sense, may not go into that much detail, but needs to acknowledge suspension and its implications. Unless we are able to say very clearly what makes trust so unique – and powerful – we run the risk of turning it into an obsolete or meaningless category that is easily dismissed as helpless or hypocritical rhetoric (about which see Chapter 1). And unless we contribute new insights into how leaps of faith are possible, we miss the point of trust and explain anything but trust.

sciences. It could also be said that we need to take the topic of trust back to where it has come from, for in the past trust was identified as an issue in many different disciplines and at different levels of our societies and economies. For example, at the level of the individual, trust has been discussed as an important factor in maintaining a stable identity and personality (see Erikson, 1965). At the interpersonal and interorganizational level, trust has been a key concept in explaining cooperation (see Gambetta, 1988a), resulting in an extensive and highly diverse literature. Last but not least, the problem of social order as one of the classic concerns of sociology has been treated as a problem of trust (see Misztal, 1996). Such connections to overarching research agendas and broader literatures have been pointed out throughout this book.

In this section, I focus on one research agenda that stretches across many disciplines and affects many practical problems, too. It is selected here because it springs directly from the definition of trust as a state of *positive expectation of others* (see also Chapter 1 and Rousseau et al., 1998). I propose that the question of how actors can form positive expectations of others is among the most basic questions that can be asked in the social sciences. Arguably, if and when actors have positive expectations of others, it will enable them to be more self-confident as a person, to engage in cooperation with others and to help maintain the social order, which in turn reinforces their expectations and their trust. And trust is interesting and relevant because it is one way of producing positive expectations of others, specifically through a leap of faith.

As already indicated above, positive expectations cannot only be reached through trust but also by other means such as control. In fact, trust and control are not the two mutually exclusive sides of a dualism but rather are so directly interrelated that they constitute a duality (Möllering, 2005a). Trust and control each assume the existence of the other, refer to each other and create each other, but remain irreducible to each other. The difference between a dualism and a duality is subtle, but important. For instance, philosophers have debated whether body and mind form a dualism (human beings have a body on the one hand and a mind on the other) or a duality (to be human, the body needs a mind and the mind needs a body).

If we assume, as I have done in this book, that social interaction as such is possible only if and when actors are embedded *and* retain their agency, then expectations of such actors by others will be based on both of these inseparable aspects. When we form expectations of others, we take influences of structure and agency into account that are strictly inseparable but can be distinguished analytically as control, on the one hand, and trust, on the other: when an actor bases positive expectations on structural influences on the embedded other, I speak of control (see Leifer and Mills, 1996). When an actor bases positive expectations on an assumption of benevolent agency on the part of the other, I speak of trust (Zand, 1972; Gambetta, 1988d; Rousseau et al., 1998) – implying that this is enabled by a leap of faith.

For reference, my concept of 'control' resembles Johannes Pennings and Jaana Woiceshyn's (1987) concept of 'systemic control', while my concept of 'trust' resembles their concept of 'trust control'. The main category for me, however, is 'positive expectations' instead of 'control' (which they define as regularity of behaviour), and I do not share Pennings and Woiceshyn's overall approach: in particular, for me trust is not a 'mode of control' (p. 85). Rather, trust and control together can lead to positive expectations of others.

By connecting research on trust and research on control directly to each other and, notably, to the bigger question of positive expectations, we will be able to deconstruct one-sided accounts (Möllering, 2005a). For instance, with the trust/control duality in mind, researchers will recognize more clearly the control elements in strong trust relationships, for example between lovers, relatives, friends or allies. In return, trust elements will be revealed in relationships apparently dominated by control, for example in prisons, factories, bureaucracies or religious cults.

When reconnecting trust to bigger research agendas, we have to make sure that we do not lose the core insight that trust involves suspension. We have to demonstrate that it is precisely the leap of faith that makes trust a powerful concept and a valuable contribution in explaining positive expectations. In particular, referring to control again, it can be argued that in most practical situations control cannot be perfect – it cannot close the gap completely – and therefore vulnerability and uncertainty remain. Control thus needs to be combined with trust and the leap of faith that it entails if truly positive expectations of others are to be reached. At the same time, though, there are forms of control that increase vulnerability and uncertainty, rather than decreasing it. This is, of course, detrimental to trust as it makes the leap of faith that much harder. The trust/control duality implies that the two sides need to correspond to each other in an ongoing process. Overall, it is important that the concept of trust contributes something special, namely the idea of the leap of faith, when it is adopted as one concept among many in answering more general questions raised by the social sciences.

8.3 AVENUES FOR FURTHER TRUST RESEARCH

While trust research continues to flourish and there is no shortage of more or less specific unresolved questions that could be addressed in the future, this book encourages researchers to focus on the role of the leap of faith (suspension). Chapter 5 outlined some fundamental conceptual ideas and some instructive applications in empirical studies on which future investigations of suspension can build. Chapter 6 discussed specific methodological implications of placing suspension at the heart of our understanding of trust. Overall, it can be concluded that future trust research has to become less detached and needs to get closer to the idiosyncratic interpretations and experiences of actors who are affected by trust as trustors, trustees or third parties (see also Chapter 7). Crucially, we need a better understanding of the 'as-if attitude' which is always implied in trust but seems to fall outside of established ways of accounting for human action. I have suggested some literatures in Chapter 5 that should be helpful in this regard, but future research needs to identify further ways of substantiating, by theory and application, what the leap of faith entails.

As pointed out in the previous section, however, future trust research should also be strongly connected to larger research agendas. This can be done in many ways, depending on different disciplines and practical problems, but the initial approach should always be that, by connecting trust to other topics, learning takes place in both directions. In other words, our understanding of trust can benefit from investigating how it is related, for example, to power, but our understanding of power is also enhanced when we realize that it in turn contains an element of trust and requires, by the same token, a leap of faith (see, for example, Bachmann, 1998, 2001). Rather than simply subsuming trust under a different question, future research will benefit from also taking seriously the original questions raised by the topic of trust. Research on social networks, institutions and processes provides three good examples of areas where our understanding of trust can be both enriched and enriching.

First, social networks clearly matter for trust as trustors and trustees are embedded in relationships with each other and with third parties who, again, may have complex relationships with further parties (see, for example, Granovetter, 1985; Coleman, 1990; Burt and Knez, 1995). Moreover, trust is considered a defining element of the social capital in a network or society (see, for example, Paxton, 1999). It is therefore a fruitful avenue for future trust research to apply the theory and methods of social network analysis (for an overview, see Wasserman and Faust, 1994; Kilduff and Tsai, 2003; Brass et al., 2004). Beyond the work that already exists in this area, I suggest that new questions emerge once the leap of faith is more clearly recognized. For example, if trust requires suspension and social networks require trust, does this not mean that the constitution of social networks rests at least as much on idiosyncratic accomplishments at the actor level as on self-reinforcing mechanisms at the structural level? If we recognize the role of agency and the issue of perceived networks (as opposed to 'real' networks), can the concept of trust, and the leap of faith in particular, help us to explain, say, how actors deal with their awareness of 'structural holes' (Burt, 1992) or other positional features (such as their own centrality in a network)? If there is a reflexive relationship between trust and network structures, then future trust research can contribute to social network research just as much as vice versa.

Second, trustors and trustees are not only embedded in social networks but also in institutional contexts. In Chapter 3 in particular, I have developed a number of important concepts around the question of how trust and institutions are connected. More research is required in this area, nonetheless. Once again, it seems that a closer examination of the leap of faith with regard to institutions should lead researchers to emphasize the role of agency. This may help us, for example, to understand better the processes underlying institutionalization and institutional change, in particular the role of the 'institutional entrepreneur', which Paul DiMaggio (1988) describes a follows: 'New institutions arise when organized actors with sufficient resources (*institutional entrepreneurs*) see in them an opportunity to realize interests that they value highly' (p. 14, emphasis in original; see also Beckert, 1999; Garud et al., 2002; Munir and Phillips, 2005). How are these actors able to do this? Beyond their resources and interests, I submit that they need to be able to make leaps of faith and have trust when they depart from existing institutional rules and look for other actors with whom they can collaborate in the process of institutional entrepreneurship (on this topic, see also Barley and Tolbert, 1997; Garud and Karnøe, 2001; Lawrence et al., 2002; Lawrence and Phillips, 2004). They probably need to be 'trust entrepreneurs' as well as 'institutional entrepreneurs'. Future research might explore this line of thinking further.

Third, I have argued for a process perspective on trust, recognizing the reflexivity of trust development in time and space (Chapter 4). And I have pointed out the long tradition of process theories in philosophy (for example, Whitehead, [1929] 1978) as well as important recent advances in this area (notably, Langley, 1999; Poole et al., 2000; Tsoukas and Chia, 2002; Van de Ven and Poole, 2005) which have the potential to enrich our analysis of trust. Equally, though, I believe that the analysis of social processes can also benefit in return from investigating the role of trust in initiating and maintaining processes. In many empirical cases, continuity may not be simply a matter of self-reinforcement, but dependent on recurrent leaps of faith that cannot be taken for granted. Without the accomplishment of leaps of faith, many processes will stop as soon as minor doubts or disturbances occur. This is implied in the concept of 'active trust' (Giddens, 1994b), which recognizes that actors have to actively work on shared understandings and expectations in their relationships with others. It will be very worthwhile to investigate further – not only at the interpersonal level – how the suspension of uncertainty and vulnerability supports important social processes.

Summarizing these suggestions for future trust research and referring once again to the overall structure of my argument, it is crucial to recognize how the leap of faith *interacts* with reason, routine and reflexivity in trust. It is not merely the case that trust rests on imperfect bases which leave a residual gap that needs to be crossed. Rather, by successfully crossing the gap, trust also validates those bases. In other words, the leap of faith helps to generate and maintain the reasons, institutions and processes from which it first springs and, hence, it is truly crucial for our understanding of trust *and* its bases. If this is generally recognized, then I have highly positive expectations as to the future benefits that trust research can bring to the social sciences.

BIBLIOGRAPHY

Abrahamson, E. 1991. Managerial fads and fashions: The diffusion and rejection of innovations. *Academy of Management Review*, 16(3), 586–612.

Abrahamson, E. 1996. Management fashion. *Academy of Management Review*, 21(1), 254–285.

Adler, P.S. 2001. Market, hierarchy, and trust: The knowledge economy and the future of capitalism. *Organization Science*, 12(2), 215–234.

Altheide, D.L., Johnson, J.M. 1994. Criteria for assessing interpretative validity in qualitative research. In: Denzin, N.K., Lincoln, Y.S. (eds.) *Handbook of Qualitative Research*. Thousand Oaks: Sage, 485–499.

Alvesson, M. 1999. *Beyond Neo-Positivists, Romantics and Localists: A Reflexive Approach to Interviews in Organization Research*. Lund Institute of Economic Research Working Paper Series 1999/3. Lund: Lund University.

Alvesson, M., Sköldberg, K. 2000. *Reflexive Methodology*. London: Sage.

Arrighetti, A., Bachmann, R., Deakin, S. 1997. Contract law, social norms and inter-firm cooperation. *Cambridge Journal of Economics*, 21(2), 171–195.

Arrow, K.J. 1973. *Information and Economic Behavior*. Stockholm: Federation of Swedish Industries (cited in Williamson, 1985, p. 405).

Arrow, K.J. 1974. *The Limits of Organization*. New York: Norton.

Arrow, K.J. 1985. The economics of agency. In: Pratt, J., Zeckhauser, R. (eds.) *Principals and Agents: The Structure of Business*. Boston: Harvard Business School Press, 37–51.

Ashworth, T. 1980. *Trench Warfare, 1914–1918: The Live and Let Live System*. New York: Holmes & Meier.

Aspers, P. 1999. The economic sociology of Alfred Marshall: An overview. *American Journal of Economics and Sociology*, 58(4), 651–667.

Aspers, P. 2001. *Markets in Fashion: A Phenomenological Approach*. Stockholm: City University Press.

Arthur, W.B. 1994. *Increasing Returns and Path Dependence in the Economy*. Ann Arbor: University of Michigan Press.

Atkinson, S. 2004. Senior management relationships and trust: An exploratory study. *Journal of Managerial Psychology*, 19(6), 571–587.

Axelrod, R. 1981. The evolution of cooperation among egoists. *American Political Science Review*, 75(2), 306–318.

Axelrod, R. 1984. *The Evolution of Cooperation*. New York: Basic Books.

Ayios, A. 2004. *Trust and Western–Russian Business Relationships*. Aldershot: Ashgate.

Bacharach, M., Gambetta, D. 2001. Trust in signs. In: Cook, K.S. (ed.) *Trust in Society*. New York: Russell Sage Foundation, 148–184.

Bachmann, R. 1998. Conclusion: Trust – conceptual aspects of a complex phenomenon. In: Lane, C., Bachmann, R. (eds.) *Trust Within and Between Organizations*. Oxford: Oxford University Press, 298–322.

Bachmann, R. 2001. Trust, power and control in trans-organizational relations. *Organization Studies*, 22(2), 337–366.

Bachmann, R., Knights, D., Sydow, J. 2001. Editorial. *Organization Studies,* 22(2), v–viii.

Bachmann, R., Zaheer, A. (eds.) 2006. *Handbook of Research on Trust*. Cheltenham: Edward Elgar, forthcoming.

Baier, A. 1986. Trust and antitrust. *Ethics*, 96(2), 231–260.

Barber, B. 1983. *The Logic and Limits of Trust*. New Brunswick: Rutgers University Press.

Barley, S.R., Tolbert, P.S. 1997. Institutionalization and structuration: Studying the links between action and institutions. *Organization Studies,* 18(1), 93–117.

Barnes, J.B. 1981. Managing the paradox of organizational trust. *Harvard Business Review*, 59(2), 107–116.

Barney, J.B., Hansen, M.H. 1994. Trustworthiness as a source of competitive advantage. *Strategic Management Journal*, 15(8), 175–190.

Beale, H., Dugdale, T. 1975. Contracts between businessmen: Planning and the use of contractual remedies. *British Journal of Law and Society*, 2(1), 45–60.

Beatt, A. (ed.) 1993. *Printing: A Market Sector Overview*. Hampton: Key Note.

Becker, G. 1976. *The Economic Approach to Human Behavior*. Chicago: University of Chicago Press.

Becker, M.C. 2004. Organizational routines: A review of the literature. *Industrial and Corporate Change*, 13(4), 643–678.

Becker, M.C. 2005. The concept of routines: Some clarifications. *Cambridge Journal of Economics*, 29(2), 249–262.

Becker, M.C., Knudsen, T. 2005. The role of routines in reducing pervasive uncertainty. *Journal of Business Research,* 58(6), 746–757.

Becker, M.C., Lazaric, N., Nelson, R.R., Winter, S. 2005. Applying organizational routines in understanding organizational change. *Industrial and Corporate Change*, 14(5), 775–791.

Beckert, J. 1999. Agency, entrepreneurs, and institutional change: The role of strategic choice and institutionalized practices in organizations. *Organization Studies*, 20(5), 777–799.

Beckert, J. 2002. *Beyond the Market: The Social Foundations of Economic Efficiency*. Princeton: Princeton University Press.

Beckert, J. 2005. *Trust and the Performative Construction of Markets*. MPIfG Discussion Paper 05/8. Cologne: Max Planck Institute for the Study of Societies.

Berger, P.L., Luckmann, T. 1966. *The Social Construction of Reality*. Garden City: Doubleday.

Bernstein, M., Potvin, D., Martin, D.K. 2004. A qualitative study of attitudes toward error in patients facing brain tumour surgery. *The Canadian Journal of Neurological Sciences*, 31(2), 208–212.

Bigley, G.A., Pearce, J.L. 1998. Straining for shared meaning in organization science: Problems of trust and distrust. *Academy of Management Review*, 23(3), 405–421.

Birch, P. (ed.) 1994. *Managing Change in the Printing and Publishing Industry: Strategic Approaches*. Leatherhead: Pira.

Bijlsma, K.M., Koopman, P. 2003. Introduction: Trust within organisations. *Personnel Review,* 32(5), 543–555.

Bijlsma, K.M., Van de Bunt, G.G. 2003. Antecedents of trust in managers: A 'bottom up' approach. *Personnel Review,* 32(5), 638–664.

Bijlsma-Frankema, K.M., Klein Woolthuis, R. (eds.) 2005. *Trust under Pressure: Empirical Investigations of Trust and Trust Building in Uncertain Circumstances*. Cheltenham: Edward Elgar.

Blau, P. 1964. *Exchange and Power in Social Life*. London: John Wiley.

Blau, P. 1968. Interaction: Social exchange. In: Sills, D.L. (ed.) *International Encyclopedia of the Social Sciences*. New York: Macmillan, 452–458.

Blois, K.J. 1999. Trust in business to business relationships: An evaluation of its status. *Journal of Management Studies*, 36(2), 197–215.

Boon, S.D., Holmes, J.G. 1991. The dynamics of interpersonal trust: Resolving uncertainty in the face of risk. In: Hinde, R.A., Groebel, J. (eds.) *Cooperation and Prosocial Behavior*. Cambridge: Cambridge University Press, 190–211.

BPIF 1995. *Information File: The Printing Industry*. London: British Printing Industries Federation.

BPIF 1996. *Facts & Figures about the Printing Industry*. London: British Printing Industries Federation.

Bradach, J.L., Eccles, R.G. 1989. Price, authority and trust: From ideal types to plural forms. *Annual Review of Sociology*, 15, 97–118.

Brandenburger, A.M., Nalebuff, B.J. 1996. *Co-opetition*. New York: Currency/Doubleday.

Brass, D.J., Galaskiewicz, J., Greve, H.R., Tsai, W. 2004. Taking stock of networks and organizations: A multilevel perspective. *Academy of Management Journal*, 47(6), 795–819.

Brenkert, G.G. 1998. Trust, morality and international business. In: Lane, C., Bachmann, R. (eds.) *Trust Within and Between Organizations*. Oxford: Oxford University Press, 273–297.

Brothers, D. 1995. *Falling Backwards: An Exploration of Trust and Self-experience*. New York: Norton.

Brownlie, J., Howson, A. 2005. Leaps of faith and MMR: An empirical study of trust. *Sociology*, 39(2), 221–239.

Burchell, B., Wilkinson, F. 1997. Trust, business relationships and the contractual environment. *Cambridge Journal of Economics*, 21(2), 217–237.

Burt, R.S. 1992. *Structural Holes*. Cambridge: Harvard University Press.

Burt, R.S. 1993. The social structure of competition. In: Swedberg, R. (ed.) *Explorations in Economic Sociology*. New York: Russell Sage Foundation, 65–103.

Burt, R.S., Knez, M. 1995. Kinds of third-party effects on trust. *Rationality and Society*, 7(3), 255–292.

Burt, R.S., Knez, M. 1996. Trust and third-party gossip. In: Kramer, R.M., Tyler, T.R. (eds.) *Trust in Organizations*. Thousand Oaks: Sage, 68–89.

Buskens, V. 2002. *Social Networks and Trust*. Dordrecht: Kluwer Academic Publishers.

Buskens, V., Raub, W. 2002. Embedded trust: Control and learning. In: Thye, S., Lawler, E.J. (eds.) *Group Cohesion, Trust and Solidarity*. Amsterdam: JAI Press, 167–202.

Butler, J.K. 1991. Toward understanding and measuring conditions of trust: Evolution of a conditions of trust inventory. *Journal of Management*, 17(3), 643–663.

Camerer, C., Loewenstein, G., Prelec, D. 2005. Neuroeconomics: How neuroscience can inform economics. *Journal of Economic Literature*, 43(1), 9–64.

Child, J. 1998. Trust and international strategic alliances: The case of Sino–foreign joint ventures. In: Lane, C., Bachmann, R. (eds.) *Trust Within and Between Organizations*. Oxford: Oxford University Press, 241–272.

Child, J. 2001. Trust – The fundamental bond in global collaboration. *Organizational Dynamics*, 29(4), 274–288.

Child, J., Faulkner, D. 1998. *Strategies of Co-operation: Managing Alliances, Networks, and Joint Ventures*. Oxford: Oxford University Press.

Child, J., Möllering, G. 2003. Contextual confidence and active trust development in the Chinese business environment. *Organization Science*, 14(1), 69–80.

Chiles, T.H., McMackin, J.F. 1996. Integrating variable risk preferences, trust, and transaction cost economics. *Academy of Management Review*, 21(1), 73–99.

Coase, R.H. 1937. The nature of the firm. *Economica*, 6, 386–405.

Cohen, M.D., Burkhart, R., Dosi, G., Egidi, M., Marengo, L., Warglien, M., Winter, S.G. 1996. Routines and other recurring action patterns of organizations: Contemporary research issues. *Industrial and Corporate Change*, 5(3), 653–698.

Cohen, W., Levinthal, D. 1990. Absorptive capacity: A new perspective on learning and innovation. *Administrative Science Quarterly*, 35(1), 128–152.

Coleman, J.S. 1982. Systems of trust: A rough theoretical framework. *Angewandte Sozialforschung*, 10(3), 277–299.

Coleman, J.S. 1990. *Foundations of Social Theory*. Cambridge, MA: Harvard University Press.

Commons, J.R. 1934. *Institutional Economics*. Madison: University of Wisconsin Press.

Cook, K.S. (ed.) 2001. *Trust in Society*. New York: Russell Sage Foundation.

Cook, K.S., Hardin, R., Levi, M. 2005a. *Cooperation Without Trust?* New York: Russell Sage Foundation.

Cook, K.S., Yamagishi, T., Cheshire, C., Cooper, R., Matsuda, M., Mashima, R. 2005b. Trust building via risk taking: A cross-societal experiment. *Social Psychology Quarterly*, 68(2), 121–142.

Cortina, J.M. 1993. What is coefficient alpha? An examination of theory and applications. *Journal of Applied Psychology*, 78(1), 98–104.

Costa, A.C. 2003. Work team trust and effectiveness. *Personnel Review*, 32(5), 605–622.

Craswell, R. 1993. On the uses of 'trust': Comment on Williamson, 'Calculativeness, trust, and economic organization'. *Journal of Law and Economics*, 36(2), 487–500.

Crowne, D.P., Marlowe, D. 1964. *The Approved Motive: Studies in Evaluative Dependence*. New York: Wiley.

Cummings, L.L., Bromiley, P. 1996. The organizational trust inventory (OTI): Development and validation. In: Kramer, R.M., Tyler, T.R. (eds.) *Trust in Organizations*. Thousand Oaks: Sage, 302–330.

Currall, S.C., Inkpen, A.C. 2002. A multilevel approach to trust in joint ventures. *Journal of International Business Studies*, 33(3), 479–495.

Currall, S.C., Judge, T.A. 1995. Measuring trust between organizational boundary role persons. *Organizational Behavior and Human Decision Making Processes*, 64(2), 151–170.

Dasgupta, P. 1988. Trust as a commodity. In: Gambetta, D. (ed.) *Trust: Making and Breaking Co-operative Relations*. Oxford: Basil Blackwell, 49–72.

David, P.A. 1985. Clio and the economics of QWERTY. *American Economic Review*, 75(2), 332–337.

Dawes, R.M. 1980. Social dilemmas. *Annual Review of Psychology*, 31, 169–193.

De Sousa, R. 1987. *The Rationality of Emotion*. Cambridge, MA: MIT Press.

Deakin, S., Lane, C., Wilkinson, F. 1997. Contract law, trust relations, and incentives for co-operation: A comparative study. In: Deakin, S., Michie, J. (eds.) *Contracts, Cooperation and Competition: Studies in Economics, Management and Law.* Oxford: Oxford University Press, 105–139.

Deakin, S., Wilkinson, F. 1998. Contract law and the economics of interorganizational trust. In: Lane, C., Bachmann, R. (eds.) *Trust Within and Between Organizations.* Oxford: Oxford University Press, 146–172.

DeFillippi, R.J., Arthur, M.B. 1998. Paradox in project-based enterprise: The case of film making. *California Management Review,* 40(2), 125–139.

Defoe, D. 1994 [1791]. *Robinson Crusoe.* London: Penguin Books.

Denzin, N.K., Lincoln, Y.S. 1994. Introduction: Entering the field of qualitative research. In: Denzin, N.K., Lincoln, Y.S. (eds.) *Handbook of Qualitative Research.* Thousand Oaks: Sage, 1–17.

Deutsch, M. 1973. *The Resolution of Conflict.* New Haven: Yale University Press.

Dibben, M.R. 2000. *Exploring Interpersonal Trust in the Entrepreneurial Venture.* Basingstoke: Macmillan.

DiMaggio, P.J. 1988. Interest and agency in institutional theory. In: Zucker, L.G. (ed.) *Institutional Patterns and Organizations.* Cambridge, MA: Ballinger, 3–22.

DiMaggio, P.J., Powell, W.W. 1983. The iron cage revisited: Institutional isomorphism and collective rationality in organizational fields. *American Sociological Review,* 48(2), 147–160.

DiMaggio, P.J., Powell, W.W. 1991. Introduction. In: Powell, W.W., DiMaggio, P.J. (eds.) *The New Institutionalism in Organizational Analysis.* Chicago: University of Chicago Press, 1–38.

Dirks, K.T., Ferrin, D.L. 2001. The role of trust in organizational settings. *Organization Science,* 12(4), 450–467.

Dirks, K.T., Ferrin, D.L. 2002. Trust in leadership: Meta-analytical findings and implications for research and practice. *Journal of Applied Psychology,* 87(4), 611–628.

Dobbins, G.H., Lane, I.M., Steiner, D.D. 1988. A note on the role of laboratory methodologies in applied behavioural research: Don't throw out the baby with the bath water. *Journal of Organizational Behavior,* 9(3), 281–286.

Dunn, J. 1988. Trust and political agency. In: Gambetta, D. (ed.) *Trust: Making and Breaking Co-operative Relations.* Oxford: Basil Blackwell, 73–93.

Durkheim, E. 1984 [1893]. *The Division of Labour in Society.* London: Macmillan.

Dwyer, R.F., Schurr, P.H., Oh, S. 1987. Developing buyer–seller relationships. *Journal of Marketing,* 51(2), 11–27.

Dyer, J.H. 2000. *Collaborative Advantage: Winning Through Extended Enterprise Supplier Networks.* Oxford: Oxford University Press.

Dyer, J.H., Chu, W. 2003. The role of trustworthiness in reducing transaction costs and improving performance: Empirical evidence from the United States, Japan, and Korea. *Organization Science,* 14(1), 57–68.

Eisenhardt, K.M. 1989. Agency theory: An assessment and review. *Academy of Management Review,* 14(1), 57–74.

Eisenstadt, S.N., Roniger, L. 1984. *Patrons, Clients and Friends: Interpersonal Relations and the Structure of Trust in Society.* Cambridge: Cambridge University Press.

Elster, J. 1983. *Sour Grapes.* Cambridge: Cambridge University Press.

Elster, J. 1984. *Ulysses and the Sirens: Studies in Rationality and Irrationality*. Revised edition. Cambridge: Cambridge University Press.

Elster, J. 1989a. *The Cement of Society: A Study of Social Order*. Cambridge: Cambridge University Press.

Elster, J. 1989b. *Solomonic Judgements: Studies in the Limitations of Rationality*. Cambridge: Cambridge University Press.

Endreß, M. 2001. Vertrauen und Vertrautheit – Phänomenologisch-anthropologische Grundlegung. In: Hartmann, M., Offe, C. (eds.) *Vertrauen: Die Grundlage des sozialen Zusammenhalts*. Frankfurt: Campus, 161–203.

Ensminger, J. 2001. Reputations, trust, and the principal agent problem. In: Cook, K.S. (ed.) *Trust in Society*. New York: Russell Sage Foundation, 185–201.

Erikson, E.H. 1965. *Childhood and Society*. Harmondsworth: Penguin.

Faulkner, D. 1995. *International Strategic Alliances: Co-operating to Compete*. London: McGraw-Hill.

Fehr, E., Gächter, S. 2002. Altruistic punishment in humans. *Nature*, 415, 137–140.

Feldman, M.S. 2000. Organizational routines as a source of continuous change. *Organization Science* 11(6), 611–629.

Feldman, M.S., Pentland, B.T. 2003. Reconceptualizing organizational routines as a source of flexibility and change. *Administrative Science Quarterly*, 48(1), 94–118.

Fennell, M.L. 1980. The effects of environmental characteristics on the structure of hospital clusters. *Administrative Science Quarterly,* 25(3), 484–510.

Ferres, N., Connell, J., Travaglione, A. 2004. Co-worker trust as a social catalyst for constructive employee attitudes. *Journal of Managerial Psychology*, 19(6), 608–622.

Ferrin, D.L., Dirks, K.T. 2003. The use of rewards to increase and decrease trust: Mediating processes and differential effects. *Organization Science*, 14(1), 18–31.

Fineman, S. 1996. Emotion and organizing. In: Clegg, S.R., Hardy, C., Nord, W.R. (eds.) *Handbook of Organization Studies.* London: Sage, 543–564.

Fontana, A., Frey, J.H. 1994. Interviewing: The art of science. In: Denzin, N.K., Lincoln, Y.S. (eds.) *Handbook of Qualitative Research.* Thousand Oaks: Sage, 361–376.

Ford, D. 1980. The development of buyer–seller relationships in industrial markets. *European Journal of Marketing*, 14(5/6), 339–353.

Fox, A. 1974. *Beyond Contract: Work, Power and Trust Relations*. London: Faber & Faber.

Frank, R.H. 1987. If homo economicus could choose his own utility function, would he choose one with a conscience? *American Economic Review*, 77(4), 593–604.

Frank, R.H. 1988. *Passions Within Reason: The Strategic Role of the Emotions*. New York: Norton.

Frankel, S.H. 1977. *Money: Two Philosophies*. Oxford: Basil Blackwell.

Fukuyama, F. 1995. *Trust: The Social Virtues and the Creation of Prosperity*. London: Hamish Hamilton.

Galaskiewicz, J., Wasserman, S. 1989. Mimetic and normative processes within an interorganizational field: An empirical test. Administrative Science Quarterly, 34(3), 454–479.

Gambetta, D. (ed.) 1988a. *Trust: Making and Breaking Co-operative Relations*. Oxford: Basil Blackwell.

Gambetta, D. 1988b. Foreword. In: Gambetta, D. (ed.) *Trust: Making and Breaking Co-operative Relations*. Oxford: Basil Blackwell.

Gambetta, D. 1988c. Mafia: The price of distrust. In: Gambetta, D. (ed.) *Trust: Making and Breaking Co-operative Relations*. Oxford: Basil Blackwell, 158–175.

Gambetta, D. 1988d. Can we trust trust? In: Gambetta, D. (ed.) *Trust: Making and Breaking Co-operative Relations*. Oxford: Basil Blackwell, 213–237.

Gambetta, D., Hamill, H. 2005. *Streetwise: How Taxi Drivers Establish Their Customers' Trustworthiness*. New York: Russell Sage Foundation.

Garfinkel, H. 1963. A conception of, and experiments with, 'trust' as a condition of stable concerted actions. In: Harvey, O.J. (ed.) *Motivation and Social Interaction*. New York: The Ronald Press Company, 187–238.

Garfinkel, H. 1967. *Studies in Ethnomethodology*. Englewood Cliffs: Prentice Hall.

Garud, R., Jain, S., Kumaraswamy, A. 2002. Institutional entrepreneurship in the sponsorship of common technological standards: The case of Sun Microsystems and Java. *Academy of Management Journal*, 45(1), 196–214.

Garud, R., Karnøe, P. 2001. Path creation as a process of mindful deviation. In: Garud, R., Karnøe, P. (eds.) *Path Dependence and Creation*. Mahwah, NJ: Lawrence Earlbaum Associates, 1–38.

Geyskens, I., Steenkamp, J.-B., Kumar, N. 1998. Generalizations about trust in marketing channel relationships using meta-analysis. *International Journal of Research in Marketing*, 15(3), 223–248.

Gibb, J.R. 1964. Climate for trust formation. In: Bradford, L.P., Gibb, J.R., Benne, D. (eds.) *T-Group Theory and Laboratory Method.* New York: John Wiley, 279–301.

Gibbons, R. 2001. Trust in social structures: Hobbes and Coase meet repeated games. In: Cook, K.S. (ed.) *Trust in Society*. New York: Russell Sage Foundation, 332–353.

Giddens, A. 1979. *Central Problems in Social Theory: Action, Structure and Contradiction in Social Analysis*. London: Macmillan.

Giddens, A. 1984. *The Constitution of Society*. Berkeley: University of California Press.

Giddens, A. 1990. *The Consequences of Modernity*. Stanford: Stanford University Press.

Giddens, A. 1991. *Modernity and Self-Identity*. Cambridge: Polity Press.

Giddens, A. 1992. *The Transformation of Intimacy*. Cambridge: Polity Press.

Giddens, A. 1993. *New Rules of Sociological Method*. Second edition. Cambridge: Polity Press.

Giddens, A. 1994a. Living in a post-traditional society. In: Beck, U., Giddens, A., Lash, S. (eds.) *Reflexive Modernization*. Cambridge: Polity Press, 56–109.

Giddens, A. 1994b. Risk, trust, reflexivity. In: Beck, U., Giddens, A., Lash, S. (eds.) *Reflexive Modernization.* Cambridge: Polity Press, 184–197.

Gillespie, N. 2003. *Measuring Trust in Work Relationships: The Behavioural Trust Inventory*. Paper presented at the Academy of Management Conference, Seattle, August 1–6.

Gillespie, N., Mann, L. 2004. Transformational leadership and shared values: The building blocks of trust. *Journal of Managerial Psychology*, 19(6), 588–607.

Gilson, L. 2003. Trust and the development of health care as a social institution. *Social Science and Medicine*, 56(7), 1453–1468.

Glaeser, E.L., Laibson, D.I., Schenkman, J.A., Soutter, C.L. 2000. Measuring trust. *Quarterly Journal of Economics*, 115(3), 811–846.

Goffman, E. 1959. *The Presentation of Self in Everyday Life*. London: Penguin.

Goffman, E. 1963. *Behavior in Public Places: Notes on the Social Organization of Gatherings*. New York: Free Press.

Good, D. 1988. Individuals, interpersonal relations and trust. In: Gambetta, D. (ed.) *Trust: Making and Breaking Co-operative Relations*. Oxford: Basil Blackwell, 31–48.

Granovetter, M. 1985. Economic action and social structure: A theory of embeddedness. *American Journal of Sociology*, 91(3), 481–510.

Green, C. 1994. *Professional Management for Printers*. London: Blueprint.

Grey, C., Garsten, C. 2001. Trust, control and post-bureaucracy. *Organization Studies*, 22(2), 229–250.

Guba, E.G., Lincoln, Y.S. 1994. Competing paradigms in qualitative research. In: Denzin, N.K., Lincoln, Y.S. (eds.) *Handbook of Qualitative Research*. Thousand Oaks: Sage, 105–117.

Gulati, R. 1995. Does familiarity breed trust? The implications of repeated ties for contractual choice in alliances. *Academy of Management Journal*, 38(1), 85–112.

Hagen, J.M., Choe, S. 1998. Trust in Japanese interfirm relations: Institutional sanctions matter. *Academy of Management Review*, 23(3), 589–600.

Hann, M.S. 1968. Die Idee des Vertrauens bei Konfuzius. In: Schwartländer, J. (ed.) *Verstehen und Vertrauen*. Stuttgart: Kohlhammer, 27–38.

Hannan, M.T., Freeman, J.H. 1977. The population ecology of organizations. *American Journal of Sociology*, 82(5), 929–964.

Hardin, R. 1991. Trusting persons, trusting institutions. In: Zeckhauser, R.J. (ed.) *Strategy and Choice*. Cambridge, MA: MIT Press, 185–209.

Hardin, R. 1993. The street-level epistemology of trust. *Politics & Society*, 21(4), 505–529.

Hardin, R. 2001. Conceptions and explanations of trust. In: Cook, K.S. (ed.) *Trust in Society*. New York: Russell Sage Foundation, 3–39.

Hardin, R. 2002. *Trust and Trustworthiness*. New York: Russell Sage Foundation.

Hardin, R. 2003. *Indeterminacy and Society*. Princeton: Princeton University Press.

Hardy, C., Phillips, N., Lawrence, T. 1998. Distinguishing trust and power in inter-organizational relations: Forms and façades of trust. In: Lane, C., Bachmann, R. (eds.) *Trust Within and Between Organizations*. Oxford: Oxford University Press, 64–87.

Hawley, A. 1968. Human ecology. In: Sills, D.L. (ed.) *International Encyclopedia of the Social Sciences*. New York: Macmillan, 328–337 (cited in DiMaggio and Powell, 1983).

Heckscher, C.C., Donnellon, A. (eds.) 1994. *The Post-Bureaucratic Organization*. Thousand Oaks: Sage.

Hegel, G.W.F. 1973 [1807]. *Phänomenologie des Geistes*. Frankfurt: Suhrkamp.

Heide, J.B., John, G. 1990. Alliances in industrial purchasing: The determinants of joint action in buyer–supplier relationships. *Journal of Marketing Research*, 27(1), 24–36.

Heimer, C.A. 2001. Solving the problem of trust. In: Cook, K.S. (ed.) *Trust in Society*. New York: Russell Sage Foundation, 40–88.

Hendry, J. 2002. The principal's other problems: Honest incompetence and the specification of objectives. *Academy of Management Review*, 27(1), 98–113.

Henslin, J.M. 1968. Trust and the cab driver. In: Truzzi, M. (ed.) *Sociology and Everyday Life*. Englewood Cliffs: Prentice Hall.

Heritage, J.C. 1987. Ethnomethodology. In: Giddens, A., Turner, J.H. (eds.) *Social Theory Today*. Stanford: Stanford University Press, 224–272.

Hill, C.W.L. 1990. Cooperation, opportunism, and the invisible hand: Implications for transaction cost theory. *Academy of Management Review*, 15(3), 500–513.

Hirsch, P.M., Levin, D.Z. 1999. Umbrella advocates versus validity police: A life-cycle model. *Organization Science*, 10(2), 199–212.

Hollis, M. 1998. *Trust Within Reason*. Cambridge: Cambridge University Press.

Holloran, J. 1994. The challenge of managing change. In: Birch, P. (ed.) *Managing Change in the Printing and Publishing Industry: Strategic Approaches*. Leatherhead: Pira, 13–26.

Holstein, J.A., Gubrium, J.F. 1994. Phenomenology, ethnomethodology, and interpretative practice. In: Denzin, N.K., Lincoln, Y.S. (eds.) *Handbook of Qualitative Research*. Thousand Oaks: Sage, 262–272.

Hosmer, L.T. 1994. Strategic planning as if ethics mattered. *Strategic Management Journal*, 15(5), 17–34.

Huberman, A.M., Miles, M.B. 1994. Data management and analysis methods. In: Denzin, N.K., Lincoln, Y.S. (eds.) *Handbook of Qualitative Research*. Thousand Oaks: Sage, 428–444.

Huemer, L. 1998. *Trust in Business Relations: Economic Logic or Social Interaction?* Umeå: Boréa.

Inkpen, A.C., Currall, S.C. 1997. International joint venture trust: An empirical examination. In: Beamish, P.W., Killing, J.P. (eds.) *Cooperative Strategies: North American Perspectives*. San Francisco: New Lexington, 308–334.

Inkpen, A.C., Curall, S.C. 2004. The co-evolution of trust, control, and learning in joint ventures. *Organization Science,* 12(5), 586–599.

James Jr., H.S. 2002. The trust paradox: A survey of economic inquiries into the nature of trust and trustworthiness. *Journal of Economic Behavior & Organization*, 47(3), 291–307.

James, W. 1948. *Essays in Pragmatism*. New York: Hafner Press.

Jensen, M.C., Meckling, W.H. 1976. Theory of the firm: Managerial behavior, agency costs, and ownership structure. *Journal of Financial Economics*, 3(4), 305–360.

Jepperson, R.L. 1991. Institutions, institutional effects, and institutionalism. In: Powell, W.W., DiMaggio, P.J. (eds.) *The New Institutionalism in Organizational Analysis*. Chicago: University of Chicago Press, 143–163.

Johnson, J.L., Cullen, J.B., Sakano, T., Takenouchi, H. 1996. Setting the stage for trust and strategic integration in Japanese–U.S. cooperative alliances. *Journal of International Business Studies*, 27(5), 981–1004.

Johnson-George, C., Swap, W.C. 1982. Measurement of specific interpersonal trust: Construction and validation of a scale to assess trust in a specific other. *Journal of Personality and Social Psychology*, 43(6), 1306–1317.

Jones, K. 1996. Trust as an affective attitude. *Ethics*, 107(1), 4–25.

Kahneman, D., Tversky, A. 1979. Prospect theory: An analysis of decision under risk. *Econometrica*, 47(2), 263–291.

Kee, H.W., Knox, R.E. 1970. Conceptual and methodological considerations in the study of trust and suspicion. *Journal of Conflict Resolution*, 14(3), 357–366.

Kelley, H.H., Thibaut J.W. 1978. *Interpersonal Relations*. New York: Wiley.

Kern, H. 1998. Lack of trust, surfeit of trust: Some causes of the innovation crisis in German industry. In: Lane, C., Bachmann, R. (eds.) *Trust Within and Between Organizations*. Oxford: Oxford University Press, 203–213.

Kierkegaard, S. 1985 [1843]. *Fear and Trembling*. London: Penguin.

Kieser, A. 1997. Rhetoric and myth in management fashion. *Organization*, 4(1), 49–74.

Kilduff, M., Tsai, W. 2003. *Social Networks and Organizations*. London: Sage.

Klein Woolthuis, R., Hillebrand, B., Nooteboom, B. 2005. Trust, contract and relationship development. *Organization Studies*, 26(6), 813–840.

Knight, F.H. 1971 [1921]. *Risk, Uncertainty, and Profit*. San Francisco: University of Chicago Press, Phoenix Books.

Kollock, P. 1994. The emergence of exchange structures: An experimental study of uncertainty, commitment, and trust. *American Journal of Sociology*, 100(2), 313–345.

Kosfeld, M., Heinrichs, M., Zak, P.J., Fischbacher, U., Fehr, E. 2005. Oxytocin increases trust in humans. *Nature*, 435, 673–676.

Kramer, R.M. 1996. Divergent realities and convergent disappointments in the hierarchic relation: Trust and the intuitive auditor at work. In: Kramer, R.M., Tyler, T.R. (eds.) *Trust in Organizations*. Thousand Oaks: Sage, 216–245.

Kramer, R.M. 2001. Identity and trust in organizations: One anatomy of a productive but problematic relationship. In: Hogg, M.A., Terry, D.J. (eds.) *Social Identity Processes in Organizational Contexts*. Philadelphia: Psychology Press, 167–180.

Kramer, R.M., Tyler, T.R. (eds.) 1996. *Trust in Organizations: Frontiers of Theory and Research.* Thousand Oaks: Sage.

Kreps, D.M. 1990. Corporate culture and economic theory. In: Alt, J.E., Shepsle, K.A. (eds.) *Perspectives on Positive Political Economy*. Cambridge: Cambridge University Press, 90–143.

Kühlmann, T.M. 2005. Formation of trust in German–Mexican business relations. In: Bijlsma-Frankema, K.M., Klein Woolthuis, R. (eds.) *Trust under Pressure: Empirical Investigations of Trust and Trust Building in Uncertain Circumstances*. Cheltenham: Edward Elgar, 37–54.

Lamming, R. 1993. *Beyond Partnership: Strategies for Innovation and Lean Supply*. New York: Prentice Hall.

Lane, C. 1997. The social regulation of inter-firm relations in Britain and Germany: Market rules, legal norms and technical standards. *Cambridge Journal of Economics*, 21(2), 197–215.

Lane, C. 1998. Introduction: Theories and issues in the study of trust. In: Lane, C., Bachmann, R. (eds.) *Trust Within and Between Organizations*. Oxford: Oxford University Press, 1–30.

Lane, C., Bachmann, R. 1996. The social constitution of trust: Supplier relations in Britain and Germany. *Organization Studies*, 17(3), 365–395.

Lane, C., Bachmann, R. (eds.) 1998. *Trust Within and Between Organizations: Conceptual Issues and Empirical Applications*. Oxford: Oxford University Press.

Lane, P.J., Salk, J.E., Lyles, M.A. 2001. Absorptive capacity, learning, and performance in international joint ventures. *Strategic Management Journal*, 22(12), 1139–1161.

Langley, A. 1999. Strategies for theorizing from process data. *Academy of Management Review,* 24(4), 691–710.

Larson, A. 1992. Network dyads in entrepreneurial settings: A study of the governance of exchange relationships. *Administrative Science Quarterly,* 37(1), 76–114.

Larzelere, R.E., Huston, T.L. 1980. The dyadic trust scale: Toward understanding interpersonal trust in close relationships. *Journal of Marriage and the Family*, 42(3), 596–604.

Lash, S. 1994. Expert-systems or situated interpretation? Culture and institutions in disorganized capitalism. In: Beck, U., Giddens, A., Lash, S. (eds.) *Reflexive Modernization.* Cambridge: Polity Press, 198–215.

Lawrence, T.B., Phillips, N. 2004. From Moby Dick to Free Willy: Macro-cultural discourses and institutional entrepreneurship in emerging institutional fields. *Organization,* 11(5), 689–711.

Lawrence, T.B., Phillips, N., Hardy, C. 2002. Institutional effects of inter-organizational collaboration: The emergence of protoinstitutions. *Academy of Management Journal,* 45(1), 281–290.

Lee-Treweek, G. 2002. Trust in complementary medicine: The case of cranial osteopathy. *Sociological Review,* 50(1), 48–68.

Leifer, R., Mills, P.K. 1996. An information processing approach for deciding upon control strategies and reducing control loss in emerging organizations. *Journal of Management,* 22(1), 113–137.

Lewicki, R.J., Bunker, B.B. 1995. Trust in relationships: A model of development and decline. In: Bunker, B.B., Rubin, J.Z. (eds.) *Conflict, Cooperation and Justice.* San Francisco: Jossey-Bass, 133–173.

Lewicki, R.J., Bunker, B.B. 1996. Developing and maintaining trust in work relationships. In: Kramer, R.M., Tyler, T.R. (eds.) *Trust in Organizations.* Thousand Oaks: Sage, 114–139.

Lewicki, R.J., McAllister, D.J., Bies, R.J. 1998. Trust and distrust: New relationships and realities. *Academy of Management Review,* 23(3), 438–458.

Lewis, J.D., Weigert, A. 1985. Trust as a social reality. *Social Forces,* 63(4), 967–985.

Liebeskind, J.P., Oliver, A.L. 1998. From handshake to contract: Intellectual property, trust, and the social structure of academic research. In: Lane, C., Bachmann, R. (eds.) *Trust Within and Between Organizations.* Oxford: Oxford University Press, 118–145.

Likert, R. 1932. *A Technique for the Measurement of Attitudes.* New York: McGraw-Hill.

Lindenberg, S. 2000. In takes both trust and lack of mistrust: The workings of cooperation and relational signalling in contractual relationships. *Journal of Management and Governance,* 4(1/2), 11–33.

Lorenz, E.H. 1988. Neither friends nor strangers: Informal networks of subcontracting in French industry. In: Gambetta, D. (ed.) *Trust: Making and Breaking Co-operative Relations.* Oxford: Basil Blackwell, 194–210.

Lowe, P. 2005. Embodied expertise: Women's perceptions of contraception consultation. *Health,* 9(3), 361–378.

Luce, R.D., Raiffa, H. 1957. *Games and Decisions.* New York: Wiley.

Luhmann, N. 1979. *Trust and Power: Two Works by Niklas Luhmann.* Chichester: Wiley.

Luhmann, N. 1988. Familiarity, confidence, trust: Problems and alternatives. In: Gambetta, D. (ed.) *Trust: Making and Breaking Co-operative Relations.* Oxford: Basil Blackwell, 94–107.

Lyles, M.A., Salk, J.E. 1996. Knowledge acquisition from foreign parents in international joint ventures. *Journal of International Business Studies,* 27(5), 877–904.

Macaulay, S. 1963. Non-contractual relations in business: A preliminary study. *American Sociological Review,* 28(1), 55–69.

Maguire, S., Phillips, N., Hardy, C. 2001. When 'silence = death', keep talking: Trust, control and the discursive construction of identity in the Canadian HIV/AIDS treatment domain. *Organization Studies*, 22(2), 285–310.

Mahoney, J. 2000. Path dependence in historical sociology. *Theory and Society*, 29(4), 507–548.

Malhotra, D., Murnighan, J.K. 2002. The effects of contracts on interpersonal trust. *Administrative Science Quarterly*, 47(3), 534–559.

March, J.G., Olsen, J.P. 1989. *Rediscovering Institutions: The Organizational Basis of Politics*. New York: Free Press.

March, J.G., Simon, H.A. 1958. *Organizations*. New York: Wiley.

Marshall, A. 1920. *Industry and Trade*. London: Macmillan.

Matthews, B.A., Shimoff, E., 1979. Expansion of exchange: Monitoring trust levels in ongoing exchange relations. *Journal of Conflict Resolution*, 23(3), 538–560.

Mauss, M. 1954 [1925]. *The Gift: Forms and Functions of Exchange in Archaic Societies*. Glencoe: Free Press.

Mauthner, N.S., Doucet, A. 2003. Reflexive accounts and accounts of reflexivity in qualitative data analysis. *Sociology,* 37(3), 413–431.

Mayer, R.C., Davis, J.H. 1999. The effect of the performance appraisal system on trust for management: A field quasi-experiment. *Journal of Applied Psychology,* 84(1), 123–136.

Mayer, R.C., Davis, J.H., Schoorman, F.D. 1995. An integrative model of organizational trust. *Academy of Management Review*, 20(3), 709–734.

Mayer, R.C., Gavin, M.B. 2005. Trust in management and performance: Who minds the shop while the employees watch the boss? *Academy of Management Journal*, 48(5), 874–888.

McAllister, D.J. 1995. Affect- and cognition-based trust as foundations for interpersonal cooperation in organizations. *Academy of Management Journal*, 38(1), 24–59.

McCloskey, D.N. 1994. *Knowledge and Persuasion in Economics*. Cambridge: Cambridge University Press.

McEvily, B., Marcus, A. 2005. Embedded ties and the acquisition of competitive capabilities. *Strategic Management Journal*, 26(11), 1033–1055.

McEvily, B., Perrone, V., Zaheer, A. 2003. Introduction to the special issue on trust in an organizational context. *Organization Science*, 14(1), 1–4.

McKneally, M.F., Ignagni, E., Martin, D.K., D'Cruz, J. 2004. The leap to trust: Perspective of cholecystectomy patients on informed decision making and consent. *Journal of the American College of Surgeons*, 199(1), 51–57.

McKnight, D.H., Cummings, L.L., Chervany, N.L. 1998. Initial trust formation in new organizational relationships. *Academy of Management Review*, 23(3), 473–490.

Mead, G.H. 1934. *Mind, Self and Society*. Chicago: University of Chicago Press.

Merton, R.K. 1949. *Social Theory and Social Structure*. New York: Free Press.

Meyer, J.W. 1983. Institutionalization and the rationality of formal organizational structure. In: Meyer, J.W., Scott, W.R. (eds.) *Organizational Environments: Ritual and Rationality*. Beverly Hills: Sage, 261–282.

Meyer, J.W., Jepperson, R.L. 2000. The 'actors' of modern society: The cultural construction of social agency. *Sociological Theory*, 18(1), 100–120.

Meyer, J.W., Rowan, B. 1977. Institutionalized organizations: Formal structure as myth and ceremony. *American Journal of Sociology*, 83(2), 340–363.

Meyerson, D., Weick, K.E., Kramer, R.M. 1996. Swift trust and temporary groups. In: Kramer, R.M., Tyler, T.R. (eds.) *Trust in Organizations*. Thousand Oaks: Sage, 166–195.

Miller, G. 2001. Why is trust necessary in organizations? The moral hazard of profit maximization. In: Cook, K.S. (ed.) *Trust in Society*. New York: Russell Sage Foundation, 307–331.

Mills, P.K., Ungson, G.R. 2003. Reassessing the limits of structural empowerment: Organizational constitution and trust as controls. *Academy of Management Review*, 28(1), 143–153.

Misztal, B.A. 1996. *Trust in Modern Societies*. Cambridge: Polity Press.

Mohr, A.T. 2002. *Erfolg deutsch-chinesischer Joint Ventures: Eine qualitative und quantitative Analyse*. Frankfurt: Peter Lang.

Mohr, J., Spekman, R. 1994. Characteristics of partnership success: Partnership attributes, communication behavior, and conflict resolution techniques. *Strategic Management Journal*, 15(2), 135–152.

Möllering, G. 2001. The nature of trust: From Georg Simmel to a theory of expectation, interpretation and suspension. *Sociology*, 35(2), 403–420.

Möllering, G. 2002. Perceived trustworthiness and inter-firm governance: Empirical evidence from the UK printing industry. *Cambridge Journal of Economics*, 26(2), 139–160.

Möllering, G. 2003. A typology of supplier relations: From determinism to pluralism in inter-firm empirical research. *Journal of Purchasing and Supply Management*, 9(1), 31–41.

Möllering, G. 2005a. The trust/control duality: An integrative perspective on positive expectations of others. *International Sociology*, 20(3), 283–305.

Möllering, G. 2005b. Rational, institutional and active trust: Just do it!? In: Bijlsma-Frankema, K.M., Klein Woolthuis, R. (eds.) *Trust under Pressure: Empirical Investigations of Trust and Trust Building in Uncertain Circumstances*. Cheltenham: Edward Elgar, 17–36.

Möllering, G., Bachmann, R., Lee, S.H. 2004. Introduction: Understanding organizational trust – foundations, constellations and issues of operationalisation. *Journal of Managerial Psychology*, 19(6), 556–570.

Morse, J.M. 1994. Designing funded qualitative research. In: Denzin, N.K., Lincoln, Y.S. (eds.) *Handbook of Qualitative Research*. Thousand Oaks: Sage, 220–235.

Morris, S. 1998. *The Handbook of Management Fads: Survival in Business – Without Taking Yourself Too Seriously*. London: Thorogood.

Munir, K.A., Phillips, N. 2005. The birth of the 'Kodak moment': Institutional entrepreneurship and the adoption of new technologies. *Organization Studies*, 26(11), 1665–1687.

Nelson, R.R., Winter, S.G. 1982. *An Evolutionary Theory of Economic Change*. Cambridge, MA: Belknap Press.

Newell, S., Swan, J. 2000. Trust and inter-organizational networking. *Human Relations*, 53(10), 1287–1328.

Nooteboom, B. 1996. Trust, opportunism and governance: A process and control model. *Organization Studies*, 17(6), 985–1010.

Nooteboom, B. 2002. *Trust: Forms, Foundations, Functions, Failures and Figures*. Cheltenham: Edward Elgar.

Nooteboom, B. 2003. *Learning to Trust*. CentER Discussion Paper No. 2005-47. Tilburg: Tilburg University Press.

Nooteboom, B., Berger, H., Noorderhaven, N.G. 1997. Effects of trust and governance on relational risk. *Academy of Management Journal*, 40(2), 308–338.

Nooteboom, B., Six. F. 2003. (eds.) *The Trust Process in Organizations: Empirical Studies of the Determinants and the Process of Trust Development*. Cheltenham: Edward Elgar.

Nunnally, J. 1978. *Psychometric Theory*. New York: McGraw-Hill.

Oliver, A.L. 1997. On the nexus of organizations and professions: Networking through trust. *Sociological Inquiry*, 67(2), 227–246.

Ortmann, G. 2004. *Als Ob: Fiktionen und Organisationen*. Wiesbaden: VS Verlag.

Ostrom, E., Walker, J. (eds.) 2003. *Trust and Reciprocity: Interdisciplinary Lessons from Experimental Research*. New York: Russell Sage Foundation.

Parsons, T. 1978. *Action Theory and the Human Condition*. New York: Free Press.

Paxton, P. 1999. Is social capital declining in the United States? A multiple indicator assessment. *American Journal of Sociology*, 105(1), 88–127.

Pennings, J.M., Woiceshyn, J. 1987. A typology of organizational control and its metaphors. *Research in the Sociology of Organizations*, 5, 73–104.

Perrone, V., Zaheer, A., McEvily, B. 2003. Free to be trusted? Organizational constraints on trust in boundary spanners. *Organization Science*, 14(4), 422–439.

Perrow, C. 1986. *Complex Organizations: A Critical Essay*. Third edition. New York: McGraw-Hill.

Poggi, G. 1979. Introduction. In: Luhmann, N. *Trust and Power*. Chichester: Wiley, vii–xix.

Poole, M.S., Van de Ven, A.H., Dooley, K., Holmes, M.E. 2000. *Organizational Change and Innovation Processes: Theory and Methods for Research*. Oxford: Oxford University Press.

Porter, D. 1994. *Print Management*. Leatherhead: Pira.

Powell, W.W., DiMaggio, P.J. (eds.) 1991. *The New Institutionalism in Organizational Analysis*. Chicago: University of Chicago Press.

Pruitt, D.G., Kimmel, M.J. 1977. Twenty years of experimental gaming: Critique, synthesis and suggestions for the future. *Annual Review of Psychology*, 28, 363–392.

Putnam, R.D. 1995. Bowling alone: America's declining social capital. *Journal of Democracy*, 6(1), 65–78.

Reynolds, L. 1997. *The Trust Effect: Creating the High Trust, High Performance Organization*. London: Nicholas Brealey.

Ring, P.S. 1997. Processes facilitating reliance on trust in inter-organizational networks. In: Ebers, M. (ed.) *The Formation of Inter-Organizational Networks*. Oxford: Oxford University Press, 113–145.

Ring, P.S., Van de Ven, A.H. 1992. Structuring cooperative relationships between organizations. *Strategic Management Journal*, 13(7), 483–498.

Ring, P.S., Van de Ven, A.H. 1994. Developmental processes of cooperative inter-organizational relationships. *Academy of Management Review*, 19(1), 90–118.

Ripperger, T. 1998. *Ökonomik des Vertrauens: Analyse eines Organisationsprinzips*. Tübingen: Mohr Siebeck.

Robinson, S.L. 1996. Trust and breach of the psychological contract. *Administrative Science Quarterly*, 41(4), 574–599.

Ross, S. 1973. The economic theory of agency: The principal's problem. *American Economic Review*, 63(2), 134–139.

Rotter, J.B. 1967. A new scale for the measurement of interpersonal trust. *Journal of Personality*, 35(4), 651–665.

Rotter, J.B. 1980. Interpersonal trust, trustworthiness, and gullibility. *American Psychologist*, 35(1), 1–7.

Rousseau, D.M., Sitkin, S.B., Burt, R.S., Camerer, C. 1998. Not so different after all: A cross-discipline view of trust. *Academy of Management Review*, 23(3), 393–404.

Rus, A. 2005. Trust and performance: Institutional, interpersonal and network trust. In: Bijlsma-Frankema, K.M., Klein Woolthuis, R. (eds.) *Trust under Pressure: Empirical Investigations of Trust and Trust Building in Uncertain Circumstances*. Cheltenham: Edward Elgar, 80–105.

Sabel, C.F. 1993. Studied trust: Building new forms of cooperation in a volatile economy. In: Swedberg, R. (ed.) *Explorations in Economic Sociology*. New York: Russell Sage Foundation, 104–144.

Sako, M. 1992. *Prices, Quality, and Trust: Inter-firm Relations in Britain and Japan*. Cambridge: Cambridge University Press.

Sako, M. 1998. Does trust improve business performance? In: Lane, C., Bachmann, R. (eds.) *Trust Within and Between Organizations*. Oxford: Oxford University Press, 88–117.

Salk, J.E. 1996. Partners and other strangers: Cultural boundaries and cross-cultural encounters in international joint venture teams. *International Studies of Management and Organization*, 26(4), 48–72.

Saunders, M.N.K., Thornhill, A. 2003. Organisational justice, trust and the management of change: An exploration. *Personnel Review*, 32(2), 360–375.

Saunders, M.N.K., Thornhill, A. 2004. Trust and mistrust in organisations: An exploration using an organisational justice framework. *European Journal of Work and Organisational Psychology*, 13(4), 493–515.

Schütz, A. 1967 [1932]. *The Phenomenology of the Social World*. Evanston: North-Western University Press.

Schütz, A. 1970a. *Reflections on the Problem of Relevance*. New Haven: Yale University Press.

Schütz, A. 1970b. *On Phenomenology and Social Relations*. Chicago: University of Chicago Press.

Schwandt, T.A. 1994. Constructivist, interpretivist approaches to human inquiry. In: Denzin, N.K., Lincoln, Y.S. (eds.) *Handbook of Qualitative Research*. Thousand Oaks: Sage, 118–137.

Scott, W.R. 2001. *Institutions and Organizations*. Second edition. Thousand Oaks: Sage.

Seligman, A. 1997. *The Problem of Trust*. Princeton: Princeton University Press.

Shapiro, D., Sheppard, B.H., Cheraskin, L. 1992. Business on a handshake. *Negotiation Journal*, 8(4), 365–377.

Shapiro, S.P. 1987. The social control of impersonal trust. *American Journal of Sociology*, 93(3), 623–658.

Shaw, B. 1997. *Trust in the Balance: Building Successful Organizations on Results, Integrity, and Concern*. San Francisco: Jossey-Bass.

Shea, G.F. 1987. *Building Trust for Personal and Organizational Success: A Self-paced, Skill-building Training Manual*. New York: John Wiley.

Sheppard, B.H., Sherman, D.M. 1998. The grammars of trust: A model and general implications. *Academy of Management Review*, 23(3), 422–437.

Shurtleff, M. 1998. *Building Trust: A Manager's Guide for Business Success.* Menlo Park, CA: Crisp Publications.

Simmel, G. 1950 [1908]. *The Sociology of Georg Simmel.* New York: Free Press.

Simmel, G. 1990 [1907]. *The Philosophy of Money.* Second edition. London: Routledge.

Sitkin, S.B., Roth, N.L. 1993. Explaining the limited effectiveness of legalistic remedies for trust/distrust. *Organization Science*, 4(3), 367–392.

Sitkin, S.B., Stickel, D. 1996. The road to hell: The dynamics of distrust in an era of quality. In: Kramer, R.M., Tyler, T.R. (eds.) *Trust in Organizations.* Thousand Oaks: Sage, 196–215.

Six, F. 2003. The dynamics of trust and trouble. In: Nooteboom, B., Six, F. (eds.) *The Trust Process in Organizations.* Cheltenham: Edward Elgar, 196–222.

Six, F. 2005. *The Trouble with Trust.* Cheltenham: Edward Elgar.

Smeltzer, L.R. 1997. The meaning and origin of trust in buyer–supplier relationships. *International Journal of Purchasing and Materials Management*, Winter 1997, 40–48.

Smith, J.A. 1995. Semi-structured interviewing and qualitative analysis. In: Smith, J.A., Harré, R., Van Langenhove, L. (eds.) *Rethinking Methods in Psychology.* London: Sage.

Smitka, M.J. 1994. Contracting without contracts. In: Sitkin, S.B., Bies, R.J. (eds.) *The Legalistic Organization.* London: Sage, 91–108.

Spence, M.A. 1974. *Market Signaling: Informational Transfer in Hiring and Related Screening Processes.* Cambridge, MA: Harvard University Press.

Stake, R.E. 1994. Case studies. In: Denzin, N.K., Lincoln, Y.S. (eds.) *Handbook of Qualitative Research.* Thousand Oaks: Sage, 236–247.

Steier, F. (ed.) 1991. *Research and Reflexivity.* London: Sage.

Stigler, G.J. 1961. The economics of information. *Journal of Political Economy*, 69(3), 213–225.

Streeck, W. 1992. *Social Institutions and Economic Performance: Studies of Industrial Relations in Advanced Capitalist Countries.* London: Sage.

Stolle, D. 2001. Clubs and congregations: The benefits of joining an association. In: Cook, K.S. (ed.) *Trust in Society.* New York: Russell Sage Foundation, 202–244.

Sydow, J. 1998. Understanding the constitution of inter-organizational trust. In: Lane, C., Bachmann, R. (eds.) *Trust Within and Between Organizations.* Oxford: Oxford University Press, 31–63.

Sydow, J. 2006. How can systems trust systems? A structuration perspective on trust-building in inter-organizational relations. In: Bachmann, R., Zaheer, A. (eds.) *Handbook of Research on Trust.* Cheltenham: Edward Elgar, forthcoming.

Sydow, J., Windeler, A. 2003. Knowledge, trust, and control: Managing tensions and contradictions in a regional network of service firms. *International Studies of Management and Organization*, 33(2), 69–99.

Sztompka, P. 1999. *Trust: A Sociological Theory.* Cambridge: Cambridge University Press.

Tillmar, M. 2002. *Swedish Tribalism and Tanzanian Agency: Preconditions for Trust and Cooperation in a Small-Business Context.* Linköping Studies in Management and Economics, Dissertation No. 58, Linköping: Linköping University.

Tillmar, M., Lindkvist, L. 2005. *Cooperation Against All Odds: Finding Reasons for Trust Where Formal Institutions Fail.* Paper presented at the Third EIASM Workshop on Trust Within and Between Organizations, Amsterdam, October 27–28.

Tsebelis, G. 1989. The abuse of probability in political analysis: The Robinson Crusoe fallacy. *American Political Science Review,* 83(1), 77–92.

Tsoukas, H., Chia, R. 2002. On organizational becoming: Rethinking organizational change. *Organization Science,* 13(5), 567–582.

Tversky, A., Kahneman, D. 1981. The framing of decisions and the psychology of choice. *Science,* 211, 453–458.

Tyler, T.R., Kramer, R.M. 1996. Whither trust? In: Kramer, R.M., Tyler, T.R. (eds.) *Trust in Organizations.* Thousand Oaks: Sage, 1–15.

Tzafrir, S.S., Dolan, S.L. 2004. Trust ME: A scale for measuring manager–employee trust. *Management Research,* 2(2), 117–134.

Uzzi, B. 1996. The sources and consequences of embeddedness for the economic performance of organizations: The network effect. *American Sociological Review,* 61(4), 674–698.

Uzzi, B. 1997. Social structure and competition in interfirm networks: The paradox of embeddedness. *Administrative Science Quarterly,* 42(1), 35–67.

Van de Ven, A.H., Poole, M.S. 1995. Explaining development and change in organizations. *Academy of Management Review,* 20(3), 510–540.

Van de Ven, A.H., Poole, M.S. 2005. Alternative approaches for studying organizational change. *Organization Studies,* 26(9), 1377–1404.

Venkatraman, N., Ramanujam, V. 1986. Measurement of business performance in strategy research: A comparison of approaches. *Academy of Management Review,* 11(4), 801–814.

Walgenbach, P. 2001. The production of distrust by means of producing trust. *Organization Studies,* 22(4), 693–714.

Warren, M.E. (ed.) 1999. *Democracy and Trust.* Cambridge: Cambridge University Press.

Wasserman, S., Faust, K. 1994. *Social Network Analysis: Methods and Applications.* Cambridge: Cambridge University Press.

Wenzel, H. 2001. *Die Abenteuer der Kommunikation.* Weilerswist: Velbrück Wissenschaft.

Whitehead, A.N. 1978 [1929]. *Process and Reality: An Essay in Cosmology.* New York: Free Press.

Whitener, E.M., Brodt, S.E., Korsgaard, M.A., Werner, J.M. 1998. Managers as initiators of trust: An exchange relationship framework for understanding managerial trustworthy behavior. *Academy of Management Review,* 23(3), 513–530.

Williams, M. 2001. In whom we trust: Group membership as an affective context for trust development. *Academy of Management Review,* 26(3), 377–396.

Williamson, O.E. 1975. *Markets and Hierarchies.* New York: Free Press.

Williamson, O.E. 1979. Transaction-cost economics: The governance of contractual relations. *Journal of Law and Economics,* 22(2), 233–261.

Williamson, O.E. 1985. *The Economic Institutions of Capitalism.* New York: Free Press.

Williamson, O.E. 1991. Comparative economic organization: The analysis of discrete structural alternatives. *Administrative Science Quarterly*, 36(2), 269–296.

Williamson, O.E. 1993. Calculativeness, trust, and economic organization. *Journal of Law and Economics*, 36(2), 453–486.

Williamson, O.E. 1996. *The Mechanisms of Governance*. Oxford: Oxford University Press.

Willmott, H.C. 1986. Unconscious sources of motivation in the theory of the subject: An exploration and critique of Giddens' dualistic models of action and personality. *Journal for the Theory of Social Behaviour*, 16(1), 105–121.

Windeler, A., Sydow, J. 2001. Project networks and changing industry practices – collaborative content production in the German television industry. *Organization Studies*, 22(6), 1035–1060.

Wrightsman, L.S. 1966. Personality and attitudinal correlates of trusting and trustworthy behaviors in a two-person game. *Journal of Personality and Social Psychology*, 4(3), 328–332.

Yamagishi, T. 2001. Trust as a form of social intelligence. In: Cook, K.S. (ed.) *Trust in Society*. New York: Russell Sage Foundation, 121–147.

Yamagishi, T., Kanazawa, S., Mashima, R., Terai S. 2005. Separating trust from cooperation in a dynamic relationship: Prisoner's dilemma with variable dependence. *Rationality and Society*, 17(3), 275–308.

Zaheer, A., McEvily, B., Perrone, V. 1998. Does trust matter? Exploring the effects of inter-organizational and interpersonal trust on performance. *Organization Science*, 9(2), 141–159.

Zaheer, A., Venkatraman, N. 1995. Relational governance as inter-organizational strategy: An empirical test of the role of trust in economic exchange. *Strategic Management Journal*, 16(5), 373–392.

Zak, P.J., Kurzban, R., Matzner, W.T. 2004. The neurobiology of trust. *Annals of the New York Academy of Sciences*, 1032, 224–227.

Zand, D.E. 1972. Trust and managerial problem solving. *Administrative Science Quarterly*, 17(2), 229–239.

Zucker, L.G. 1977. The role of institutionalization in cultural persistence. *American Sociological Review*, 42(5), 726–743.

Zucker, L.G. 1983. Organizations as institutions. In: Bacharach, S.B. (ed.) *Advances in Organizational Theory and Research*, Vol. 2. Greenwich, CT: JAI Press, 1–43.

Zucker, L.G. 1986. Production of trust: Institutional sources of economic structure, 1840–1920. In: Staw, B.M., Cummings, L.L. (eds.) *Research in Organizational Behavior*, Vol. 8. Greenwich, CT: JAI Press, 53–111.

Zucker, L.G. 1987. Institutional theories of organization. *Annual Review of Sociology*, 13, 443–464.

INDEX

AUTHOR INDEX

Abrahamson, E. *5–6*
Adler, P.S. *2–3*
Altheide, D.L. *134–35, 153*
Alvesson, M. *152–54*
Arrighetti, A. *146–49*
Arrow, K.J. *29–31, 60*
Arthur, M.B. *107*
Arthur, W.B. *92–93*
Ashworth, T. *78*
Aspers, P. *2*
Atkinson, S. *144*
Axelrod, R. *14, 36–39, 78–83, 133, 136*
Ayios, A. *150–51*

Bacharach, M. *34, 41–43, 46–47, 113*
Bachmann, R. *4–5, 7–8, 18, 48, 66–67, 127–28, 130–31, 134–35, 138, 145–50, 156, 196*
Baier, A. *3, 7, 21*
Barber, B. *2–3, 47, 67–68, 71, 133*
Barley, S.R. *197*
Barnes, J.B. *84–85*
Barney, J.B. *25, 27*
Beale, H. *65–66*
Beatt, A. *156–57*
Becker, G. *24*
Becker, M.C. *52–53, 70*

Beckert, J. *41, 70–71, 75, 79, 99–100, 112–13, 119–20, 122, 197*
Berger, H. *79, 93*
Berger, P.L. *9, 55–56, 58–62, 68–69, 95–96, 98*
Bernstein, M. *122, 144*
Bies, R.J. *48–49*
Bigley, G.A. *7–8, 27, 47*
Bijlsma-Frankema, K.M. *2–3, 5, 130, 144*
Birch, P. *156–57*
Blau, P. *85–86, 88, 187*
Blois, K.J. *131–32, 156*
Boon, S.D. *89*
Bradach, J.L. *7, 25, 110*
Brandenburger, A.M. *78–79*
Brass, D.J. *196–97*
Brenkert, G.G. *8*
British Printing Industries Federation *156–57*
Brodt, S.E. *30*
Bromiley, P. *27, 138*
Brothers, D. *2*
Brownlie, J. *73, 123–24, 144*
Bunker, B.B. *49–50, 89–90, 92–93*
Burchell, B. *147–49*
Burkhart, R. *53*
Burt, R.S. *7–9, 47, 85, 130–31, 153, 194–97*

Buskens, V. *84–85*
Butler, J.K. *48*

Camerer, C. *7–9, 47, 130–31, 139,*
    194–95
Cheraskin, L. *89*
Chervany, N.L. *47, 50, 57, 64, 79*
Cheshire, C. *94, 146*
Chia, R. *102–03, 198*
Child, J. *3–4, 52–53, 72–74, 90,*
    100, 150–51, 154
Chiles, T.H. *26–29*
Choe, S. *66*
Chu, W. *48, 146*
Coase, R.H. *26*
Cohen, M.D. *53*
Cohen, W. *128–29*
Coleman, J.S. *2–3, 10, 14–23, 25–*
    26, 71, 83–84, 131, 196–97
Commons, J.R. *26*
Confucius *2*
Connell, J. *137–38*
Cook, K.S. *2–3, 5, 78, 94, 119, 133,*
    146
Cooper, R. *94, 146*
Cortina, J.M. *137*
Costa, A.C. *137–38*
Craswell, R. *7–8, 25–26, 77–78*
Crowne, D.P. *139–40*
Cullen, J.B. *150–51*
Cummings, L.L. *27, 47, 50, 57, 64,*
    79, 138
Currall, S.C. *130–32, 134, 150–51,*
    186

D'Cruz, J. *122–23, 144*
Dasgupta, P. *7–8, 17, 33–37, 40–42*

David, P.A. *92–93*
Davis, J.H. *7–9, 14, 47–50, 79, 130,*
    137–39
Dawes, R.M. *38*
Deakin, S. *42, 66–67, 146–50*
DeFillippi, R.J. *107*
Defoe, D. *77–78*
Denzin, N.K. *140–41, 152–54*
Deutsch, M. *1–2, 33, 35, 38–39,*
    49–50, 135–36
Dibben, M.R. *102–03*
DiMaggio, P.J. *9, 60–65, 70–71,*
    74–75, 197
Dirks, K.T. *113, 128, 130, 135–36,*
    140
Dobbins, G.H. *136*
Dolan, S.L. *139*
Donnellon, A. *70*
Dooley, K. *102–03, 152, 198*
Dosi, G. *53*
Doucet, A. *154*
Drescher, M. *32–33*
Dugdale, T. *65–66*
Dunn, J. *71*
Durkheim, E. *60, 97–98*
Dwyer, R.F. *156*
Dyer, J.H. *27, 48, 146*

Eccles, R.G. *7, 25, 110*
Egidi, M. *53*
Eisenhardt, K.M. *30–32*
Eisenstadt, S.N. *4, 67–68, 141,*
    145–46
Elster, J. *10, 18–20, 22–23, 80, 188*
Endreß, M. *56*
Ensminger, J. *30–31*
Erikson, E.H. *69–70, 113, 116,*
    129–30, 193–94

Faulkner, D. *3–4, 150–51*
Faust, K. *196–97*
Fehr, E. *36, 139*
Feldman, M.S. *52–54, 70*
Fennell, M.L. *62–63*
Ferres, N. *137–38*
Ferrin, D.L. *113, 128, 130, 135–36, 140*
Fineman, S. *45–46*
Fischbacher, U. *139*
Fitz-James, S. *121*
Flood, M. *32–33*
Fontana, A. *153–54, 159*
Ford, D. *156*
Fox, A. *4, 62, 145–46*
Frank, R.H. *35, 45*
Frankel, S.H. *109*
Freeman, J.H. *62–63*
Frey, J.H. *153–54, 159*
Fukuyama, F. *71, 129–30, 146*

Gächter, S. *36*
Galaskiewicz, J. *64, 196–97*
Gambetta, D. *1–8, 14, 34, 41–43, 46–47, 77–79, 81–85, 93, 112–13, 142, 144–45, 193–95*
Garfinkel, H. *10, 55–61, 69–69, 74, 116, 141*
Garsten, C. *70*
Garud, R. *93, 197*
Gavin, M.B. *139*
Geyskens, I. *128*
Gibb, J.R. *85–87*
Gibbons, R. *33–34, 36*
Giddens, A. *2–3, 9–11, 55–56, 58, 69–70, 73–74, 79–80, 98–102, 108–09, 113, 116–18, 125–26, 151, 153, 187–88, 198*

Gillespie, N. *113, 139*
Gilson, L. *121–22*
Glaeser, E.L. *71, 132, 135, 137*
Goffman, E. *68–70, 113, 116*
Good, D. *37, 41, 80, 83–84, 114*
Granovetter, M. *9, 29, 36, 153, 196–97*
Green, C. *156–57*
Greve, H.R. *196–97*
Grey, C. *70*
Guba, E.G. *153–54*
Gubrium, J.F. *55–57*
Gulati, R. *27, 90–91, 94–95*

Hagen, J.M. *66*
Hamill, H. *46–47, 84–85, 112–13, 142, 144–45*
Hann, M.S. *2*
Hannan, M.T. *62–63*
Hansen, M.H. *25, 27*
Hardin, R. *7, 10, 13, 20–23, 31, 37, 40, 41, 46–47, 49, 78, 81–85, 88, 112, 114–15, 119, 125*
Hardy, C. *61–62, 113, 143, 197*
Hawley, A. *62–63*
Heckscher, C.C. *70*
Hegel, G.W.F. *116*
Heide, J.B. *156*
Heimer, C.A. *7–8*
Heinrichs, M. *139*
Hendry, J. *30–31*
Henslin, J.M. *46–47, 68, 84–85, 112–13, 141, 144–45*
Heraclitus *102–03*
Heritage, J.C. *56, 58*
Hill, C.W.L. *26*
Hillebrand, B. *55, 93*
Hirsch, P.M. *127*

Hobbes, *71*
Hollis, M. *13, 39–40, 50*
Holloran, J. *157*
Holmes, J.G. *89*
Holmes, M.E. *102–03, 152, 198*
Holstein, J.A. *55–57*
Hosmer, L.T. *32*
Howson, A. *73, 123–24, 144*
Huberman, A.M. *159*
Huemer, L. *30, 32, 93–94, 129–30,
     134, 142–43, 153–54, 156,
     158, 185*
Husserl, E. *55–56*
Huston, T.L. *138–40*

Ignagni, R. *122–23, 144*
Inkpen, A.C. *130–32, 150–51, 186*

Jain, S. *197*
James Jr., H.S. *4, 31, 33–36, 38,
     40–41, 43–44, 46, 48*
James, W. *111, 119–21*
Jensen, M.C. *30–31*
Jepperson, R.L. *9, 54–55, 59, 61,
     121, 126*
John, G. *156*
Johnson, J.L. *150–51*
Johnson, J.M. *134–35, 153*
Johnson-George, C. *44–45, 138*
Jones, K. *45*
Judge, T.A. *131–32, 134*

Kahneman, D. *15, 20*
Kanazawa, S. *41, 135–36*
Karnøe, P. *93, 197*
Kee, H.W. *41, 135–36*

Kelley, H.H. *34*
Kern, H. *93*
Kierkegaard, S. *110, 117–18*
Kieser, A. *5–6*
Kilduff, M. *196–97*
Kimmel, M.J. *36*
Klein Woolthuis, R. *2–3, 5, 66, 93,
     144*
Knez, M. *85, 196–97*
Knight, F.H. *8*
Knights, D. *4–5*
Knox, R.E. *41, 135–36*
Knudsen, T. *52*
Kollock, P. *135*
Koopmann, P. *2–3*
Korsgaard, M.A. *30*
Kosfeld, M. *139*
Kramer, R.M. *2, 5, 22, 53–54,
     67–68, 106–08, 112, 130–33,
     136, 141, 159*
Kreps, D.M. *33–34, 36*
Kühlmann, T.M. *150–51*
Kumar, N. *128*
Kumaraswamy, A. *197*
Kurzban, R. *139*

Lafontaine, O. *124*
Laibson, D.I. *71, 132, 135, 137*
Lamming, R. *156–57*
Lane, C. *2–3, 5, 7–8, 18, 66–67, 73,
     85, 105, 109, 146–50, 156*
Lane, I.M. *136*
Lane, P.J. *128–29, 150–51*
Langley, A. *102–03, 198*
Larson, A. *84–85, 90*
Larzelere, R.E. *138–40*
Lash, S. *99*
Lawrence, T.B. *61–62, 197*

Lazaric, N. *52–53*
Lee, S.H. *48, 135, 138*
Lee-Treweek, G. *121–22*
Leifer, R. *194–95*
Levi, M. *78, 119*
Levin, D.Z. *127*
Levinthal, D. *128–29*
Lewicki, R.J. *48–50, 89–90, 92–93*
Lewis, J.D. *7–8, 44–46, 49–50,*
   83–84, 93, 109, 112
Liebeskind, J.P. *78–79, 143*
Likert, R. *137*
Lincoln, Y.S. *140–41, 152–54*
Lindenberg, S. *24, 35, 48–49*
Lindkvist, L. *124–25*
Locke, J. *71*
Loewenstein, G. *139*
Lorenz, E.H. *27*
Lowe, P. *73*
Luce, R.D. *21–22, 32–33, 37, 82*
Luckmann, T. *9, 55–56, 58–62,*
   68–69, 95–96, 98
Luhmann, N. *3, 5, 7–8, 65–67,*
   71–74, 82–90, 94–99, 108–09,
   112–13, 116, 118–19, 149,
   152, 187
Lyles, M.A. *128–29, 150–51*

Macaulay, S. *65–66*
Maguire, S. *113, 143*
Mahoney, J. *92–93*
Malhotra, D. *66, 135*
Mann, L. *113*
March, J.G. *52, 64*
Marcus, A. *130*
Marengo, L. *53*
Marlowe, D. *139–40*
Marshall, A. *2*

Martin, D.K. *122–23, 144*
Mashima, R. *41, 94, 135–36, 146*
Matsuda, M. *94, 146*
Matthews, B.A. *135*
Matzner, W.T. *139*
Mauss, M. *88*
Mauthner, N.S. *154*
Mayer, R.C. *7–9, 14, 47–50, 79,*
   137–39
McAllister, D.J. *44–45, 48–49, 90,*
   138–40
McCloskey, D.N. *114*
McEvily, B. *1–2, 110, 130–32, 134,*
   138, 156, 186
McKneally, M.F. *122–23, 144*
McKnight, D.H. *47, 50, 57, 64, 79*
McMackin, J.F. *26–29*
Mead, G.H. *68*
Meckling, W.H. *30–31*
Merton, R.K. *87*
Meyer, J.W. *9, 61–63, 68, 74, 121,*
   126
Meyerson, D. *67–68, 106–08, 112*
Miles, M.B. *159*
Miller, G. *31–32*
Mills, P.K. *31–32, 194–95*
Misztal, B.A. *2–3, 15, 18–19, 52,*
   54, 69–71, 73, 109, 133,
   193–94
Mohr, A.T. *151*
Mohr, J. *138*
Morris, S. *5–6*
Morse, J.M. *157–58*
Munir, K.A. *197*
Murnighan, J.K. *66, 135*

Nalebuff, B.J. *78–79*
Nelson, R.R. *26, 52–53*

Newell, S. *143, 152*
Noorderhaven, N.G. *79, 93*
Nooteboom, B. *1–2, 7, 25, 27, 66,
    79–81, 93, 130–32*
Nunnally, J. *137*

Oh, S. *156*
Oliver, A.L. *70, 78, 143*
Olsen, J.P. *64*
Ortmann, G. *114–15*
Ostrom, E. *136*

Parsons, T. *73–74, 121–22*
Paxton, P. *71, 137, 196–97*
Pearce, J.L. *7–8, 27, 47*
Pennings, J.M. *195*
Pentland, B.T. *52–54, 70*
Perrone, V. *1–2, 110, 131–32, 134,
    138, 156, 186*
Perrow, C. *32*
Phillips, N. *61–62, 113, 143, 197*
Plato *16–17*
Poggi, G. *116*
Poole, M.S. *102–03, 152, 198*
Porter, D. *156–57*
Potvin, D. *122, 144*
Powell, W.W. *9, 60–65, 74–75*
Prelec, D. *139*
Pruitt, D.G. *36*
Putnam, R.D. *2–3, 71, 137*

Raiffa, H. *21–22, 32–33, 37, 82*
Ramanujam, V. *140*
RAND Corporation *32–33*
Raub, W. *84–85*
Reynolds, L. *100*

Ring, P.S. *25, 78–79, 90–93*
Ripperger, T. *29–30*
Robinson, S.L. *152*
Roniger, L. *4, 67–68, 141, 145–46*
Ross, S. *30–31*
Roth, N.L. *49, 87*
Rotter, J.B. *49–50, 137*
Rousseau, D.M. *7–9, 47, 130–31,
    194–95*
Rowan, B. *61–63, 68, 74*
Rus, A. *146*

Sabel, C.F. *84–85, 152*
Sakano, T. *150–51*
Sako, M. *7, 130, 133, 138, 146, 156*
Salk, J.E. *128–29, 150–51*
Saunders, M.N.K. *118–19, 143*
Schenkman, J.A. *71, 132, 135, 137*
Schoorman, F.D. *7–9, 14, 47–50, 79,
    137–38*
Schurr, P.H. *156*
Schütz, A. *10, 54–57, 95–96, 98,
    114–15*
Schwandt, T.A. *153–54*
Scott, W.R. *57–58, 64–65, 69*
Seligman, A. *2–3, 68–69, 73, 95,
    97–99, 102, 108, 110, 118, 153*
Shapiro, D. *89*
Shapiro, S.P. *30–31, 36, 54, 72–73*
Shaw, B. *100*
Shea, G.F. *100*
Sheppard, B.H. *29, 89*
Sherman, D.M. *29*
Shimoff, E. *135*
Shurtleff, M. *100*
Simmel, G. *2, 4, 11, 51–52, 71, 107,
    109, 111–12, 114–15, 118,
    121, 123*

Simon, H.A. *52*
Sitkin, S.B. *7–9, 47, 49, 87, 128–31, 141–42, 153–54, 194*
Six, F. *93–94, 142–43*
Sköldberg, K. *152–54*
Smeltzer, L.R. *156*
Smith, J.A. *153–54, 159*
Smitka, M.J. *90*
Sousa, R. de *10, 45–46, 49–50*
Soutter, C.L. *71, 132, 135, 137*
Spekman, R. *138*
Spence, M.A. *41–42*
Stake, R.E. *159*
Steenkamp, J.-B. *128*
Steier, F. *154*
Steiner, D.D. *136*
Stickel, D. *87, 128–29, 141–42, 153–54*
Stigler, G.J. *16–17*
Stolle, D. *132, 146*
Streeck, W. *145–46*
Swan, J. *143, 152*
Swap, W.C. *44–45, 138*
Sydow, J. *4–5, 71, 100–02, 107, 131–32, 153, 188*
Sztompka, P. *1–3, 10, 22–23, 71, 83–84, 94–95, 110, 112*

Takenouchi, H. *150–51*
Terai, S. *41, 135–36*
Thibaut, J.W. *34*
Thornhill, A. *118–19, 143*
Tillmar, M. *124–25, 140–42, 144–45*
Tolbert, P.S. *197*
Tocqueville, A. de *145–46*
Travaglione, A. *137–38*
Tsai, W. *196–97*

Tsebelis, G. *77–78*
Tsoukas, H. *102–03, 198*
Tucker, A. *32–33*
Tversky, A. *15, 20*
Tyler, T.R. *5, 53–54, 130–31*
Tzafrir, S.S. *139*

Ungson, G.R. *31*
Uzzi, B. *128–29, 140–42, 153*

Van de Bunt, G.G. *130*
Van de Ven, A.H. *25, 78–79, 90–93, 102–03, 152, 198*
Venkatraman, N. *138, 140*

Walgenbach, P. *72–73*
Walker, J. *136*
Warglien, M. *53*
Warren, M.E. *71*
Wasserman, S. *64, 197*
Weber, M. *145–46*
Weick, K.E. *67–68, 106–08, 112*
Weigert, A. *7–8, 44–46, 49–50, 83–84, 93, 109, 112*
Wenzel, H. *113*
Werner, J.M. *30*
Whitehead, A.N. *102–03, 198*
Whitener, E.M. *30*
Wilkinson, F. *42, 66, 146–50*
Williams, M. *46, 151*
Williamson, O.E. *25–29, 35, 41, 48, 80*
Willmott, H.C. *125–26*

Windeler, A. *100–01, 107*
Winter, S.G. *26, 52–53*
Woiceshyn, J. *195*
Wrightsman, L.S. *49–50, 137*

Yamagishi, T. *38, 41, 94, 135–35, 146*

Zaheer, A. *1–2, 110, 127–28, 131–32, 134, 138, 156, 186*
Zak, P.J. *139*
Zand, D.E. *49–50, 85–88, 92, 187, 194–95*
Zucker, L.G. *10, 47, 51–55, 59–61, 63–64, 67, 71, 88–89, 93, 113, 187*

SUBJECT INDEX

ability, *see* competence
access point *73–74*
active trust *10–11, 79, 98–100, 108, 125–126, 142, 151, 187–88, 198*
affect *44–46, 139–40*
agency *8–9, 52–54, 62–63, 70–71, 79, 99, 102–03, 110, 119, 121, 125–26, 162–63, 194–95, 197*
agency theory, *see* principal–agent theory
alliance, *see* interfirm alliance
altruism *19, 36*
ambiguity *64, 114, 189*
ambivalence *6–7, 11–12, 155–56*
appropriateness *45–46, 64*
as if *6–7, 11, 21–22, 81–84, 97–98, 102, 111–15, 117, 121, 125, 196*
autobiographical narrative *141, 144, 159*

backward induction *21–22, 37, 81–82*
Bayesianism *22, 47, 25–26*

behavioural economics *136*
Belfast *46–47, 144–45*
benevolence *14, 47, 194–95*
bet *16, 22–23*
blind trust *80, 83–84, 98–99, 187*
boundary *150–51*
bounded rationality *26, 29, 31*
bracketing *111, 115–18, 123–24*
business cycle *164, 169–70*
business relationships, *see* inter-organizational relationships
buyer *146–47, 150, 155–57, 185*

calculation *8, 22–26, 106*
calculativeness *25–26, 45, 64, 80, 89*
Cambridge Contracting Study *66–67, 146–50*
Canada *113, 143*
chance *16, 87*
child labour *59*
China *52–53, 72–73, 90, 100, 150–51*
cognition *44–46, 139–40*
coincidence *78, 81*
commitment *19, 22, 30, 87, 91–92, 100*

communication *17, 38–39, 99–100, 108, 162, 187–88*
community *17, 40, 124–25*
comparative research *145–151*
competence *14, 23, 47, 70, 73–74, 139, 147–48, 165–66, 183*
complaint *162, 164–65, 172–73, 178–79, 187–89*
complexity *11–12, 67, 82, 84–85, 96–97, 116, 149, 154–56, 169, 185, 189*
confidence *51–53, 68–69, 41, 74, 123, 150*
confidentiality *154, 159–60, 163–64, 167, 184–86*
connectability *5–6, 66–67*
constitutive expectancies *57–58*
context *62–63, 100, 134–35, 138–39, 145, 159*
contingency *97, 99–100, 102*
continuity *52–53, 96–97, 114–15, 198*
contract *35–36, 65–66, 90–91, 146–50, 168*
control *12, 71–72, 74, 79, 85–87, 110, 122, 124, 143, 192–95*
cooperation *19–20, 38–44, 78–82, 124–25, 135–36, 147–49, 156, 193–94*
cost *24–26, 35–36, 41–43, 156–57, 160–64*
credibility *18–19*
creditworthiness *172, 182–83*
cross-level effect *132*
culture *23–24, 151, 182*

descriptive research *132*
dialectic *67–68, 116, 127*

disembedding *73*
disposition, *see* predisposition
distrust *36, 38, 45, 48–49, 51–52, 62–63, 72, 85–87, 124–25, 152, 157, 162–63, 182–83*
doubt *122–23*
drama *68, 114*
duality *45–46, 49–50, 100–01, 124, 194–96*

economic theory *10, 14, 24–26, 29, 43–44, 48–49*
effort *29–30, 32, 36*
embeddedness *9, 13, 27–28, 50, 54, 84–85, 121–24, 134–35, 142, 151–53, 159, 169, 186, 194–96*
emotion *10, 44–46, 83, 93, 182*
empathy *93, 113, 123, 153*
empirical research *11, 127–89*
enactment *7*
encapsulated interest *20–22, 31, 81–82, 107, 182*
equity *78–79, 91–92*
estimate *16–18, 22–24*
ethnographic research *67–68, 140–45, 152*
ethnomethodology *10, 53, 58*
evolutionary theory *26, 34–35, 53, 79, 81*
exception *186*
exchange *30–31, 55, 60, 88, 143*
expectation *7, 11–13, 25, 49, 51–52, 55, 59, 64, 91–92, 97–98, 110–11, 179–81, 191–95, 198*
expected value *14, 16–18, 43–44*
experience *11–12, 22, 27, 71–72, 84, 88–97, 108, 121–24, 139–56,*

159, 165–67, 174–75, 179–82,
  187, 189, 196
experiment 36–41, 57, 59, 69, 134–36
expert 72, 74, 107
explorative research 132, 156–89

façade 61–62, 114, 121
fairness 139
faith 109, 117–21, 165–68, 188–89,
  see also leap of faith
familiarity 52–53, 56, 94–99, 114,
  123–24, 142
familiarization 10–11, 94–99, 187
fear 122–23
feedback 79, 85–87, 91–92, 111,
  130
fiction 112–15, 124–25
flexibility 70, 141–42, 145, 147–48,
  156–57, 162
formality 92
frame 89–90
friendship 142, 166
functionality 80, 82–83

game theory 4, 32–33, 38–41, 78,
  81–82, 106, 134–36, 186
gap 73–74, 115, 120–21, 123, 193,
  195, 198
General Social Survey 71, 137
generalization 132, 145
Germany 72–73, 93, 124, 145–51
gift 88
globalization 151
governance 26–29, 93
grounded theory 141–42, 144
guile 25–26
guilt 34–35

habit 58, 100
helplessness 2–4
heuristic 40, 128–36, 142, 166–67,
  192
history 145–46, 152, 162–63, 165–
  66, 174, 181–82, 185
HIV/AIDS 113, 143
homo oeconomicus 38, 49–50
honesty 47, 139
Hong Kong 52–53, 72–73, 100
hope 43–44, 192–93

idealization 114–15
identification 89, 93, 143
identity 40, 51–53, 64, 113, 116,
  193–94
ignorance 97–98, 109, 116–17
illusion 112
imitation 125, see also mimicry
imposed relevance 95–96
impression management 68, 113
incentive 14, 20, 31–35, 38–39, 10
incompetence 31
inconsistency 185
indeterminacy 22, 38
indifference 116
infancy 116–17
information 16–17, 23–24, 48,
  85–87, 112–13, 118–19,
  123–24, 163–64
institution 18, 51, 53–55, 58–61,
  66–75, 106, 124–25, 132, 145,
  149–50, 186, 197
institutional entrepreneur 74–75, 197
institutionalization 53, 58–61, 73, 197
instrumentalism 19, 62
integrity 14, 47, 99
intention 30, 47

interdisciplinarity *5*
interest *4–5, 114, 197*
interfirm alliance *3–4, 27, 90,*
 150–51
interfirm network *93, 101–02,*
 142
intermediary *17–18, 60–61, 160,*
 169–70
international business *150–51*
interorganizational relationship
 11–12, 72–73, 78–79, 90–94,
 131–33, 138, 142, 147–51,
 155–89
Interpersonal Trust Scale *137*
interpretation *59, 121, 143, 151–56,*
 189, 196
interpretative research *11,*
 151–154
intersubjectivity *56, 112*
interview *140–47, 153, 156–60,*
 184–86, 189
intuition *45*
irrationality *19, 24*
isomorphism *10, 53–54, 61–65*
Italy *146–50*

Japan *145–46, 150–51*
joint venture *3–4, 90, 128–29,*
 150–51
just do it *4, 11, 82, 84, 94, 115, 118,*
 125
just-in-time *171, 176–77*

knowledge *20–22, 51, 89, 96, 109,*
 124–25, 153, 188

leadership *113*
leap of faith *11–12, 83, 110–11,*
 114-15, 117–26, 140, 151, 167,
 191–98
learning *49, 81, 84–85, 93, 111,*
 116–17, 168, 196
legitimacy *61–65, 126*
legitimation *58–59, 101–02*
level of analysis *130–32, 169, 182*
Leviathan *71*
lifeworld *56, 95, 114*
Likert scale *137–40*
lock-in *92–96*
loyalty *180–83*

management *14, 53–54, 128,*
 145–46, 150–51
manager *31, 52–53, 73, 100,*
 131–32, 144, 155–56
measurement *44–45, 48, 135,*
 138–40, 152–53, 159
medical professional *73, 123*
medical system *73–74, 114, 121–23,*
 144
membership *60*
methodological individualism *13, 26*
methodology *132–35, 140–41,*
 143–45, 151–54
mimicry *42, 64*
mistrust *172, see also* distrust
modernity *51–52, 68–69, 71–72, 95,*
 97–100, 145–46
money *71–72*
monitoring *117, 152*
moral obligation *73–74*
motivation *38, 49–50, 70, 125–26*
myth *61–62, 113–14*

natural attitude *10, 53–61, 64–65,
    68–69, 74, 95–96, 107–08,
    114–16*
negotiation *91–92*
neoinstitutionalism *10, 53–55, 59–
    61, 66–67, 74–75*
Netherlands *93–94, 143*
network effect *142*
network, *see* interfirm network,
    social network
neuroscience *139*
New York *46–47, 142, 144–45*
norm, *see* social norm, technical
    standard
normalizing *57, 74, 114*
normative research *133*

ontological security *69–70, 100, 116*
openness *99–100, 139, 167*
operationalization *29, 48, 133–35,
    141*
opportunism *24–32, 67, 93, 133, 156*
organization *44, 59–62, 70, 106–07,
    131–32, 143–46*
organization studies *53–54, 102–03,
    110, 128, 131–32*
organizational field *74–75*
Organizational Trust Inventory *138*

paper trade *157–89*
paradox *10, 16–17, 43–44, 132–33*
parents *116–17, 123–24*
path creation *93*
path dependence *79, 92–93*
patient *73, 121–23*
pay-off *19, 24–25, 33–37, 39, 40,
    42–43*

penalty *32–36*
performance *29–30, 48, 140, 142,
    147–50*
personality *49–50, 69, 137, 193–94*
phenomenology *10, 53, 55, 116*
political science *71, 137*
power *114, 196*
pragmatist philosophy *119–20*
precondition, *see* trust, precondition
predictability *47, 69–70, 89, 149*
predictive research *132–33*
predisposition *13–14, 23–24, 38–39,
    49–50, 137–38, 182*
principal–agent theory *29–32*
principle of gradualness *84–87, 106,
    108, 167–68, 187*
printing industry *155–89*
prisoner's dilemma *32–37, 135*
probability *8, 14, 16, 18, 22–24, 37*
problem solving *162, 165, 173, 175,
    180, 188*
process *10–11, 49, 59, 77–79, 84,
    87–95, 99–100, 102–03, 106,
    108, 142, 151–53, 159, 185,
    195, 198*
project *107–08*
prosperity *129–30, 146*
prudence *22–23, 36, 38, 43–44,
    88*
psychological contract *91–92*
psychology *14, 137*

qualitative research *140–45, 153–89*
quality management *72–73, 87,
    141–42, 156–57*
quantitative research *135–40, 156–
    57*
questionnaire *137, 139–40, 158*

rapport *167–69, 174–75, 187, 189*
rational choice *4, 10, 15–26, 44, 49, 83–84, 186*
rationalization *118–19*
reason *10, 13–15, 45, 50, 107–11, 186*
reciprocity *19–20, 39–40, 85, 88, 157, 169–70*
recursiveness *100–01*
reflexivity *10–11, 77, 79, 102–03, 108–11, 151–54, 159, 187–89, 198*
reliability *139, 147–48, 172–73, 178–81*
reputation *17, 37, 60, 88, 147–49*
research agenda *12, 193–96*
research process *145, 151–54, 189*
resignation *117, 123, 192–93*
respect *165–66, 174*
responsibility *126*
responsiveness *178–82, 183*
reward *29–30, 32, 136*
rhetoric *3–5, 191*
risk *8, 15, 17–18, 22–23, 25–26, 66–67, 85, 94, 149*
Robinson Crusoe *77–78*
role *64, 67–69, 107–08, 186*
routine *10, 51–54, 69–70, 75, 96, 100, 107–11, 117, 186*
rule *52–53, 57–58, 60, 65–67, 91–92, 101–02, 107–08, 124–25, 142, 186*

sacrifice *117*
safeguard *24–25, 27–29, 133*
sanction *19–20, 36, 63–66*
scruple *34–35*
security *129–30*

self-fulfilling prophecy *87*
self-interest *13, 18–26, 30, 33–36, 47*
self-reinforcement *79, 81, 85, 92–93, 106, 108, 120, 198*
service *176–83*
shadow of the future *36–37, 107, 169–70*
signalling theory *41–43, 113*
social capital *137, 146, 196–97*
social construction *58, 114, 121, 126*
social desirability effect *139–40*
social network *23, 107, 123–24, 134, 196–97*
social norm *18–20, 24, 27–28, 34–35, 36, 64, 147–49*
social order *71, 193–94*
social structure *60, 126*
socialization *167–68, 175*
society *2, 58–59, 69, 193–94*
sociology *14, 54, 193–94*
solidarity *19, 60, 73–74*
specific investment *26–29*
stability *52–53, 70, 149*
structural hole *196–97*
structuration *10–11, 99–102*
supplier *142, 146–47, 150, 155–58, 185*
survey *132, 137–140, 144, 153, 156–57*
suspension *12, 72, 74, 96, 102, 110–11, 115–26, 140, 155, 174–75, 179–80, 182, 188–89, 191–93, 195–96, 198*
Sweden *93–94, 142, 144–45*
swift trust *67, 106–08, 112*
system trust, *see* trust, system

taken-for-grantedness *10, 51–60, 65, 95, 97, 114–15, 186*

Tanzania *124–25, 144–45*

taxi driver *46–47, 68, 112–13, 144–45*

technical standard *148–49*

temporary work group *106–08*

test *167–68, 187–88*

text *140–41*

third party *17–18, 34–36, 38–39, 133–34*

tit-for-tat *39, 81, 133, 181*

trade association *148–49*

transaction cost economics *26–29, 48*

trench warfare *78, 81*

triangulation *134–35, 153*

trouble *93–94, 143*

trust
  – active, *see* active trust
  – antecedent *7, 129–30, 137, 192–93*
  – blind, *see* blind trust
  – crisis *2–3, 133*
  – definition *6–9, 14, 25, 45, 55, 57, 111, 116, 139*
  – dynamic *85–87, 93–94, see also* process
  – game *33–34, 36, 38–42, 46, 135*
  – manifestation *7, 105, 129–30, 152*
  – politics *4–5, 114*
  – precondition *15–16, 37, 41, 129–30, 193*
  – swift, *see* swift trust
  – system *71–74, 97, 99–100, 149*
  – topicality *1–6*
  – types *23, 60, 88–89*

Trust Wheel *110–11, 125, 185, 189*

trustee *3, 7, 14–15, 33–34, 113, 133–34*

trustor *3, 7, 14–15, 33–34, 133–34*

trustworthiness *10, 13–14, 17–24, 29, 31, 41–42, 46–49, 85–87, 93–94, 112–13, 138–39, 147, 158, 162, 165, 172, 178–80*

truthfulness *173–75*

typification *56, 58, 96*

uncertainty *6–8, 11, 21, 25–26, 30–32, 38, 40–41, 46–48, 52, 64, 66–67, 82, 94, 97–98, 106, 108–10, 114, 116, 118, 149, 167, 169–70, 191–93, 195, 198*

unconditionality *69, 97–99, 102*

unfamiliarity *56, 94–96, 187*

United Kingdom *143, 145–50, 155–57*

United States *60, 71, 88, 137, 145–46, 150–51*

utility *13, 15, 19–20, 25, 27–28, 38, 50, 51, 64–65, 84–85, 186*

vaccination *123*

validity *135–38, 145*

vulnerability *6–9, 11, 21, 30–32, 38, 40–41, 43–44, 46–48, 51, 69–70, 94, 97–98, 106, 108–10, 116, 118, 156–57, 173, 191–93, 195, 198*

will *111, 119–21*

witchcraft *124–25*

work relationship *89, 144*